# THE TWENTY MOST EFFECTIVE LANGUAGE TEACHING TECHNIQUES

From leading scholar and applied linguist Paul Nation, this book describes and explains the 20 most effective and efficient language teaching techniques and why they work. Backed by decades of research and expertise, Nation examines the principles of learning connected to these techniques, as well as the factors affecting their choice and usage.

These techniques are organized around the four skills of listening, speaking, reading, and writing. For each skill, there is an opportunity for learning through meaning-focused use, an opportunity for learning through deliberate study, and a window for fluency development through working with easy material. Each technique is described and analyzed to demonstrate its learning goals and the principles of learning in use.

In demonstrating key techniques and methods for language learning, this book is particularly useful for pre-service teachers and students in applied linguistics, TESOL, and language teaching. Each chapter also has a substantial list of research topics for projects or theses.

**I.S.P. Nation** is Professor Emeritus in Applied Linguistics at Victoria University of Wellington, New Zealand.

# ESL & Applied Linguistics Professional Series
Eli Hinkel, Series Editor

**Doing Reflective Practice in English Language Teaching**
120 Activities for Effective Classroom Management, Lesson Planning, and Professional Development
*Thomas S. C. Farrell*

**Creating Classrooms of Peace in English Language Teaching**
*Edited by Barbara M. Birch*

**Shaping Learners' Pronunciation**
Teaching the Connected Speech of North American English
*James Dean Brown and Dustin Crowther*

**Handbook of Practical Second Language Teaching and Learning**
*Edited by Eli Hinkel*

**English L2 Vocabulary Learning and Teaching**
Concepts, Principles, and Pedagogy
*Lawrence J. Zwier and Frank Boers*

**Praxis-oriented Pedagogy for Novice L2 Teachers**
Developing Teacher Reasoning
*Karen E. Johnson, Deryn P. Verity and Sharon S. Childs*

For more information about this series, please visit: www.routledge.com/ESL-Applied-Linguistics-Professional-Series/book-series/LEAESLALP

# THE TWENTY MOST EFFECTIVE LANGUAGE TEACHING TECHNIQUES

*I.S.P. Nation*

NEW YORK AND LONDON

Designed cover image: © Getty Images

First published 2025
by Routledge
605 Third Avenue, New York, NY 10158

and by Routledge
4 Park Square, Milton Park, Abingdon, Oxon, OX14 4RN

*Routledge is an imprint of the Taylor & Francis Group, an informa business*

© 2025 I.S.P. Nation

The right of I.S.P. Nation to be identified as author of this work has been asserted in accordance with sections 77 and 78 of the Copyright, Designs and Patents Act 1988.

All rights reserved. No part of this book may be reprinted or reproduced or utilised in any form or by any electronic, mechanical, or other means, now known or hereafter invented, including photocopying and recording, or in any information storage or retrieval system, without permission in writing from the publishers.

*Trademark notice*: Product or corporate names may be trademarks or registered trademarks, and are used only for identification and explanation without intent to infringe.

ISBN: 9781032802725 (hbk)
ISBN: 9781032802718 (pbk)
ISBN: 9781003496151 (ebk)

DOI: 10.4324/9781003496151

Typeset in Times New Roman
by codeMantra

# CONTENTS

*List of Figures*   viii
*List of Tables*   ix
*Acknowledgements*   xi

   Introduction   1

1 Language teaching techniques and the four strands   6

2 A system of tasks for language learning   17

3 Group work and language learning   31

4 The principles of learning   39

**PART 1**
**Listening**   **57**

5 Extensive listening and viewing   59

6 Dictation   71

7 Easy listening   89

## PART 2
## Speaking 99

  8  Informal conversation    101

  9  Problem-solving speaking    110

10  Prepared talks    126

11  Hearing and pronunciation practice    136

12  4/3/2    147

## PART 3
## Reading 157

13  Extensive reading    159

14  Intensive reading    176

15  Speed reading    190

## PART 4
## Writing 203

16  Extensive writing with feedback    205

17  Information transfer    219

18  Guided writing    229

19  Substitution tables    238

20  10-minute writing    246

## PART 5
## General purpose 255

21  Linked skills activities    257

| 22 Projects | 269 |
|---|---|
| 23 Vocabulary flash cards | 277 |
| 24 Learner training | 286 |

## PART 6
## Research                                                                295

| 25 Researching language teaching techniques | 297 |
|---|---|

*Appendix 1: A feedback system for writing
    and self-checking procedures*                                          *303*
*References*                                                               *306*
*Author index*                                                             *317*
*Subject index*                                                            *321*

# FIGURES

| | | |
|---|---|---|
| 6.1 | Variants of dictation | 80 |
| 6.2 | Variants of dicto-comp | 83 |
| 15.1 | A learner's graph showing a gradual increase in reading speed | 200 |
| 19.1 | A substitution table based around the negative imperative pattern (George, 1967) | 239 |
| 19.2 | Table 10 on question forms from George (1967) | 239 |
| 19.3 | Substitution table 18 from George (1967) | 241 |

# TABLES

| | | |
|---|---|---|
| 0.1 | The 20 most useful language teaching techniques | 2 |
| 0.2 | The goals of language learning | 3 |
| 2.1 | Experience tasks in the four skills | 19 |
| 2.2 | Examples of control and focus in experience tasks in listening | 21 |
| 2.3 | Guided tasks for listening activities | 22 |
| 2.4 | Experience tasks involving reading | 27 |
| 2.5 | Experience tasks involving speaking | 28 |
| 4.1 | Bygate's types of repetition | 45 |
| 4.2 | Activities involving immediate and delayed verbatim repetition | 46 |
| 4.3 | Challenges to motivate repetition | 47 |
| 4.4 | The most common topic types and the texts they occur in | 50 |
| 4.5 | The different types of repetition activities | 51 |
| 4.6 | Applying principles in language teaching techniques with a focus on vocabulary | 52 |
| 5.1 | The learning goals of extensive listening and viewing | 60 |
| 6.1 | The learning goals of dictation | 72 |
| 7.1 | How easy listening meets the five fluency criteria | 90 |
| 7.2 | The goals of easy listening | 90 |
| 8.1 | The goals of informal conversation | 102 |
| 9.1 | The goals of problem-solving speaking | 111 |
| 9.2 | Topics for problem-solving tasks | 113 |
| 10.1 | The goals of prepared talks | 127 |
| 11.1 | The goals of hearing and pronunciation practice | 137 |
| 12.1 | The goals of 4/3/2 | 148 |
| 13.1 | The goals of extensive reading | 160 |

| | | |
|---|---|---|
| 14.1 | The goals of intensive reading | 177 |
| 14.2 | Useful focuses in intensive reading | 181 |
| 15.1 | How speed reading meets the fluency criteria | 191 |
| 15.2 | The goals of speed reading | 192 |
| 16.1 | The goals of extensive writing | 206 |
| 16.2 | Supporting extensive writing | 208 |
| 16.3 | Types of written texts organized according to text types and genre | 209 |
| 16.4 | How do you give effective formative feedback? | 212 |
| 17.1 | The goals of information transfer | 221 |
| 18.1 | The goals of guided writing | 232 |
| 19.1 | The goals of learning from substitution tables | 240 |
| 20.1 | The goals of 10-minute writing | 247 |
| 21.1 | The goals of linked skills activities | 258 |
| 21.2 | Five sets of linked skills activities | 260 |
| 21.3 | Examples of four linked skills activities | 264 |
| 22.1 | The goals of projects | 270 |
| 23.1 | The goal of the flash card strategy | 278 |
| 23.2 | The CEFR levels with suggested vocabulary and word family levels | 281 |
| 24.1 | The goals of learner training | 287 |
| 24.2 | Principles and their applications for language learning | 290 |

# ACKNOWLEDGEMENTS

The original version of Chapter 2 A system of tasks appeared as Nation, I. S. P. (1990). A system of tasks for language learning, in *Language Teaching Methodology for the Nineties* Sarinee Anivan (ed), RELC Anthology Series No 24, 51–63. The original version of Chapter 3 Group work appeared as Nation, P. (1989a). Group work and language learning. *English Teaching Forum*, *27*(2), 20–24. A small part of Chapter 4 Group work comes from Chapter 10 of Newton and Nation (2021) Teaching ESL/EFL listening and speaking. Parts of Chapter 6 Dictation appeared in Nation, I. S. P. (1991a). Dictation, dicto-comp and related techniques. *English Teaching Forum*, *29*(4), 12–14. Parts of Chapter 14 Intensive reading appeared in Nation, P. (2004). Vocabulary learning and intensive reading. *EA Journal*, *21*(2), 20–29. Parts of Chapter 17 Information transfer appeared in Nation, P. (1988). Using techniques well: Information transfer. *Guidelines*, *10*(1), 17–23. Parts of Chapter 21 Linked skills appeared in Nation (2013b) *What Should Every ESL Teacher Know?* Compass Publishing. Parts of Appendix 1 appeared in Nation (2024) *What Should Every EFL Teacher Know?* Compass Publishing.

# INTRODUCTION

The aim of this book is to show teachers and learners what needs to be done to learn a language. The book describes and explains the 20 most effective and efficient teaching techniques, and shows what kind of techniques they are and why they work. Some of the techniques are very well known, although they may not be well understood. Some of the techniques have unfortunately fallen out of favour, usually because they do not fit with current theories or trends. The choices and justifications for the techniques dealt with in the book are supported by research wherever this is possible. After reading through the book, you should have a good understanding of each of the techniques as well as a good understanding of the nature of teaching techniques in general and how they achieve their purposes.

## The 20 most useful language teaching techniques

In Table 0.1 column 3, the term "Meaning-focused strands" includes meaning-focused input, meaning-focused output, and fluency development, because these three strands involve communicative use of the language.

This book is not only about teaching techniques but is also about language courses, because part of course design involves deciding what language teaching techniques will be used in the course. The 20 techniques described in this book cover the four strands in a balanced way, making sure that each strand has roughly equal time.

Part of this book brings together articles and chapters that I wrote several years ago. Early in my career as a teacher-trainer, I had a strong interest in language teaching techniques. This was partly because around half of our academic

DOI: 10.4324/9781003496151-1

**TABLE 0.1** The 20 most useful language teaching techniques

| Skill area | Technique | Strand |
|---|---|---|
| Listening | Extensive listening and viewing | Meaning-focused input |
| | Dictation | Language-focused learning |
| | Easy listening | Fluency development |
| Speaking | Informal conversation | Meaning-focused output |
| | Problem-solving speaking | Meaning-focused output |
| | Prepared talks | Meaning-focused output |
| | Hearing and pronunciation practice | Language-focused learning |
| | 4/3/2 | Fluency development |
| Reading | Extensive reading | Meaning-focused input |
| | Intensive reading | Language-focused learning |
| | Speed reading | Fluency development |
| Writing | Extensive writing with feedback | Meaning-focused output |
| | Information transfer | Meaning-focused strands |
| | Guided writing | Language-focused learning |
| | Substitution tables | Language-focused learning |
| | Ten-minute writing | Fluency development |
| General purpose | Linked skills | Meaning-focused strands |
| | Projects | Meaning-focused strands |
| | Word cards | Language-focused learning |
| | Learner training | Language-focused learning |

year involved training teachers and the other half involved teaching English. Sometimes this involved teaching English to the same people who would be on our teacher-training courses, so we had to put our money where our mouth was. I decided I would read every article written about language teaching techniques and would make a book containing a description of all the language teaching techniques that I could find. The result was an unpublished book called *Language Teaching Techniques*. It quickly became clear to me, from my collection of techniques and reading articles by Earl Stevick (1959), Alun Rees and others, that techniques could be analysed, and that the parts of techniques could be combined in various ways to make other techniques. I wrote several articles (Nation, 1976, 1977, 1989a, 1989b) about the parts of language teaching techniques, plus many articles about particular language teaching techniques. In 2000, I wrote an occasional publication called *Creating, using and adapting language teaching techniques*, which in some ways is the precursor for this book. It was much later in my career that I figured out how the various techniques fitted together, using the principle of the four strands. In Webb and Nation (2017), we analysed 23 different vocabulary learning activities. Thirteen of these are covered in chapters in this book. Several of the other ten (guessing from context, word parts, keyword, and glossing) appear briefly in this book as a part of other techniques.

Most teachers will have techniques that they use regularly but which do not appear in the book. I hope that the analysis in this book will help in the analysis of those techniques I have not included. I included techniques that I felt could be used almost every week. There are many techniques which are effective and fun, but which are typically used only once or twice in a course. My favourites like this include Alibi (Woolrich, 1963), Marketplace, Headlines, the Strip story, and Dicto-gloss. In one of my favourite books that I have written, I devoted a chapter to such techniques (Nation, 2024, Chapter 11). They certainly could be included in a course, and they should certainly be analysed to see their learning goals, how they work, and how they can be used well.

The motivation to write this book came from work I was doing rethinking the principles of learning. This is briefly described in Chapter 4. I was interested in seeing how the principles of learning applied to the most useful language teaching techniques.

Using well thought out techniques is the easiest way to put the findings of research into practice. If a technique has been designed to use research findings, then using the technique well will apply these findings. In each chapter, the section called *How can this technique be done well?* describes the best application of this technique.

## The goals of language learning

The goals of language learning can be easily remembered using the mnemonic LIST (see Table 0.2).

If we relate language learning goals to the different strands of a course, the strands of meaning-focused input and meaning-focused output generally have the primary goal of developing skill in language use. That is, they have skill goals, namely developing skill in listening, speaking, reading, or writing. A

**TABLE 0.2** The goals of language learning

| Goals | Explanation |
|---|---|
| Language | Language goals can include pronunciation, spelling, word parts, vocabulary, multiword units, and grammar. |
| Ideas | Ideas goals include learning about the world (subject matter learning), cultural understanding, and learning about how to learn. |
| Skill | Skill goals involve the four skills of listening, speaking, reading, and writing. Developing a language skill, involves developing accuracy, fluency, and complexity in the use of that skill, and involves being able to draw on a range of language resources in real time to use the skill. |
| Text | Learning text or discourse involves learning how language is used in interaction with others and in forming and understanding appropriate texts beyond the sentence level. |

secondary goal may be learning language features, such as vocabulary or grammar. Such language learning goals are secondary goals in these meaning-focused strands partly because they involve incidental learning. Such incidental learning can be made more deliberate through the use of enhancement (bolding or highlighting words or multiword units), or through planning, but if this is overdone, then the activity will no longer fit into the meaning-focused strands and will become part of the language-focused learning strand.

The language-focused learning strand of a course typically has specific language learning goals, that is, it focuses on pronunciation, spelling, word parts, vocabulary, multiword units, or grammar. The language-focused learning strand can also include the content goals of learning how to learn and understanding the principles of learning. The teaching of language learning strategies, which is considered as ideas or content learning, also fits into the language-focused learning strand.

The fluency development strand has skill goals, primarily fluency of course, but fluency should be accompanied by accuracy which involves comprehension of input and comprehensibility of output. A secondary goal of fluency development is the development of complexity in that the development of fluency can push learners to work with larger units of language and to restructure their language knowledge to allow more fluent use. In the principle of the four strands, fluency is basically measured by speed as in words per minute or standard words per minute. The word "fluency" is used with many meanings, such as being able to speak a language well, or being able to use exactly the right expression, but in the four strands it is used with the very limited meaning of speed.

In each of the chapters on language teaching techniques (Chapters 5–24), the section on learning goals uses the Language, Ideas, Skills, and Text classification.

Most of the chapters are organized around the four skills of listening, speaking, reading, and writing. For each skill, there should be an opportunity for learning through meaning-focused use, an opportunity for learning through deliberate study, and an opportunity for fluency development through working with easy material. If you look at the table of contents for the book, you will see this three-part organization (use, deliberate attention, fluency) in the arrangement of Chapters 5–20. This three-part organization is based on the four strands, with meaning-focused input and meaning-focused output representing language use.

The terms *techniques*, *tasks*, and *activities* are used interchangeably throughout this book. Activities and tasks are techniques put into practice. I would not dream of attempting to define what a technique is. As can be seen from the various chapters in the book, I use the term *technique* very loosely indeed to include activities such as extensive writing which probably includes several techniques rather than just one, activities such as information transfer which is really a way of supporting some other technique, such as listening or writing, and I even include learner training as a technique, which certainly does not fit with task-based language learning writers' idea of a task.

The early chapters of this book look more generally at language teaching techniques. They look at how techniques can fit together to make a course providing a balance of opportunities for language learning (Chapter 1, the four strands), how techniques can be used to make learning easier (Chapters 2 and 3, experience, shared, guided, and independent tasks), and how techniques put the basic principles of learning into use (Chapter 4).

## Using the techniques in large classes

Many of the activities can be done as individual, pair, and group, or whole class activities, making them suitable for large classes. The major issue with pair and group activities in large classes is the amount of noise created by many people talking at once. A partial solution to this is to have a signal for getting learners to speak more quietly, and to give learners responsibility for keeping the noise level of their own group as low as possible.

Another issue in rooms with fixed seating is to get a seating arrangement for each group so that the members of the group are equal distance from each other.

Providing detailed feedback on writing is a problem in large classes because of the amount of marking the teacher has to do. We look at this problem in the chapter on prepared talks.

Each of the 20 chapters from Chapters 5 to 24 follow a set format of describing a particular technique, its learning goals, how it helps learning occur, requirements for using the technique (including how much time to spend on it), the steps to follow when using the technique well, how to monitor the technique, variations of the technique, digital applications, building repetition into its use, and existing and future research on the technique. Chapters 5–24 need not be read in order, but in Chapter 5, the aims of the parts of the chapter are signalled much more explicitly than in the later chapters.

# 1
# LANGUAGE TEACHING TECHNIQUES AND THE FOUR STRANDS

### What is the principle of the four strands?

The principle of the four strands (Nation, 2007, 2024) says that a well-balanced language course provides opportunities for learning through four equal strands – meaning-focused input, meaning-focused output, language-focused learning, and fluency development. An equal amount of time should be spent on each strand (each making up one-quarter of the total course time), and ideally the material used in these strands should be similar, so that the language features covered are much the same and get plenty of repetition. The four strands need not all occur in every lesson, but over the period of a month or more, there should be a roughly equal amount of time spent on each strand.

Let us now look at each of these four strands.

### *Meaning-focused input*

The meaning-focused input strand involves learning through listening and reading. The material used for listening and reading should only contain a small proportion of unfamiliar language items. This is so that the learners can do listening and reading focusing on comprehending the input without being burdened by a lot of unknown words or unknown grammatical constructions. From a vocabulary perspective, around 2% of the running words (tokens) should be unfamiliar. This means that for every 50 running words or for every five lines of text, there should be only one unfamiliar or partly familiar word.

The meaning-focused input strand involves extensive reading and extensive listening, and this listening and reading should take up around one-quarter

DOI: 10.4324/9781003496151-2

of the total course time. The total course time includes work done in class and out of class.

Each strand has criteria that can be used to decide if an activity fits into that strand. The criteria for meaning-focused input are (1) there is a focus on successfully comprehending the message, (2) there are some unfamiliar language items but not enough to disrupt comprehension, and these language items can be largely dealt with by guessing from context and a small amount of dictionary look-up, and (3) there are large amounts of input. The meaning-focused input strand should largely involve individual, independent work, and each learner should be working at the language level that most suits them. To make this clearer, let us look at the definition of extensive reading used by Nation and Waring (2020, p. 3):

> Extensive reading ... involves each learner independently and silently reading a lot of material which is at the right level for them.

This definition fits well with the criteria for the meaning-focused input strand. The "silently reading" part of the definition relates to criterion 1, focusing on the message. The "independently" and "at the right level" parts relate to criterion 2, a small number of unfamiliar items. The "a lot of material" part of the definition relates to criterion 3, large amounts of input. It is useful to note that extensive reading is not wholly meaning-focused input. Around one-third of the time in an extensive reading programme should involve another strand, fluency development.

The definition for extensive listening is largely the same as the definition for extensive reading, although extensive listening is likely to involve more interaction between learners, and between the teacher and the learners, than extensive reading does. The same three criteria that applied to extensive reading apply to extensive listening.

The meaning-focused input strand is largely the same as Krashen's (1985) comprehensible input. The major difference between comprehensible input and the meaning-focused input strand is that the meaning-focused input strand makes up one-quarter of a well-balanced course, while some advocates of comprehensible input see it as making up the whole course.

The learning in the meaning-focused input strand involves learning to make use of language that is already known, learning new items through meeting them in context or through a small amount of look-up, and strengthening and enriching knowledge of partly known items. The primary goal of the meaning-focused input and meaning-focused output strands is developing skill in language use. The secondary goal is developing language knowledge through incidental learning. In this book, the techniques covered in the meaning-focused input strand include extensive reading for meaning-focused input, extensive listening and viewing for meaning-focused input, information transfer, linked skills, and projects.

The major kind of learning in the meaning-focused input, meaning-focused output, and fluency development strands is incidental learning, that is, learning that occurs when the learner's main focus is on something else, in this case understanding or producing messages.

## Meaning-focused output

The meaning-focused output strand involves learning through speaking and writing. The speaking and writing should largely be near the limits of learners' language knowledge so that they have the opportunity to expand small parts of their knowledge through language use. This expansion can involve turning receptive knowledge of language features into productive knowledge, learning unfamiliar items through language-focused episodes and negotiation, and strengthening knowledge of partly familiar items through productive use. In terms of Skill Acquisition Theory (DeKeyser, 2015), the meaning-focused input and meaning-focused output strands involve the proceduralization of declarative knowledge. That is, learners become proficient at using what they know across the four skills of listening, speaking, reading, and writing.

Just as we have extensive reading and extensive listening, it is possible to talk about extensive speaking and extensive writing, and the definitions of these activities would be somewhat similar to the definitions of extensive reading and extensive listening. Most of the learning in the meaning-focused input and meaning-focused output strands is incidental learning, and this is one of the reasons why they both contain the criterion of large amounts of language use. These large amounts of language use are necessary to provide the repetition that is needed for the small gains, that each incidental meeting with a language feature involves, to become larger gains. In this book, the techniques covered in the meaning-focused output strand include problem-solving speaking, informal conversation, prepared talks, extensive writing, information transfer, linked skills, and projects.

## Language-focused learning

The language-focused learning strand involves deliberate learning, that is, studying the language. One of the major effects of the principle of the four strands is to provide a clear role for deliberate learning within a course and to place limits on it so that it does not dominate the course. Language-focused learning should take up no more than one-quarter of the total course time. Similarly, the principle of the four strands provides a major role for meaning-focused communicative language use across the four skills, allocating three-quarters of the course time to language use (meaning-focused input, meaning-focused output, and fluency development).

The language-focused learning strand involves a deliberate intentional focus on language features, language skills, and strategy development. This is the sole criterion for this strand. The success of this deliberate attention will depend on the focus of attention, the quantity of attention (including repetition), and the quality of attention. These same aspects of attention also apply to the three meaning-focused strands of meaning-focused input, meaning-focused output, and fluency development, and we will look more closely at them in Chapter 4 of this book.

The language-focused learning strand should take up around one-quarter of the total learning time. In this book, the techniques covered in the language-focused learning strand include dictation, hearing and pronunciation practice, intensive reading, feedback on writing, guided writing, substitution tables, vocabulary flash cards, and learner training. For each of the four skills of listening, speaking, reading, and writing, there is a relevant language-focused learning technique.

## Fluency development

The fluency development strand involves the learners making the best use of what they already know. There need to be fluency development activities for each of the four skills of listening, speaking, reading, and writing. So, there needs to be focused fluency development for reading, focused fluency development for speaking and so on.

There are five criteria for fluency development activities. (1) The material used for fluency development should be easy with no unknown language features. (2) A fluency development activity should involve accurate language use. Accurate language use means that there should be a reasonable level of comprehension in listening and reading, and a reasonable level of language accuracy in speaking and writing. (3) A fluency development activity should involve some pressure to go faster. That is, a fluency development activity should push the learner to use the language at a speed getting near that of native speakers. (4) A fluency development activity should be meaning-focused. That is, it should be focused on receiving or communicating messages. (5) There should be plenty of opportunity for fluent language use. An effective way of developing fluency is simply to repeat the same communicative tasks, but there are also other ways of developing fluency.

The fluency development strand should take up around one-quarter of the total time in a language course, and each language skill should get around one-quarter of the time in the fluency development strand. So, reading fluency development, for example, should take one-quarter of the time devoted to fluency development. This means that around one-sixteenth of the time (one-quarter of one-quarter) should be devoted to reading fluency development in a language course. Similarly, one quarter of the time in the fluency development strand should be given to speaking fluency development, making up around one-sixteenth of the time in the whole course. In this book, the techniques covered in the fluency development strand include easy listening, 4/3/2, speed reading, 10-minute writing, linked skills and projects. Linked skills and projects also involve the meaning-focused input, meaning-focused output, and language-focused learning strands.

## How can you apply the principle of the four strands?

The principle of the four strands is a curriculum design principle which focuses on the allocation of time in a language course. One way to apply the principle to an existing course is to list the activities in the course along with the amount of time given to each activity. Each activity should then be classified into the four strands using the criteria described above and the amount of time given to each activity in a strand added up. If each strand occupies roughly one quarter of the course time, then the four strands principle has been well applied. If the time given to each strand is not roughly equal, then adjustments need to be made.

Most language courses do not have an extensive reading programme that includes reading fluency development and which in total occupies around three-sixteenths of the course time (one-eighth for meaning-focused input in reading, plus one-sixteenth for reading fluency development). The addition of a well thought out extensive reading programme is the most effective change that a teacher could make to a language course.

The principle of the four strands can also be used to evaluate the techniques used in the course, looking at how well each technique fits the criteria for the strand it occurs in. Some activities fit into more than one strand. For example, pair and group conversation activities involve both meaning-focused input and meaning-focused output. The project work and linked skills activities can involve meaning-focused input, meaning-focused output, language-focused learning, and fluency development. In such cases, when looking at the allocation of time across the four strands, a decision needs to be made about what proportion of the activity fits into a particular strand.

The principle of the four strands can be applied to courses that focus on only one or two language skills, such as a reading course, or a conversation course. In such courses, fluency development and language-focused learning should each make up one-quarter of the course time, and the other 50% should focus on the particular skills that are the goal of the course. That is, the meaning-focused part of a reading course should focus on reading, and not on listening, or speaking and writing, with reading taking up around 50%. Having said that, however, it is worth considering, for example, what roles listening, speaking, and writing should play in a reading course. Similarly, it is worth considering what role reading and writing should play in a speaking course.

## How do teaching techniques fit into the four strands?

The four strands are simply a classification system for teaching techniques. It is the techniques that put the strands into practice.

To fit into a strand, each teaching technique needs to meet most of criteria for the strand. In the descriptions of the criteria given above, the criteria for each strand are ranked so that the most important criterion is given first, the next most important criterion is listed second, and so on. So, for meaning-focused input, the criterion of a focus on the message is the most important criterion, and the next most important criterion is having some but only a small amount of unfamiliar items. The criteria for each strand can be a useful way of evaluating the teaching techniques used in a course. Some reading courses do not involve extensive reading but instead focus on intensive reading, or they involve short pieces of text followed by comprehension questions which hardly qualify as meaning-focused input.

The teaching techniques used in each strand of a course are in competition with each other for the time available in that strand. This is most apparent in the language-focused learning strand where there is a wide variety of ways of giving deliberate attention to language features. It is well worth looking at each of the techniques used in a course to see if they are meeting the criteria for the strand they are in and if a better technique could be used instead. Fortunately, there is now a growing interest in researching language teaching techniques. This research has suggested that fluency development techniques need to involve some preparation so that errors are not practised. It has also underlined the value of repetition as a way of developing fluency. Similarly, techniques involving trial-and-error have been shown to be not as effective as those providing accurate models to follow.

## How can the four strands be used to allocate time to teaching activities?

The allocation of equal time to each of the four strands is an arbitrary decision, but it is one that has useful applications when deciding what techniques to use and how much time to give to each technique.

The justifications for the arbitrary decision of equal time are that there is plenty of research evidence and common-sense evidence for the value of each strand, and the allocation of equal time makes sure that language-focused learning is not over-emphasized (under the four strands it occupies only a quarter of the course time), that proper attention is given to fluency (one-quarter of the course time), and that the emphasis is on using the language (three-quarters of the course time). Some critics of the four strands have suggested that the proportional allocation of time to the strands should change as the learners' proficiency develops, with less time given to fluency initially (and more to language-focused learning) and more time being given to fluency later in the learning programme. I do not agree with this as fluency development should occur in even the very early stages of language learning, for example, when learning the 120-item spoken survival vocabulary (Nation & Crabbe, 1991) or when learning to read very simple books.

If the idea of equal time for each strand is accepted, it is then possible to allocate time for each technique within a particular strand. The most obvious cases of this are with extensive reading and extensive listening. Giving equal time in the meaning-focused input strand to reading and listening makes sense, although the allocation could be done on words-per-minute (equal amounts of input) which would give more time to listening than to reading. Because extensive listening and extensive reading programmes should involve fluency development, the ratio of meaning-focused input to fluency development can be calculated by seeing what proportion of the meaning-focused input strand and fluency development strand focus on each of these two skills. The result is one-eighth of the total course time on meaning-focused input for listening, and one-sixteenth of the total course time for listening fluency, so a ratio of 2:1 for input and fluency.

Similarly, we can ask the question: How much time should be spent on intensive reading? Intensive reading is part of the language-focused learning strand which should take up one-quarter of the course time. Intensive reading needs to share this time with the study of pronunciation, spelling, vocabulary, collocation, grammar, discourse, and language learning strategies. At the most, intensive reading should occupy one-quarter of the time in the language-focused learning strand, making up one-sixteenth of the total course time.

The study of word parts is worth including in a language course. It would be part of the language-focused learning strand because it involves deliberate attention to language features and would fit into the vocabulary part of the language-focused learning strand. The vocabulary part of the language-focused learning strand should occupy less than one-quarter of the time in that strand. The study of word parts needs to share time with learning from flash cards, studying multiword units, and vocabulary learning strategies. This means that the study of word parts should make up about one-quarter of the vocabulary learning part, which makes up around one-quarter of the language-focused learning strand which makes up one-quarter of the total course time. That is, one-quarter of one-quarter of one-quarter which makes up about one-sixty-fourth of the course time. In a language course of roughly four hours a week for 40 weeks of the year, that means $\frac{1}{64}$th of about 160 hours (4 times 40) which is something over two hours spread over the school year. That seems a reasonable amount of time for a focus on a small number of important word parts and some practice in cutting words into parts.

This calculation of quarters of quarters and so on should not be taken too seriously. The seeming precision of the calculation is based on several arbitrary judgements, but nonetheless it provides a rational and useful way of deciding where to spend time and how much time to spend. In each of the chapters on teaching techniques, we look at how much time should be spent using a particular technique.

In this section, we have looked at how the principle of the four strands can be used to answer questions, such as How much time should we spend studying grammar? How much time should be spent on extensive reading? How much time should be spent on vocabulary flash cards? We have also briefly looked at how the four strands can be used to answer questions, such as Is it worth giving time to blank-filling exercises to study grammar? Should we do grammar translation? Is dictation a useful activity? The answers to these questions involve looking at what strand the technique fits into, how well it meets the criteria of that strand, and what other techniques would need to be excluded to make time for this technique and whether these excluded techniques would do a better or worse job than the one replacing them. It is also worth noting that the four strands can be used to answer questions, such as How do you teach vocabulary? How do you teach grammar? How do you teach reading? Such questions are better expressed as How should vocabulary be learned? How should grammar be learned? How should reading be learned? The answer is "The four strands". Vocabulary should be learned through meaning-focused input. It should also be learned through meaning-focused output. It should also be learned through using vocabulary learning strategies, such as vocabulary flash cards, the word part strategy, and dictionary use. That is through language-focused learning. Vocabulary should also be learned through fluency development, that is through learning to make the best use of vocabulary that is already known.

### How does repetition fit into the four strands?

The principle of the four strands says that ideally the material used in the four strands should be similar, so that the language features covered are the same. This part of the four strands principle is concerned with repetition, namely coming back to the same texts or language features in different ways so that they have an opportunity to be learned and become part of the learners' receptive and productive fluent language use.

Zipf's Law describes the frequency of vocabulary and grammatical features within texts. In many ways, the learning of a language is a battle against Zipf's Law. A broad view of Zipf's Law says that in any text or collection of texts, a small number of language items will occur very frequently, accounting for a large proportion of the text. In the same texts, a large number of language items will occur very infrequently accounting for a small proportion of the text. A large number of these items will occur only once in the text(s). For the sake of simplicity, let us call these two groups of items high-frequency items and low-frequency items, although in reality there is not an abrupt separation between the two.

This frequency distribution has important implications for language learning. The high-frequency items should be learned early in a language course, although that could take a few years. We have very useful lists of high-frequency word parts, high-frequency word families, high-frequency multiword units, and high-frequency grammatical items. The major problem lies with the low-frequency items, although in courses where there are only small amounts of input, the same problem lies with the high-frequency items. The problem is that repetition is needed for learning, and in most courses low-frequency items do not get enough repetition for learning to occur. In addition, because there are many low-frequency items, they become a burden and distraction for learners who should be focusing on the high-frequency items. For example, if a learner with a vocabulary size of 2,000–3,000 words is trying to read a novel written for native speakers of English, there will be at least one unknown word in every line, and most of those unknown words will not occur again in the novel resulting in a total of at least 1,000 unknown words in whole novel (Nation, 2018). This is a heavy burden indeed, and one of the great values of graded readers is that almost every word in them is a useful word for learners at that level, and well worth learning.

Because the nature of language does not readily provide repetition to help learning, teachers need to build repetition into their courses, and meeting the same material and language features again across the four strands is a very helpful and straightforward way of doing this. This simply means integrating the four strands across the language programme by making sure they cover similar content. In addition, it is important to revisit the previous parts of the course again either for verbatim or varied repetition. We will look at this in more detail in Chapter 4.

## Commonly asked questions about the four strands

### Should each lesson contain the four strands?

No. The balance of activities across the four strands should be worked out for the whole course, not lesson by lesson. Alternatively, the balance of the strands could be worked out based on a month's lessons plus homework. There just need to be sufficient lessons to make a reliable analysis.

### Should the strands be covered in a certain order?

There is a logic to moving from declarative knowledge (language-focused learning) to procedural knowledge (meaning-focused input and meaning-focused output) to automatization (fluency development), but this is simply a practical requirement and not a requirement of the four strands. It is possible to develop fluency with memorized expressions before understanding their parts. The principle of the four strands does not dictate the order of covering the strands.

*Can an activity fit into more than one strand?*

Different parts of an activity can fit into different strands. For example, informal conversation activities involve meaning-focused input and meaning-focused output because they involve speaking and listening. Complex activities that involve various steps, such as linked skills and project work can involve a different strand at each step. Activities involving repetition, such as when learning a spoken dialogue, may begin by involving language-focused learning, then move to meaning-focused input or meaning-focused output as the learner gets more practice, and then become fluency development as the number of repetitions makes the task easier and easier. Different learners doing the same activity may be working in different strands. For example, a particular extensive reading text may be meaning-focused input for one learner but fluency development for another. The criteria for each strand usually involve the difficulty level of the task. For meaning-focused input, for example, unknown language items should make up a small proportion of the input, around 2% for vocabulary. Fluency tasks involve easy material.

*Should homework and opportunities to use the language outside class be included when working out the balance of the four strands?*

Yes. This is particularly important where English is taught as a second language, as there are many opportunities in such a situation to make use of the language. When considering learning outside the foreign language classroom, it is important not to over-estimate the opportunities for learning. Computer games may involve some use of English, but in many games, it is very limited use.

*Can the four strands be applied to learning without a teacher?*

Definitely. The Nation and Yamamoto (2012) article gives an account of using the four strands for independent learning. This article is freely available from Paul Nation's web resources page under Publications.

*Does the four strands principle apply only to language learning, or can it be applied more widely?*

The principle of the four strands says that there should be learning from observation or input, learning from doing, and learning from study and explanation, as well as the opportunity to get really good (fluent) by easy repeated practice. If we apply the four strands to learning to drive a car, meaning-focused input would involve watching someone drive and thoughtfully observing what they do. Meaning-focused output would involve doing the driving yourself, initially under the guidance of a teacher. Language-focused learning should involve studying the road code (the rules of the road), learning safety tips, learning something about the nature of cars and how they work, and getting carefully guided practice when beginning to drive and when learning difficult manoeuvres like parking, reversing, using a trailer, and changing a tyre. There should also be lots of easy driving (fluency development) on different kinds of roads so that driving well becomes to a large degree automatic.

It is useful to consider the four strands when learning something new and to consider if you are getting opportunities to learn through each of the strands. In learning some skills, like driving, it is likely that each of the strands should not get the same amount of time. This may be because that skill is an input type of skill or an output type of skill. It is always useful to consider what kind of balance of time is the best for that particular skill and why.

# 2
# A SYSTEM OF TASKS FOR LANGUAGE LEARNING

This chapter sets out a system for describing language teaching tasks which has supporting the learner as its primary consideration. The major categories in this system, of experience, shared guided and independent tasks, are deliberately based on categories used in the description of first language education. The aim of the chapter is to show how the demands of a learning task and the learners' knowledge can be brought together. In other words, it shows how teachers can help learners manage the various activities that they may meet in a language course.

Language learning, like most learning, involves learners working on tasks that require them to cope with items or skills that are new to them or that they have only partly mastered. The way that they are helped to cope with the tasks will affect the tasks and will have a major effect on the kind of learning that occurs.

Imagine that a teacher wishes to help learners improve their writing skills. To do this the teacher will get them to work on writing tasks that will take them beyond their present level of proficiency. But to make sure that the learners are successful in doing the tasks, the teacher may have to provide some help. There are several ways of doing this.

1. The teacher could think of a topic that the learners are very familiar with, such as a recent exciting event. The teacher then gets the learners talking about the event so that the ideas and the organization of the ideas are clear and so that the learners have an oral command of the language needed to describe the event. When all this previous knowledge has been stimulated, the learners are then told to put it in writing. Because the ideas, organization,

and necessary language are now all familiar to them and are at the front of their minds, the learners have only to concentrate on turning these ideas into a written form (see Kessler, Ma & Solheim [2022] for a useful investigation of the effects of topic familiarity).
2  The teacher could think of a topic and then put the learners into groups of three or four. Each group has to plan and produce one piece of writing. By helping each other, the learners in each group are able to produce a piece of writing that is better than what any of them could have produced by working alone. In this kind of activity, the learners learn from each other.
3  The teacher finds or makes a guided composition exercise, such as a series of pictures with accompanying questions and language items.
4  The teacher chooses a topic and then lets the learners get on with their writing. They may ask for help if they need it, but they are mainly left to work independently.

These four kinds of tasks are called (1) experience tasks, (2) shared tasks, (3) guided tasks, and (4) independent tasks. These tasks can focus on a range of learning goals. For simplicity, these learning goals will be described as mastering language items, ideas, skills, and text types (discourse).

Most tasks in the meaning-focused input, meaning-focused output, and fluency development strands of a course are experience tasks or independent tasks. Sometimes shared tasks are used in the meaning-focused input and meaning-focused output strands to practice communication skills and to make the activity interesting and more manageable. Guided tasks fit into the language-focused learning strand. The categories of experience, shared/independent, and guided are not mutually exclusive categories. It is possible for a task to be an experience, shared, guided task as, for example, with pair dictation where the text has been chosen to be largely within the learners' knowledge (experience), the learners work in pairs to write the dictation (shared), and the nature of dictation with the spoken input provided makes it a guided task. However, typically a task predominantly uses one kind of support as its major support.

Let us look at the kinds of tasks to see how they suggest a large number of particular tasks, and to see the features of each kind of task.

## Experience tasks

Experience tasks closely resemble the uses that learners will make of the language. They rely on top-down processing, that is, background knowledge and experience rather than building up knowledge of the text by piece-by-piece study of the items that make it up. The gap between the known and the unknown is reduced by maximizing the known parts of the task. Then learners are given large quantities of practice with the unknown part. An essential feature is that the help with the task occurs before learners do the task. This help can be of several kinds. For example, before the learners do a task, the teacher can help them recall any previous learning that will make the task easier. Alternatively, the teacher can pre-teach language items, concepts, etc., which will be needed in the task, or can simplify aspects of the task so that the learner is not overloaded with difficulties. Thus, the learner is able to do the task in a reasonably fluent and trouble-free way without having to continually seek help. For example, in a reading task, learners can work with known content written in familiar language with a known text structure. In this task, the only unfamiliar part is the reading skills required by the task. This kind of task is a very common one in language learning. It includes reading graded readers, speed reading (Quinn & Nation, 1974), and various reading exercises like scanning, answering comprehension questions, and doing cloze exercises. In all of these, the focus is on improving reading skills while other factors are held within the learners' previous experience.

However, the focus could be on a different aspect of the task. Table 2.1 lists the four areas of focus (the learning goals) with several examples.

**TABLE 2.1** Experience tasks in the four skills

| Area of focus | Listening | Speaking | Reading | Writing |
|---|---|---|---|---|
| Language | Listen to a description of a familiar ceremony or celebration | Present an item read in a newspaper | Read a familiar folk story written in the new language | Interview a native speaker and write it up |
| Ideas | Listen to classmates give talks | Report on a new piece of learning | Learners read texts they wrote for each other | Write a description of an experiment in your own words |
| Skills | Read and then listen / Dictation of learners' own stories | Repeat the same talk to different listeners / Read aloud | Do an experiment then read about it | Record yourself telling a story and then write it |
| Text | Listen to the news | Give a prepared speech | Read a known story written as a newspaper article | Write a formal report of an experiment |

Let us look at four of these tasks in Table 2.1 in more detail.

1. When learners listen to a description of a familiar ceremony or celebration, such as a wedding from their own culture or a religious celebration, all the ideas that they hear will be familiar to them. Similarly, the organization of the description (text type) is familiar. The speaker would need to be careful to present the material at an acceptable rate for the listeners. Because of the familiar content, familiar organization of ideas and controlled presentation, the learners would be able to cope with new vocabulary and constructions. The familiar features provide a helpful context for dealing with new language items.
2. When learners report on a new piece of learning, they are able to use their own words, organize the material in a way that suits them, and be in control of the presentation. This allows them to use their speaking to become more familiar and confident with the new ideas they are dealing with. These reports can be based on practical work done in class, learning from others in the class (especially multicultural classes) and through discussion, and learning from reading.
3. Doing an experiment and discussing it while doing it make the ideas and language familiar. If the written account of the experiment follows the steps of the experiment, then only the reading skills will be the area of focus while reading an account of that kind of experiment.
4. If the learners write about one of their own experiences in the form of a newspaper report, they are writing about familiar ideas in their own words and at their own speed. The unusual format of newspaper articles is the aspect outside their experience.

Table 2.2 shows how experience-based activities can have a range of focuses.

Good experience tasks have the following characteristics. (1) The learners receive a large quantity of experience in the aspect that is focused on. (2) Other aspects of the task are kept well within the learners' present proficiency. (3) The task closely resembles the kind of task that learners might meet outside the classroom. That is, it does not include specially constructed exercises to make the task easier, although the preparation for the task is particularly directed at making the task easier by using the learners' previous experience.

Language learning through experience tasks is largely incidental. The model of learning corresponds to Krashen's input theory where the necessary conditions for learning require the learners to understand and be interested in understanding messages which contain some unfamiliar items which can be understood from context. Context in experience tasks is provided by the three features of the task which are kept within the learners' previous experience. Experience tasks also include those involving output.

TABLE 2.2  Examples of control and focus in experience tasks in listening

| Activity | Language | Ideas | Skill | Text type |
|---|---|---|---|---|
| Dictation of learners' own stories | The language items come from the learners | The learners who produce the stories are told to use ones that are familiar to their classmates | The listening skill is the area of focus | The text type is produced by the learners and so is familiar to them |
| Listening to the news | The teacher may need to produce a language-controlled version of the news | The ideas in the news are likely to be familiar to learners. If they are not, some previous discussion or reading may be necessary | The material would have to be presented at a manageable rate with a familiar pronunciation | The text type is the area of focus. Learners have to deal with the rather unusual way in which the information is arranged |

## Shared tasks

Shared tasks involve learners working together in a supportive way. In this way the learners as a group model the language use that they aim to achieve as individuals. For example, one shared reading activity involves each learner in the group having a different job to do (Palincsar & Brown, 1986). These jobs include predicting what will come next in the text, summarizing, question generating, and clarifying. Other well-known shared tasks include group composition, information gap activities, and ranking exercises. Shared tasks can be used over the four language skills. The four types of sharing are *co-operating* where learners have equal access to the same information, *combining* or *split information* where each learner has unique information which all the others in the group need to complete a task, *superior-inferior* where one learner has all the information that the others need, and *individual* where each learner does an individual performance for the group. Chapter 3 describes these kinds of group work in more detail. It is also possible to have the same range of learning goals in shared tasks as in experience tasks, namely language, ideas, skills, and text type.

Good shared tasks have the following characteristics. (1) Learners work together in pairs or groups to help each other on the task. (2) The organization of the tasks ensures that the various features of group work are properly matched, i.e., the spread of information amongst the members of the group, the seating arrangement of the group, the social relationships amongst the group members, the type of outcome, and the learning goal (see Chapter 3).

## Guided tasks

Guided tasks involve learners doing exercises or using support materials which are often not like activities or support which are present in normal language use. Guided tasks differ from experience tasks in that guided tasks involve specially constructed exercises that are used *during* the task. When experience tasks involve specially constructed exercises, the help occurs *before* the task begins. The purpose of this guidance is to help use unfamiliar items in ways that provide the greatest chance of success. Typically, such exercises require the learners to repeat models, complete sentences or texts, transform sentences, or put items in the correct order. A detailed description of such activities can be found in Nation (1976). A danger in the use of guided tasks is that they become an end in their own right instead of being a way to help in the normal use of language (Table 2.3).

A good guided task has the following characteristics: (1) It provides help with unfamiliar items in the material. (2) It enables learners to do the task with a minimum of errors.

Guided tasks encourage deliberate learning. They generally isolate language items, subskills, or text features for learners to focus on, rather than focusing on the communication of messages. Whereas experience tasks encourage top-down processing, guided tasks encourage bottom-up processing.

**TABLE 2.3** Guided tasks for listening activities

| Guided activity | Listening activity |
| --- | --- |
| Distinguishing | Learners read a written version of the talk and note the differences |
| Identification | While listening to a talk, learners fill in an information transfer diagram |
| Completion | While listening, learners fill in the blanks in an incomplete summary of the talk |
| Ordering | The learners have a set of written statements that summarize the talk. While listening they put the statements in order |
| Following instructions | The learners have a set of instructions that guide them in what to notice and take notes on in the talk |
| Answering questions | The learners have a list of questions that they answer while they listen to the talk |
| Classifying | The learners have a set of statements, items, or situations that they sort into given groups while they listen |

## Independent tasks

Independent tasks require the learners to work alone without any planned help. Learners can work successfully on independent tasks when they have developed some proficiency in the language and when they have control of helpful strategies. These strategies can develop from experience, shared, or guided tasks. Let us look at learners faced with a difficult independent reading task, such as reading part of a science text.

1 The learners could read the text several times. During each rereading, the learners have the experience gained from the previous readings. (experience)
2 The learners could ask the teacher or classmates for help when they need it. (shared)
3 The learners could guide their reading of the text by asking themselves questions, or by using a notetaking or information transfer strategy. (guided)

A good independent task has the following features. (1) It provides a reasonable challenge, that is, it has some difficulty but the learners can see that with effort they can do it. (2) It is a task that learners are likely to face outside the classroom.

The difference between an experience and independent task lies in the control and preparation that goes into an experience task. Experience tasks are planned so that learners are faced with only one aspect of the task that is outside their previous experience. Independent tasks do not involve this degree of control and learners may be faced with several kinds of difficulty in the same task.

## Using the system

The aim in describing this system of learning tasks is to make teachers aware of the range of possible approaches to dealing with the gap between the learners' knowledge and the knowledge required to do a task, and to make them aware of the very large number of activities that can be made to help learners. When teachers are able to think of a variety of ways of dealing with a problem, they can then choose the ones that will work best in their class and for their learners. Let us now apply the system.

Your learners need to read a text about land use in the Amazon basin. For several reasons, this text will be difficult for them. There are new concepts to learn, there is new vocabulary, and the text is written in a rather academic way. What can the teacher do to help the learners with this task?

The first step is to think of whether an experience approach is feasible. Can the teacher bring the language, ideas, needed reading skills, or text organization within the experience of the learners? For example, is it possible to bring the language within the learners' proficiency by pre-teaching vocabulary or discussing the topic before going on to the reading? Is it possible to bring the ideas within the learners' experience by getting them to collect pictures and short articles about the Amazon basin? Can the way the text is organized be outlined and explained to the learners? Can the text be simplified so that it contains largely known vocabulary? If these things are not possible or if more help is needed, then the teacher should look at making the reading a shared task.

The reading could be made into a shared task in several ways. The text could be divided up with each learner having a part of the text to read and explain to the others. Alternatively, pairs of learners could read and discuss the text together section by section. If this is not possible or further help is needed, guided help can be given.

Some of the simpler guided tasks could involve answering a detailed set of questions based on the text, completing a set of statements that summarize the text, filling in an information transfer grid based on a topic type analysis of the text (Franken, 1987), or labelling a diagrammatic representation of the text.

The distinctions made here between experience, shared and guided tasks are for ease of description. Clearly, experience or guided tasks can be done in small groups as shared tasks, just as experience tasks may have some guided elements.

Let us now look more closely at experience tasks. It could be argued that experience tasks are the most important kinds of language learning tasks because they are the most common means of learning from meaning-focused input and meaning-focused output, and they are essential for fluency development across the four skills of listening, speaking, reading, and writing.

## The classic experience task

Let us begin by looking at the classic example of an experience task that is involved in the experience approach to reading with young learners as described by Sylvia Ashton-Warner (1963) in relation to what was largely a first language learning environment.

The reading class begins with the young children each drawing a picture of something that happened to them during the weekend. As each learner completes their picture, they come to the teacher to describe what is happening in it. The teacher listens carefully to the learner's description and then, in clear teacherly printing, writes *exactly* what the learner said underneath the picture. This then becomes the learner's reading text for the day. The learner then takes the picture away and works on reading the written text. The learner reads it to themselves, and then to other learners, and then to parents and family. Day by day these illustrated, highly meaningful texts are gathered together to make the child's personalized reading book.

This reading activity is an experience task because most of the knowledge needed to do the task is already within the learner's experience. The language needed to do the task comes from the learner (it is their story), the ideas in the reading text come from the learner, and the organization of the text comes from the learner. The only new, partly unknown features in the task are the learning goals of the task. They are the recognition of the written form of the story and turning that written form into ideas by reading. This important learning goal of learning to read is brought within the learners' capability by the rest of the aspects of the task being well within their previous experience. Imagine the difficulties the beginning learner would face if the language, ideas, and text organization were all unfamiliar.

The essence of an experience task then is that most of the knowledge and skill needed to do the task is already within the learners' experience. When learners do experience tasks, to an outsider, they seem to perform quite fluently without any obvious support. What the outsider might not realize is that the support has occurred before the task is done.

## Making experience tasks

There are two major ways of making experience tasks – (1) by bringing the task to the learner, or (2) by bringing the learner to the task.

### *Bringing the task to the learner*

In the example given above, the task is largely brought within the learner's present knowledge. That is, the reading task uses language that the learner already knows, uses ideas the learner already knows, and uses a text structure the learner already knows. In second or foreign language learning, the most obvious experience task of this type is the use of graded readers for extensive reading. Graded reader series like Oxford Bookworms, Cambridge English Readers, Penguin Readers, the Foundations Reading Library from Thomson ELT, and the Heinemann English Readers are made up of books especially written within a controlled vocabulary and a controlled set of grammatical structures. This means that learners can choose books to read that contain vocabulary and grammatical structures that are completely or largely within their previous experience. They can then focus on the learning goal of reading more fluently or of picking up the few vocabulary and grammatical items that are outside their experience. The availability of graded readers at a variety of proficiency levels means that learners can read largely within their previous language experience at most levels of proficiency. This is very important in a language course for several reasons. Firstly, it is through such experience tasks that most of the kind of learning needed for normal language use occurs. This learning adds to implicit knowledge which is the knowledge needed for unmonitored use of the language (Ellis, 2005). Secondly, learners can engage in authentic receptive language use with such texts. They can experience the same kinds of understanding, feelings, and reactions that a native speaker would have while reading. These include comprehension, enjoyment (or boredom if it is not a good story), and some kind of evaluative reaction to the story. That is, they can have an authentic reading experience. Thirdly, reading at the right level of difficulty can result in successful reading and can result in the strong motivation that can come from success. Finally, reading at the right levels and near a native speaker's reading speed can result in large quantities of language input. The greater the language input, the greater the possible language learning.

There are several ways of bringing the level of the task to the learners' present level of proficiency. One way is to use the learners' output as a source of input. This is the method used in Sylvia Ashton-Warner's experience approach to reading. It is also possible to use other learners' output as a source of input for others. This happens when learners read other learners' stories. Another way is for the teacher or course designer to deliberately control the level of the task as in graded readers. This can also be done through the careful selection and sequencing of material (Ghadirian, 2002).

### Bringing the learner to the task

The second major way of setting up an experience task is to bring the learner to the task. That is, to provide the learner with knowledge and experience *before* the task so that the task will then be within their experience. There are two ways of doing this, through pre-teaching or some form of pre-teaching, and through reminding the learners of the relevant ideas that they already know and helping them organize these in a useful way, as in semantic mapping.

When checking an experience task, it is useful to ask these two questions.

1  What is the learning goal of the task?
2  Are the three other aspects of the task within the learners' experience?

Table 2.4 shows how various aspects of a reading task can be brought within the learners' experience, either through control which brings the task to the learner, or through recall and pre-teaching which brings the learner to the task. Table 2.4 summarizes the ways of making experience tasks with a focus on reading. The same table can be made for the skills of listening, speaking, and writing.

In Table 2.4 the suggestions are organized under the goals of Language, Ideas, Skills, and Text. The suggestions in the section on control all deal with ways in which the text can be written and adapted. The suggestions in the other two sections, recall and pre-teaching, describe how the learners can be prepared for the text. All of the suggested activities occur *before* the learners read the text, so that the actual reading of the text will become an experience task.

A system of tasks for language learning  27

**TABLE 2.4** Experience tasks involving reading

| Ways of bringing the task within the learners' experience | Goals | Typical procedures for reading activities |
|---|---|---|
| *Bringing the task to the learner:* Control through selection or simplification | L | A reading text is written within a controlled vocabulary and a controlled list of structures |
|  | I | Learners describe their experience to the teacher who writes it to become the learners' reading texts |
|  | S | The learners read texts which are closely based on the texts they read in their first language |
|  | T | The teacher writes informative science texts as stories or personal accounts |
| *Bringing the learner to the task:* Recall or sharing of personal experience | L | The learners work together to label diagrams and pictures based on the text they will read |
|  | I | The learners are asked to predict what will occur in a text after they know the topic of the text |
|  | S | The learners discuss how they take notes and summarize when they read in their first language |
|  | T | The learners share their predictions of which kinds of information will occur in what order in the text |
| *Bringing the learner to the task:* Pre-teaching | L | The teacher explains vocabulary that will occur in the reading text |
|  | I | The learners collect and display pictures and articles relating to the topic of the text |
|  | S | The learners do guided exercises or first language reading activities to develop the needed reading skills |
|  | T | The learners are helped with a discourse analysis of a text of the same topic type as the text they will read |

Table 2.4 focuses on a receptive task, reading. Table 2.5 shows how a productive task, speaking, can be brought within the experience of the learners.

Although the suggestions in Table 2.5 are organized under control, recall and pre-teaching, it is possible to combine suggestions from different categories. For example, the teacher can choose a topic that the learners know a lot about from first language experience, such as how weddings are celebrated in their country.

**TABLE 2.5** Experience tasks involving speaking

| Ways of bringing the task within the learners' experience | Goals | Typical procedures for speaking activities |
|---|---|---|
| Control through selection or simplification | L | A topic is chosen that allows the learners to use vocabulary and structures they already know |
| | I | A topic is chosen that the learners know a lot about from first language experience |
| | S | The learners are not put under time pressure during the talk |
| | T | The task involves kinds of speaking, such as telling stories, that are already familiar from first language use |
| Recall or sharing of personal experience | L | The teacher helps the learners build up a semantic map around the topic, based on useful vocabulary and phrases |
| | I | The learners work in groups to list all the things they know about the topic |
| | S | The learners recall relevant sentences and collocations they have used before |
| | T | The learners work in groups to order the points they will talk about |
| Pre-teaching | L | The learners write about the topic before they talk about it. The teacher provides needed vocabulary for the writing |
| | I | The learners go on a visit to some place related to the topic they will talk about |
| | S | The learners do a 4/3/2 activity on the topic with the 2-minute talk being the experience task, and the 4- and 3-minute talks are a kind of pre-teaching |
| | T | The learners practice supporting main points with examples |

Then, the class builds up a semantic map of the relevant second language vocabulary. Finally, they perform a 4/3/2 activity in pairs on the topic. The two-minute talk is the experience task. All the rest, the semantic mapping (a shared task), and the four-minute and three-minute speaking (shared tasks) are preparation for the two-minute experience task.

Let us now look at research on experience tasks and vocabulary learning.

## Vocabulary control

The research on vocabulary density for second language learners (Hu & Nation, 2000; Schmitt, Jiang & Grabe, 2011) and first language learners (Carver, 1994) suggests that in order for learners to gain adequate comprehension of a text, no more than 1–2% of the running words (tokens) in a text should be outside their present knowledge. This assumes that proper nouns are considered as known items or at least items that do not require much or any previous knowledge. This is an unknown word density of around one unknown word in every 50 running words and fits with Michael West's (1955, p. 21) suggestion based on experience of writing and using graded readers for learners of English as a foreign language.

One unknown word in 50 still means that there is one unknown word in every five ten-word lines and six unknown words on every 300-word page. Thus, even with the vocabulary control typical of graded readers, there can still be a substantial unknown vocabulary load (Nation & Wang, 1999).

It has been suggested that using books written for young native speakers of English could reduce the unknown vocabulary load. Elley and Mangubhai (1981), for example, used children's books written for native speakers in their book flood in rural Fiji. Cho and Krashen (1993) recommend the Sweet Valley series, written for young native speakers, as texts for extensive reading programmes for non-native speakers. However, research by Macalister and Webb (2019) suggest that children's literature also requires quite a large vocabulary knowledge, although McQuillan (2019) notes that careful selection of children's books can yield more accessible texts. Young native speakers beginning school already have a vocabulary of several thousand words and the books written for them make use of a correspondingly rich vocabulary (Nation, 1997). The attractive presentation of such books and their interesting stories may help sustain interest and motivation and encourage the effort to read, but the amount non-native learners could read would be greatly reduced by the vocabulary load of such difficult texts.

The ideal for non-native-speaking learners of English is that there are attractive, engaging texts written in a controlled vocabulary that takes account of their initially low levels of vocabulary knowledge when they begin reading. There are many books like these, and with initiatives to encourage the production of high-quality texts, such as the Extensive Reading Foundation awards, the number should grow.

For learners of English with a vocabulary size over 2,000 words, the careful sequencing of texts written for native speakers may be a feasible way of making listening and reading become experience tasks.

The major resource, however, for learners of English at elementary and intermediate levels has to be text written within a controlled vocabulary. Without this, there can be few if any experience tasks in a foreign language programme.

## Pre-teaching vocabulary

The research on pre-teaching vocabulary shows that for pre-teaching to have an effect on comprehension, each pre-taught word has to get substantial attention (Graves, 1986), what some call "rich instruction". Rich instruction involves spending several minutes teaching a word, drawing attention to several aspects of what is involved in knowing a word (its spoken and written forms, its word parts, its meaning, its grammar, and its collocations). This is time-consuming and in effect only a few words can get this kind of attention before learners read a text. Nonetheless, for a few important topic-related words, pre-teaching may be a useful option.

## Stimulating previous knowledge

There has been very interesting research on first language readers by Stahl and his colleagues to see the relative effects on comprehension of vocabulary knowledge and learners' background knowledge of the topic of the text (Stahl, Hare, Sinatra & Gregory, 1991; Stahl, Jacobson, Davis & Davis, 1989). Their findings have been that vocabulary knowledge and topic knowledge have different effects. Vocabulary knowledge increases the comprehension of sentence and proposition level detail (the microstructure), while topic knowledge affects global comprehension of the text (the macrostructure) including seeing an organization behind the facts in the text.

Because vocabulary knowledge and topic knowledge have different effects, one is not a satisfactory compensation for lack of the other. This is supported by Laufer's (1992) findings with foreign language learners.

For learners of English as a second or foreign language, vocabulary knowledge is clearly a dominating factor in determining whether a task will be an experience task or not. Background knowledge cannot substitute for lack of vocabulary knowledge, and pre-teaching is limited in the number of words that can be satisfactorily covered in a reasonable amount of time. It is thus essential to make use of controlled material if a course is to have a suitable number of the experience tasks that are needed for developing proficiency through meaning-focused input, meaning-focused output, and fluency development.

At the beginning of each chapter, from Chapter 5 on, when a technique is introduced, part of the description of the technique will involve saying whether it is an experience, shared or guided technique. This description is not particularly revealing, because all meaning-focused input, meaning-focused output, and fluency development techniques should be experience tasks, because the material needs to be at the right level for the learners.

The main reason for understanding the four kinds of tasks is so that the teacher can adjust tasks so that the learners are able to successfully complete them.

# 3
# GROUP WORK AND LANGUAGE LEARNING

In Chapter 2, we looked at a range of tasks for language learning, giving special attention to experience tasks. In this chapter, we focus on shared tasks, or in other words, group work. There are several group work techniques among those focused on in this book. While most involve listening and speaking, there are reading and writing activities that can be made easier and more engaging through the use of group work. The discussion of group work in this chapter involves what McCarthy et al. (2022) would call task groups, as opposed to group work with psychological goals.

Like all learning activities, group work is more likely to go well if it is properly planned. Planning requires an understanding of the principle which lies behind successful group work.

## The principle of group work

Several factors work together to result in group work where *everyone* involved is interested, active, and engaged. If these factors agree with each other, then group work is likely to be successful. If they are not in agreement, group work is likely to be unsuccessful. The five factors are (1) the learning goals of group work, (2) the task, (3) the way information is distributed, (4) the seating arrangement of the members of the group, and (5) the social relationships between the members of the group.

Let us look first at the learning goals of group work before seeing how the factors work together.

DOI: 10.4324/9781003496151-4

## The goals of group work

The following description of the goals of group work focuses on the spoken use of language. There are several reasons for this focus. Firstly, group work is most commonly used to get learners talking to each other. Secondly, much research on group work in language learning has studied spoken activity partly because this is the most easily observed and recorded. Thirdly, most teachers use speaking activities in unprincipled ways. One of the aims of this chapter is to suggest how such activities can be used and adapted to achieve goals in language learning classes.

Group work can help learning in the following ways.

1. Negotiation of input: Group work provides an opportunity for learners to get exposure to language that they can understand (negotiate comprehensible input) and which contains unknown items for them to learn. There has been considerable research on the possible sources of this input and the processes of negotiation (Long & Porter, 1985), with the general recommendation that group work properly handled is one of the most valuable sources.
2. New language items: Group work gives learners exposure to a range of language items and language functions. This will sometimes require pre-teaching of the needed language items. Group work provides more opportunities for the use of the new items compared to the opportunities in teacher-led classes. Group work may also improve the quality of these opportunities in terms of individualization, motivation, depth of processing, and affective climate.
3. Fluency: Group work allows learners to develop fluency in the use of language features that they have already learned (Davies, 1982). The arguments supporting group work for learning new items also apply to developing proficiency in the use of these items.
4. Communication strategies: Group work gives learners the opportunity to learn communication strategies. These strategies include negotiation strategies to control input (seeking clarification, seeking confirmation, checking comprehension, repetition), strategies to keep a conversation going (Holmes & Brown, 1976; Nation, 1980), strategies to make up for a lack of language items or a lack of fluency in the use of such items (Tarone, 1981) and strategies for managing long turns in speaking (Brown et al., 1984).
5. Content: Particularly where English is taught through the curriculum, a goal of group work may be the mastery of the content of the curriculum subject the learners are studying. For example, a communicative task based on the water cycle may have as one of its goals the learning of the processes involved in the water cycle and the development of an awareness of how the water cycle affects our lives. In addition, the teacher may expect the learners to achieve one or more of the language learning goals listed above.

## Types of group work

A useful way of classifying group work activities is to look at the distribution of the information needed to do the activity. In many group work activities, learners have equal access to the same material or information and co-operate to do the task. In the following discussion, this is called the co-operating arrangement. In the superior-inferior arrangement, one member of the group has information that all the others need. In the split information arrangement, each learner has a different piece of information that all the others need. In the individual arrangement, each learner has access to the same information but must perform or deal with a different part of it. These four different types of group work achieve different learning goals, are best suited to different kinds of tasks, require particular kinds of seating arrangement, and draw on or encourage different kinds of social relationships. In order for group work to be successful, each type of group work must have its most suitable choice of these other factors. Let us now look at each type in turn to see how the principle of group work applies.

### *The split information arrangement*

The split information arrangement has been called the combining arrangement (Nation, 1977) and two-way tasks (Long & Porter, 1985). The split information arrangement is a very effective arrangement for group work, because it ensures interest and participation. It may be noticed that ways of making other group work arrangements more effective often involve adding an element of split information. The essential feature of a split information arrangement is that each learner has unique, essential information. This means that each learner in a group has a piece of information that the others do not have, and each piece of information is needed to complete the task. Here is an example involving a group of three learners.

Each learner has a map of an island. However, on one learner's map only some of the towns are named and only some of the roads are indicated. On the second learner's map, some of the other towns are named, the railway system is given, and the airport is shown. On the third learner's map the remaining roads and towns are shown, the central mountain is named, and the forest is indicated. Each learner's map is, therefore, incomplete, and each learner has information that the other two do not have. By combining this information each learner can make a complete map. They do this by keeping their map hidden from the others and by describing what is on their map for the others to draw on theirs. It helps if two or three pieces of information are the same on all of the maps, as this helps the learners use common reference points.

The best seating arrangement of the members of the group during this activity supports the essential features of the arrangement. Each learner needs to have equal access to the other learners to get the essential information while preserving the uniqueness of their own information. This means that when working in pairs, the learners should face each other, because that allows good communication while hiding their written or pictorial information. When working in a group, it is best if the learners sit in a circle so that each learner is an equal distance from any other learner. Equal access to each other is the most important element in the seating arrangement of split information arrangement groups.

The social relationship amongst the members of a split information group needs to be one of equality. For this reason, it is usually unwise for the teacher to become a member of a group, unless the learners are prepared to treat the teacher as an equal and the teacher is willing to take a non-dominant role. Some teachers find this difficult to do. In addition, various status relationships among learners may upset the activity. Research by Philips (1972) with the Warm Springs Indians found that the way in which the local community's group activities were organized had a strong effect on learners' participation in classroom activities. Just as social relationships can affect the group activity, participation in the group activity can have effects on the social relationships of learners. Aronson et al. (1975) and Lucker, Rosenfield, Sikes and Aronson (1976) found that working in split information arrangements increased the liking that members of the group had for each other and resulted in a relationship of equality.

Research on the split information arrangement as a means of achieving learning goals has focused on acquiring language through negotiating comprehensible input (Doughty & Pica, 1986; Long & Porter, 1985, p. 222) and mastering content (Lucker, Rosenfield, Sikes & Aronson, 1976). Long and Porter call split information arrangement activities "two-way tasks" to distinguish them from superior-inferior activities ("one-way tasks"). This research indicates a superiority for split information arrangement activities over teacher-fronted activities and "one-way tasks". Long and Porter's excellent article goes into this in detail.

The most suitable tasks for split information arrangement group work include:

1 completion, e.g., completing a picture by exchanging information, completing a story by pooling ideas.
2 providing directions, e.g., describing a picture for someone to draw, telling someone how to make something.
3 matching, classifying, distinguishing, e.g., deciding if your partner's drawing is the same as yours, arranging pictures in the same order as your partner's unseen pictures (Nation, 1977).
4 ordering, e.g., putting the sentences or pictures of a story in order (Gibson, 1975).

Split information arrangement activities do not usually present problems for the teacher, and group size is not a restricting factor. Strip story exercises

(Gibson, 1975) involving the ordering of pictures or sentences can be done with groups of 15 or more, as long as learners can sit in a large circle or move about to have easy access to each other. One difficulty that may occur is maintaining the uniqueness of each learner's information. This can be done by getting learners to memorize their information at the beginning of the task, or in pair work, setting up a physical barrier between learners. This physical barrier may be a cardboard screen about 30 cm high. Should split information groups be made up of learners with mixed proficiency or with roughly similar proficiency? In assessing the spread of participation in the activity, Nation (1985) found that learners in a homogeneous, low-proficiency group had more equal spoken participation than learners in mixed groups. Varonis and Gass (1983, reported in Long & Porter, 1985) found that most negotiation of meaning occurred when learners were of different language backgrounds and of different proficiency levels. Clearly, different goals will require different group membership.

## *The co-operating arrangement*

The co-operating arrangement is the most common kind of group work. Its essential feature is that all learners have equal access to the same information and have equal access to each other's view of it. This is because the purpose of a co-operating activity is for learners to share their understanding of the solutions to the task or of the material involved. Here is an example.

The learners are shown a picture and have several questions to answer about it, such as

> If you had to write a one-word title for this picture, what would it be?
> What happened before the event in this picture?
> What are the characters' feelings towards each other?

The learners discuss their answers to the questions. Maley, Duff, and Grellet's (1980) book *The Mind's Eye* consists of many activities like this. George Jacobs has done a lot of work implementing co-operative learning in English language teaching (Jacobs, Power & Loh., 2002; McCafferty, Jacobs & DaSilva Iddings, 2006).

The best seating arrangement for the members of the group is to sit in a horseshoe with the material in the open end of the horseshoe, or in a circle if there is no material to look at. Similarly, in a pair, the learners should sit facing the same direction with the material in front of them. As much as possible, all the learners in a group should be the same distance from the material and the same distance from each other. If the information is a text or a picture, then it is best not to give each learner a copy, because this would encourage individual rather than co-operative activity.

Co-operating requires some degree of equality between learners, particularly a rough equality of skill. Research shows that group performance is often inferior to the best individual's performance, if there is an exceptional individual in the group (Hill, 1982). Thus, for co-operating activities, it is best to put exceptional learners in one group rather than to spread them across groups The considerable amount of research on co-operating activities with native speakers (Hill, 1982; Johnson et al., 1981; Sharan, 1980; Slavin, 1980) shows the good effects that such work has on improving social relationships among learners, including learners from different ethnic backgrounds.

The most suitable tasks for co-operating arrangement group work include:

1 ranking, ordering, choosing, e.g., choosing the best candidate for a job, ranking a list of items needed for survival, or a list of actions open to you.
2 finding implications, causes or uses, e.g., brainstorming the uses of a paperclip on a desert island, interpreting a picture.
3 solving problems, e.g., answering *Dear Abby* letters, solving logical puzzles, simulations.
4 producing material, e.g., making a radio programme, preparing for a debate or play.

The major problem with co-operating arrangements is encouraging each learner to play an active part in the group. Because all learners have equal access to the same information, no individual is essential to the activity as occurs in the split information arrangement. Various strategies have been used to deal with non-participation. One way is to introduce elements of the split information arrangement by giving each learner in the group a different job to do. For example, one acts as the secretary to keep a record of decisions. One has the job of encouraging each learner to offer an opinion. One controls the various steps in the discussion procedure. Another way is to have a reward structure which gives the group responsibility for each individual's learning by rewarding the winning group rather than any individual in the group (Bejarano, 1987). A third way to deal with non-participation is to change group size or the people in the groups to provide the optimum climate in each group for participation to occur.

## *The superior-inferior arrangement*

The superior-inferior arrangement in group work is a parallel to traditional class teaching. The essential feature of the arrangement is that one or more learners have all the information that the others in the group need. Here are two examples.

> One learner has a complete text. The other learners have some important words from the text. By asking yes/no questions using those words as clues, the learners try to reconstruct the text.

One learner has a dictation text which she dictates to the others in the group. They write the dictation.

The best seating arrangement of the members of the group is with the person in the superior position facing the others. All the others should be an equal distance from the person with the information. Notice that this arrangement has parallels with the split information arrangement. The split information arrangement may be viewed as a set of superior-inferior arrangements with every learner in the group having the chance to be in the superior position, that is, having information that others need and do not have.

The social relationship amongst the members of a superior-inferior group is one of inequality. The person with the information is in a superior position. This person may gain status from being in this position or may need to be a person with such status.

Research on peer teaching with native speakers (Allen, 1976) shows that the superior-inferior arrangement can result in a lot of useful learning, particularly in pair work.

The most suitable tasks for superior-inferior group work include:

1 data gathering, e.g., interviews, questioning (Nation, 1980).
2 providing directions, e.g., telling how to get to a place on the map, providing instructions about how to arrange parts to make a complete item.
3 completion.

## The individual arrangement

In the individual group work arrangement, each learner has the same information but must perform individually with a part of that information. The *Say it!* activity is a good example of this.

In the *Say it!* activity, all the learners in a group can see a grid. Each section of the grid has a different task. The learners take turns to name a section of the grid, e.g., B1 and the next learner in the group has to carry out the task. The exercise is based on an article called "The world of a tree" (*NZ School Journal*, 1, 1, 1988). The learners would read it before doing the exercise.

|   | 1 | 2 | 3 |
|---|---|---|---|
| A | What animals help the tree? | What animals hurt the tree? | What animals are helped by the tree? |
| B | Explain why the tree is like a small world. | Explain what a twig is. | Name five parts of a tree. |
| C | What is the biggest tree near your home? | How do trees help us? | What is your favourite part of a tree? Why? |

Notice that unlike the superior-inferior arrangement and split information arrangement, no learner has information that the others do not have. Unlike the co-operating arrangement, each learner makes an individual performance which is not necessarily helped by the others in the group. The major effects of the individual arrangement are to increase the time each learner can spend on a task, and to ensure that each learner participates.

The learners in the group need to have equal access to the material and be in sight of each other. Sitting in a circle is usually the most convenient.

The most suitable tasks for the individual arrangement in group work include:

1 solving problems, e.g., role play activities where each individual must perform in a certain way.
2 repetition, e.g., a chain story where learners retell the story to each other and see the changes that occur in retelling.
3 completion, e.g., each learner has to add a part to complete a story.

## Applying the principle

Teachers sometimes feel uncertain about aspects of group work. Typical questions are "How many people should there be in a group?", "Is it best to have learners of mixed proficiency or equal proficiency in a group?", "What sort of material do I need to prepare for group work?" The answers to these questions all depend on the principle of group work, that is, the five features must all be in agreement with each other. For example, the size of a group depends on the particular goal of group work, the type of information distribution which most suits the goal and the seating arrangement which suits the information distribution. If the learning goal is to learn through negotiation of input, then a split information arrangement distribution of information is most suitable, and learners should work in pairs or groups of four or less, with learners sitting near and facing each other.

Similarly, the question of mixed or equal proficiency is best answered by applying the principle. If the goal of learning is to master new language items, a superior-inferior arrangement with a more proficient learner in the superior position would be a useful choice. If, however, the goal is to develop fluency, groups could be made up of learners of equal proficiency in a co-operating arrangement.

If the principle is not applied, then group work will probably not go smoothly. For example, a co-operating arrangement with four or more learners sitting in a row is unlikely to result in equal participation. Similarly, a group with two high-proficiency and two low-proficiency learners is unlikely to result in equal participation in a co-operating task.

Research on group work provides useful guidelines in applying the principle. Experience and experimentation in the classroom are equally valuable.

# 4
# THE PRINCIPLES OF LEARNING

The aim of teaching techniques is to provide opportunities for learning. In order for learning to occur, there needs to be a focus on what is to be learned, sufficient quantity of attention, and at least a minimal quality of attention. The effectiveness of a teaching technique depends on how well these three aspects of attention are put into practice. These three aspects of attention are all affected by motivation. See Nation (2024b) for further discussion of these principles.

### The principles of learning

Motivation and these three aspects of attention can be understood more clearly if they are expressed as principles of learning.

#### *Motivation principles (Engagement)*

For learning to occur, there needs to be a willingness to focus on what needs to be learned, and to give it quantity and quality of attention.

1 Motivation: The degree of engagement with the task affects the likelihood of learning occurring.
2 Self-efficacy: Our confidence in our own skills of learning affects our success in learning.

## Focus principles (Usefulness)

Learning requires giving attention to what needs to be learned.

3 Focus: We learn what we focus on, and in addition, our learning is more useful if it closely resembles the use that we need to make of what we learn (transfer-appropriate). In order for incidental learning activities to have a strong effect on learning, it may be necessary to accompany them with some deliberate focus on language features.
4 Accuracy: Our learning is more efficient if the information we are focusing on is complete, accurate, and comprehensible.

## Quantity principles (Amount)

The greater and longer the attention, the stronger the learning.

5 Repetition: The more repetitions, the stronger the learning.
6 Time-on-task: Quantity of attention is increased by desirable difficulty, also called the deficient processing account. Spacing, expanding spacing, the lag effect (greater spacing rather than shorter spacing), retrieval, deliberate attention, testing (rather than re-studying), multiple-choice glosses, interleaving, production, form recall versus meaning recall, and variation ensure a greater amount of attention and a better quality of attention resulting in better long-term retention.

## Quality principles (Connections)

Elaboration and analysis increase and strengthen connections between the item to be learned and other knowledge making it easier to access the item. Note the overlap between quantity and quality principles.

7 Elaboration: This includes enriching the encoding of an item through variation of different modalities (spoken, written, pictorial/visual), through variation in type of use (receptive, productive), through variation of form (meeting different family members), through variation in meaning and reference, through variation in grammatical use, and through embedding in larger language units.
8 Analysis: This involves relating familiar parts to an unfamiliar whole. Analysis can include looking at the components of sounds, the sounds that make up words, sound-spelling correspondences, spelling patterns and rules, word parts, parts of multiword units, parts of speech, grammatical constructions, topic type components, rhetorical analysis, and discourse analysis.

## Applying the principles of learning

Let us look at how these principles apply to some of the teaching techniques covered in this book. While all the principles can be used to analyse a particular technique, typically one or two principles will be most strongly affecting learning in the use of that technique.

Learning vocabulary using flash cards (Chapter 23) is part of the language-focused learning strand of a language course. A very large body of research carried out over the last 130 years strongly supports this deliberate learning technique. The technique is effective because it applies several principles of learning. Learning from word cards is not a popular activity with most learners (Principle 1 Motivation), but it does quickly result in successful learning (Principle 2 Self-efficacy). It involves a deliberate focus on what is to be learned – the form and the meaning of the word (Principle 3 Focus). Because the meaning is typically expressed as an L1 translation, it is comprehensible and accurate enough (Principle 4 Accuracy). Flash cards are used several times, and this repetition provides quantity of attention (Principle 5 Repetition). This is the principle most affecting learning from flash cards. Because the form of the word is written on one side of the flash card and the translation is written on the other side, learners have the opportunity to do retrieval of the meaning which adds to the quantity of attention given to the form and meaning (Principle 6 Time-on-task). Giving deliberate attention to what is to be learned also increases the quantity of attention. If learners receive some training in how to use flash cards, they may say the word as they focus on it, or may use the Keyword technique for difficult words, thus increasing the quality of attention (Principle 7 Elaboration). If they have had some training in word part analysis, then they may break some of the words into parts in order to relate the new learning to previous knowledge (Principle 8 Analysis). As this analysis of the flash card technique shows, using flash cards provides many useful opportunities to apply the principles of learning. Let us now analyse another technique – extensive reading.

Extensive reading (Chapter 13) is a technique that involves incidental learning, and this is likely to be less effective than deliberate learning. However, extensive reading provides opportunity for many different things to be learned – the reading skill, spelling, vocabulary, multiword units, grammar, as well as the content matter of what is read. If large quantities of reading are done, then there can be substantial learning. What principles of learning occur during extensive reading? In extensive reading, the focus of attention is on the content (the message) of what is read. If learners choose an interesting book to read, this can increase engagement with the task (Principle 1 Motivation). Because graded readers involve vocabulary control, learners will quickly discover that they can read successfully and can experience the joy of reading their first complete book in English (Principle 2 Self-efficacy). In order to access the content of the book, learners need to focus on words and their meanings, multiword units and grammar. The kind of focus is transfer-appropriate in that it involves normal language use (Principle 3 Focus). In order to increase vocabulary learning from extensive reading, learners could be encouraged to note the unfamiliar words they meet while reading on word cards or enter them into a flash card programme. This small deliberate learning intervention will have a major effect on learning (Principle 3 Focus). If learners are reading at the right level for them, which is a requirement for extensive reading, then their recall and guessing from context of word meanings is likely to be largely accurate (Principle 4 Accuracy). If the learners do lots of reading, then they are likely to meet many of the words, multiword units, and grammatical constructions several times (Principle 5 Repetition). The quantity of attention given to any particular language item, however, is rather brief because it is incidental attention. Extensive reading, therefore, does not provide very strong application of Principle 6 (Time-on-task) for language items, although it does provide plenty of time-on-task for improving the reading skill. When learners meet vocabulary and grammatical features again while reading, these are met in varied contexts which provide a reasonable level of elaboration (Principle 7 Elaboration). If learners meet various members of the same word family in their reading, then there may be a small amount of analysis occurring (Principle 8 Analysis). Overall, extensive reading provides good opportunities for learning to occur in that many of the principles of learning have a chance to be applied well. The weakness of extensive reading is that the learning is largely incidental. The strength of extensive reading is that large quantities of reading provide many opportunities for the cumulative learning of many different language items and language use skills.

As a final example to help understand the principles of learning, let us look at learning through problem-solving speaking (Chapter 9). Problem-solving speaking involves learners talking to each other and this can increase engagement with the task (Principle 1). In addition, the task involves finding an answer to a problem. Like extensive reading, problem-solving speaking largely involves incidental learning. However, problem-solving speaking provides opportunities for language-related episodes (LREs) to occur, where there is a short deliberate focus on a language feature. This deliberate focus typically occurs because there is some barrier to understanding or some uncertainty about the message. Let us look at these language-related episodes first before considering incidental learning.

One of the most useful kinds of language-related episodes involves the negotiation of meaning of unfamiliar words. This occurs when one of the learners uses a word that the others do not know, or when an unknown word occurs in the written input to the activity. One learner may then try to explain the meaning of the word to the others in the group so that they can then get on with doing the activity (Principle 2). The explanation focuses on the meaning of the word and in most researched examples of negotiation is likely to be accurate or accurate enough for the present needs (Principles 3 & 4). The negotiation involves spending some time on the word (Principle 6) and the word and its meaning may be repeated a few times during the negotiation (Principle 5). During the explanation of the word, the word is put in a meta-linguistic context ("What does *shed* mean?" "A *shed* is a kind of small house ...") which provides a kind of elaboration for the word (Principle 7). If the word is a complex word, the learner may analyse it (Principle 8), but this rarely occurs. Negotiation provides reasonable conditions for learning but does not provide spaced repetition.

In the normal communication which occurs in problem-solving speaking, language learning is incidental, with the main learning being on the development of the speaking skill through transfer-appropriate meaning-focused use (Principle 3), and comprehensible input (Principle 4). Because such activities involve plenty of spoken use there is time-on-task (Principle 6), and there may be repetition of vocabulary and grammatical features during the task (Principle 5). Elaboration may occur through the varied contexts involved in conversation (Principle 7), but there is unlikely to be any analysis of language features or discourse.

What should be clear from this analysis of three techniques is that each principle might be applied to some degree. For example, the principle of repetition might not be applied, or it might be applied in a small way within the activity, or it could be moderately applied as in extensive reading with unplanned incidental varied repetition, or it could be strongly applied as in the flash card technique with deliberate, spaced repetition. The strength of the application will directly affect the strength of learning.

Although deliberate attention increases the quantity and quality of attention, the majority of learning in a language course should be largely incidental, that is, through the three strands of meaning-focused input, meaning-focused output, and fluency development. Incidental learning typically occurs in the most transfer-appropriate conditions and has powerful cumulative effects. However, incidental learning depends on large quantities of language use.

## Incidental learning and deliberate learning

Incidental learning is the main kind of learning in the three strands of meaning-focused input, meaning-focused output, and fluency development. Research of various kinds on incidental learning has shown that a small deliberate learning intervention may have a positive effect on learning. Using a dictionary and noting unfamiliar words on word cards for later study can enhance vocabulary learning from reading. Research on spoken and written fluency development activities has shown that although they increase fluency, some small intervention is needed to bring about improvements in accuracy. This intervention may involve the opportunity to plan, time to reflect on previous, current, or future performance, the chance to review or get feedback, or the deliberate setting of small, easily achievable language goals. Such interventions need to be small so that they do not greatly change the nature of the incidental learning activity. In terms of the principles described above, the interventions involve Principle 3 (Focus of attention), Principle 5 (Repetition), and Principle 7 (Elaboration). A lot of the research in task-based language learning involves looking at the effects of such interventions.

In the following section, we will look at one of the most important principles, repetition. We give particular attention to this principle because it is a very powerful principle, but it is largely neglected in the design of course books and in course work.

## Repetition and learning

Progress through a language course should not be about covering the material in the coursebook or syllabus. It should be about learning. The old material in a lesson is much more important than the new, because that old material contains language features that are on the way to being learned, and further attention to them can bring them to the stage of being learned. The new material is just at the first step of being learned and so does not deserve a lot of time or attention. Learning is a cumulative process with the later steps towards knowledge being most important because of the time already invested and the nearness of reaching the goal. This section, therefore, focuses on repetition and how to build it into a course.

A well-designed course book should take learners back to the same material several times in different ways so that it has a chance of being learned. The different ways should include verbatim repetition (doing exactly the same thing again) and varied repetition (revisiting the same material in a new way). Varied repetition can include doing the same activity using a different skill (for example, listening instead of reading, speaking instead of writing), doing the same activity with a different group size, changing a part of the content of the activity, or using recall to do the activity.

Varied repetition involves a deeper quality of processing than verbatim repetition, but it is useful to use both kinds of repetition. Repetition is most effective when it is spaced, that is when several days and eventually several weeks have passed before the material is revisited. At least one-third of the time in a language course should be spent revisiting old material.

While it is important for a teacher to develop the skill of revisiting previously met material, course book designers should also build revisiting into the course book. That is, learners should be directed back to previously met material with instructions about how to deal with it. Here are some examples of how this could be done in a course book. The material in the boxes would be a part of the coursebook, with each unit involving several such opportunities for repetition.

> Re-read the reading passage in Unit 3 and tell your partner about it. Your partner should re-read the reading passage in Unit 2 and tell you about it.

> Use the reading passage in Unit 2 as a dictation passage. Work in pairs with one learner giving the dictation and the other writing it. Check the writing together.

> Use the passage in Unit 3 as the information for a 4/3/2 activity. Work in pairs with one learner being the speaker and the other being the listener.

> Re-read the passage in Unit 2 as quickly as you can.

Bygate (2018, pp. 13–15; Table 4.1) has a useful and suggestive classification of types of repetition. Type 1 typically involves verbatim repetition while the other types typically involve varied repetition.

Types 2 and 3 are probably best joined together as they both involve using much the same material in a different arrangement. Keeping type 3 as a separate type could be justified if there was a large number of content areas covered by this type of task.

**TABLE 4.1** Bygate's types of repetition

| Type 1 | Doing the same task again | 4/3/2 |
| Type 2 | Using a different arrangement of the same material | Following a route on a map, arranging items in an array |
| Type 3 | Doing the same task adapting the information to current circumstances | A daily weather report, it's my word, what is it?, keeping a diary |
| Type 4 | Using the same material with different speakers highlighting different aspects | A poster presentation, different roles relating to the same material |
| Type 5 | Following the same schedule or plan | Interviews, marketplace, book reports |
| Type 6 | Using the same material across different skills | Linked skills, read and retell, listen and report |

**TABLE 4.2** Activities involving immediate and delayed verbatim repetition

|  | *Immediate repetition* | *Delayed repetition* |
| --- | --- | --- |
| Listening | Speeded listening | Relistening |
| Speaking | 4/3/2 Headlines | Repeating the same speech |
| Reading | Repeated reading | Rereading |
| Writing | Writing with a decreasing time limit | Rewriting |

In Listen and report in Type 6 in Table 4.1, learner A addresses half of the class and learner B the other half. Then learners pair up with one learner from each half to report to their partner what they heard.

## *Verbatim repetition*

Verbatim repetition involves doing the same task again. Verbatim repetition is involved in activities such as repeated reading and 4/3/2, and in these activities the repetition occurs immediately within a single task. Verbatim repetition also occurs when exactly the same task is done again several days or weeks later, as, for example, when re-reading a graded reader, or when delivering the same talk again to a different audience. This delayed repetition is most suited to longer tasks. Table 4.2 has a range of tasks involving verbatim repetition.

Speeded listening involves listening to the same material again but using a faster playback speed. Several apps including YouTube support speeded playback without distorting the sound. The Headlines activity is described in Chapter 10.

Repeating an activity can be boring, although the challenge of doing the task may be enough to get one or two repetitions with attention. In tasks involving immediate repetition, the motivation of decreasing time (as in 4/3/2, repeated reading, writing with a decreasing time limit, and speeded listening) and the motivation of having a new audience (as in 4/3/2 and Headlines) provide enough challenge to keep the task interesting. In tasks involving delayed repetition, the delay itself may be enough of a challenge to keep the task interesting. Table 4.3 includes other possible challenges (Nation, 1976).

The noisy input challenge in column 2 involves the teacher covering their mouth or speaking through a mask, or tapping on the desk while speaking. Background music can also act as noise. In communication theory, noise is defined as anything that interferes with the wanted message.

Decreasing written support in Table 4.3 involves providing written support keywords or phrases rather than the complete written text. A very entertaining activity is to write a short text on the whiteboard about 50 words long and then get one of the learners to read it aloud. Then a few words are erased, and another

**TABLE 4.3** Challenges to motivate repetition

|  | *Challenges* |
|---|---|
| Listening | Increasing speed |
|  | Noisy input |
|  | Memory (as in say the poem once) |
| Speaking | Increasing speed |
|  | New audience |
|  | Decreasing written support |
| Reading | Increasing speed |
|  | Decreasing dictionary support |
| Writing | Increasing speed |
|  | Decreasing written support |

learner has to read it filling in the gaps from memory. Then a few more words are erased, and another learner reads it aloud. This continues until nothing is left on the whiteboard and the learners are repeating the text aloud purely from memory.

The activity involving saying a poem only once (in the listening row in Table 4.3) involves the teacher saying to the class, "I will say a poem for you, but I will say it only once. After I have said it, I want you to repeat it back to me exactly as I said it". The teacher then says the poem. The learners are not allowed to take notes or to record it. Two really good poems for this activity are *Sand Dunes* by Robert Frost (the first two stanzas are enough), and *The Wind* by James Stephens. Both are available on the internet. They are both short enough and written in simple regular English. After saying the poem, the teacher says "Now, what was the first line?" Each time the learners make a correct suggestion, the teacher repeats the suggestion. This continues with the learners making suggestions and the teacher repeating the previously recalled lines and the suggestions. If necessary, the teacher gives some help, using lines for the number of letters in a word, or giving the first letter, or suggesting the meaning in the first language. By the time the whole poem has been recalled, the learners have heard it many times and have largely memorized it. This activity works particularly well with a large class.

The challenge of delay can be made a manageable challenge for the learner by providing some support such as initial prompted recall (stimulating background knowledge), brief notes, or some time for quiet recall and preparation either individually or in pairs.

Lambert, Kormos, and Min (2017) found that learners were generally positive about tasks being repeated in immediate succession, and they found that there was improvement in various markers of fluency through as many as five or six repetitions.

Ellis (2018, p. 96) concluded that

> task repetition by itself is beneficial in enhancing fluency and complexity – especially if the task is completed several times. However, for it to have a marked effect on accuracy, on either the repeated task or in the performance of a new task, something more is needed – the opportunity for unpressured online planning and/or some kind of form-focused intervention.

## *Varied repetition*

Varied repetition involves meeting or using the same language items again but in different contexts from previous meetings or uses. Varied repetition has been called *generative use* (Joe, 1998), and *creative use* (Nation, 2013a). Varied repetition within a task occurs in tasks like linked skills activities (Chapter 21) where the learners focus on the same content three times, one after the other, each time in a different skill. For example, they may read a text, then listen to a version of it, and then talk about it with a partner (Nation, 2013b, Chapter 15). Varied repetition can also occur when the content of a task is not repeated, for example, when learners do extensive reading or extensive listening, or when they engage in conversation activities. In this book, however, we focus on activities where the content is largely repeated.

The problem facing the teacher is to find ways to vary the repetition of the content enough to encourage varied meetings and use, but to keep the content much the same so that repetition of the language features occurs. Here is a list of possibilities for varying the focus on the same content.

*Varying across the four skills:* The four skills of listening, speaking, reading, and writing are the main means of variation in linked skills activities. The three steps of a linked skills activity involve three different skills, for example, listen to some information, then speak about it, and then write about it. Linked skills activities are easy to make and provide excellent opportunities for repetition and thoughtful processing to occur. In a linked skills activity, the three steps occur within the same lesson, but it is also possible to delay the occurrence of the following step or steps. Linked skills activities involve receptive versus productive variation (listening, reading versus speaking, writing), and oral versus written variation (listening, speaking versus reading, writing). In addition, there is the variation of context that is likely to occur when the focus of the task varies, for example, read to understand, then speak to clarify, and then write to summarize (Bygate type 6).

*Varying across the four strands:* The four strands of meaning-focused input, meaning-focused output, language-focused learning, and fluency development (Nation, 2007, 2024) represent four different kinds of opportunities for language learning. The major difference between varying across the four strands and varying across the four skills is that one of the strands (language-focused learning) involves deliberate attention. This means that pre-teaching, reflection, and recall of language items just met, deliberate analysis and deliberate study can be one of the opportunities for focusing or refocusing on the content or language. For example, before the learners do the task, the teacher does some pre-teaching of target language features or stimulates previous knowledge through questioning or semantic mapping. Alternatively, after the learners have completed a task, they recall vocabulary and multiword expressions that were involved in the task. A more deliberate content-focused repetition could involve applying a topic-type framework to the information used in the task (see Nation [2024], and Nation & Macalister [2021, Chapter 10] for a list and examples).

Another difference is that fluency development is one of the four strands, and so repetition of the task could involve the same skill but simply aim at being faster. This, however, is more likely to involve verbatim repetition.

*Varying across group size:* The pyramid procedure (Jordan, 1990) involves doing the same task across different group sizes. It is most commonly used in ranking activities where learners make individual decisions about the ranking of given solutions to a problem or of items to use such as what to take for survival in the forest, and then revise their decisions in pairs, then in groups of four, and then finally as a whole class. A simplified version of the pyramid procedure would be to do a task individually and then in small groups. For example, learners could individually prepare a plan for a piece of writing and then revise their plan in small groups before actually doing the writing. Delivering a talk could be done in a similar way. Prepare the talk individually, deliver it to a single critic and get feedback, and then deliver it to a group. In each step of the pyramid procedure, the revisions are likely to result in varied repetition rather than verbatim repetition (Bygate type 1).

*Varying across genre or topic type:* The same content can be experienced or delivered in different genres. A common way of making description interesting is to personalize it by turning it into narrative. For example, the description of the characteristics of a coconut can be embedded in a story of someone walking on the beach and finding a coconut and examining it. So, after writing a description of an object (perhaps using the physical structure topic type or the characteristics topic type), learners can then later write on the same topic in narrative form. Similarly, after telling how to make something, the object itself and its use can be described (Bygate type 4).

The most useful topic types and the kinds of texts they occur in are listed in Table 4.4. Moving from one topic type to another (column 1), or one kind of text to another (column 2) will provide opportunities for varied repetition.

*Varying by including interaction:* One way of varying in spoken presentations is to turn monologue into conversation. That is, instead of delivering an

**50** The principles of learning

**TABLE 4.4** The most common topic types and the texts they occur in

| Topic type | Texts |
| --- | --- |
| Characteristics (What is it like?) [Features, proof, category, other information] | Consumer reports, magazine articles, poems, application forms, curriculum vitae, letters of recommendation, course outlines |
| Physical structure (What is it like?) [Parts, location, features, function] | |
| State/situation (What happened?) [Who, time, place, background, event, effects] | Letters, newspaper reports, stories, historical accounts, diary reports |
| Instruction (How do you do it?) [Steps, materials, equipment, cautions, result] | Recipes, operating instructions, shopping lists, help manuals, articles for teachers' journals, methods section of experimental reports |
| Process (What happens to it?) [Stages, material, time and place, length of time, agent, features, action] | Science texts |
| Principle (Why does it happen?) [Principle, conditions, examples, tests, application] | Science texts |
| Theory (Why does it happen?) [Hypothesis, reasons, tests, results, significance] | |

uninterrupted monologue, the speaker can invite questions which are likely to result in considerable variation in the talk.

*Varying across viewpoint:* If the same story is told by a different character in the story, or if the same description is done by someone with a different knowledge background, varied repetition is likely to occur. For example, the effects of pollution can be described by a child, by a person whose job it is to keep the environment clean, and by giving the environment itself a voice, such as a river speaking. Similarly, a car accident can be described from the varying viewpoints of the different characters involved in the accident. For immediate repetition, the different viewpoints can be presented by different learners. For delayed repetition, the different viewpoints on the same topic can be presented by the same learner (Bygate type 4).

*Varying across outcomes:* Nation (1991b) describes various series of outcomes that can occur in problem-solving tasks (Chapter 9). When faced with a problem such as making people appreciate the work done by the police, the learners can work together to come up with a list of suggestions (suggest), choose the best suggestions (choose) and then rank the short list of suggestions (rank). Each different outcome (suggest, choose, rank) requires further discussion of the same topic. Other outcomes include decide, locate, and arrange. For example, the learners can decide whether the town should have a shopping mall, and then where it might be located in the town. Varying across outcomes typically involves immediate repetition (Bygate type 5).

*Varying across time or particular focus through narrow reading:* Narrow reading involves reading on the same topic in the same subject area preferably following the same writer. The major effect of narrow reading is to greatly reduce the number of different words involved. There is a small effect on the repetition of topic-related words (Hwang & Nation, 1989; Schmitt & Carter, 2000). Examples of narrow reading include following the same story through a series of newspaper reports, reading on a very narrowly defined topic such as reading cake recipes or houses for sale advertisements, or reading within a specialized technical field, such as building or anatomy. Reading cake recipes, for example, allows the same vocabulary of preparing, mixing, and cooking to reoccur (Bygate type 3).

Table 4.5 summarizes the various ways of getting repetition.

To check how well you have learned from this part of the chapter, consider the following task.

You want to come back to the same topic of *The importance of regular exercise* five times using a mixture of verbatim and varied repetition, and

**TABLE 4.5** The different types of repetition activities

|  | *Immediate repetition* | *Delayed repetition* |
|---|---|---|
| Verbatim repetition | Speeded listening<br>Unexploded dictation<br>4/3/2<br>Headlines<br>The best recording<br>Repeated reading<br>Rewriting with less time | Relistening<br>Retelling<br>Rereading<br>Rewriting |
| Varied repetition | Pyramid procedure<br>Linked skills<br>Discuss and report<br>Mind map and write<br>Pre-teaching and listening<br>Varying across outcomes | Varying across group size<br>Recalling through a different skill (listening, speaking, reading, and writing)<br>Varying across genre or topic type<br>Varying across the strands with deliberate attention and fluency development<br>Varying across viewpoint (role play)<br>Narrow listening or reading |

immediate and delayed repetition. List the five ways in order, indicating the amount of time between each repetition, and the type of repetition (verbatim, varied, immediate, delayed).

The idea behind this focus on repetition is that time should be spent repeating the same activities and doing activities that recycle the same language and ideas content. Such repeated activities could make up perhaps a third of the total course time. The justification for this proposal is that repetition is essential for most learning and teachers and course designers thus must build repetition into their courses. The easiest way to do this is through repeating tasks and through recycling the same content and language through varied tasks. A useful goal would be to make sure that the same significant piece of content occurs five times in the course, involving two or three verbatim repetitions and two or three varied repetitions. Some of these five repetitions should be delayed repetitions.

## Applying the principles

Techniques do not usually bring their own motivation with them, but the way the techniques are used can increase motivation. One of the major motivators is success (Principle 2 Self-efficacy), and when techniques are used as experience tasks which are at the right level for the learners, motivation is likely to increase and endure. As we have seen above with verbatim repetition, challenges can be built into activities to increase engagement with the task (Principle 1). Table 4.6

TABLE 4.6 Applying principles in language teaching techniques with a focus on vocabulary

| Principle | Application in techniques |
| --- | --- |
| 1 Motivation | Learn obviously useful words |
|  | Set challenging but achievable goals |
|  | Use puzzle-like and test-like tasks |
|  | Record successful learning using graphs |
| 2 Self-efficacy | Use vocabulary control in listening and reading materials |
|  | Do pre-study training |
|  | Work with small numbers of words |
| 3 Focus | Have a clear vocabulary learning goal |
| 4 Accuracy | Don't use trial-and-error, use study and test |
|  | Use dictionaries |
|  | Use L1 meanings |
| 5 Repetition | Use peer testing |
|  | Use related tasks |
|  | Encourage quantity of graded reading |
|  | Encourage opportunities for negotiation of meaning |

(*Continued*)

**TABLE 4.6** (Continued)

| Principle | Application in techniques |
|---|---|
| 6 Time-on-task | Use spaced retrieval |
| | Use self-testing |
| | Use larger groups of cards as skill at learning increases |
| 7 Elaboration | Find members of the same word family |
| | Look for the core meaning of various senses |
| | Look at collocations |
| | Do plenty of extensive reading to see examples of use |
| | Focus on both written and spoken forms |
| | Visualize examples of use |
| | Use the words |
| | Use pictures of the meaning as well as translations |
| | Do receptive and productive learning |
| 8 Analysis | Use the keyword technique |
| | Learn word parts |
| | Do multiword unit analysis |
| | Use analogy or patterning of form, meaning and use. For example, look at spelling regularities and irregularities, look for a core meaning among various uses, look for similarities among collocates |

brings together a number of ways in which the principles of learning can be applied in language teaching techniques.

Although there are many teaching techniques and many ways of applying principles, the number of principles is small, and they can be reduced to the four aspects of motivation, focus, quantity, and quality.

In each of the following chapters in this book, when we look at teaching techniques in the section looking at how each technique helps learning, we will look at how the principles of learning work with each technique and how the technique can be used to maximize the effects of the principles. To emphasize this, that section of each chapter uses the sub-headings *Motivation, Focus, Quantity,* and *Quality*. The section on revisiting in each chapter gives particular attention to repetition.

## Training learners to understand and apply the principles of learning

Learners should know how to learn, and understanding the principles of learning and how to apply them is an essential part of any language course. The principles of learning that are described in this chapter are few in number and easy enough to understand and apply. Part of the language-focused learning strand of a course should involve learning these principles and getting practice in applying them. The principles apply beyond the learning of language, and it is useful practice to apply them to other kinds of learning, such as remembering people's names, learning the road code, and studying for a physics exam.

Learners should understand why the teaching techniques described in this book are useful for them, because if learners know why they are doing something and how it will help them, they are more likely to be engaged with the learning. Learning how to learn can change people's lives. Chapter 24 looks more closely at learning how to learn.

There is a free book on Paul Nation's resources pages called *What do you need to know to learn a foreign language?* (Nation, 2014a), which is an attempt to apply principles of learning to learning another language.

## Principles and research

Teaching techniques are effective because of the learning conditions that they create. These conditions are described in the eight principles. An important area of research on language teaching techniques involves looking at how well those principles are at work when techniques are used. This kind of research is best done through case studies which involve looking at techniques in use.

To make this connection between principles of learning and researching language teaching techniques clearer, at the end of each of the following chapters, we will look at possible areas for future research on each technique, using the framework of the eight principles to organize the suggestions. The following general research questions show the kinds of questions that can be asked.

### *Motivation principles (Engagement)*

For learning to occur there needs to be a willingness to focus on what needs to be learned, and to give it quantity and quality of attention.

1 *Motivation: The degree of engagement with the task affects the likelihood of learning occurring.* Do learners want to do this task? Do they think that this should be a regular activity in their course? Do they enjoy it when they do it? Does their enjoyment when doing the task increase their willingness to do similar tasks? What factors encourage the learners to do the task – choice of content, the challenge of the task, obvious value outside the course, pair or group work, signs of progress (a graph, a record of work done, success in the task?).
2 *Self-efficacy: Our confidence in our own skills of learning affects our success in learning.* What difficulties do learners encounter during the task? What

support helps them be successful? Which support is the most effective? Does vocabulary control increase self-efficacy? Do learners successfully complete the task?

## Focus principles (Usefulness)

Learning requires giving attention to what needs to be learned.

3 *Focus: We learn what we focus on, and in addition, our learning is more useful if it closely resembles the use that we need to make of what we learn (transfer-appropriate).* What do learners focus on during the task? Do some aspects of the task result in unwanted focuses? Do learners improve in doing the task during repeated performance of the task? What do learners learn from doing the task? Does learning transfer outside the task to different material? Does doing the task result in improvement in related tasks and skills? What are the most useful topics to cover?
4 *Accuracy: Our learning is more efficient if the information we are focusing on is complete, accurate, and comprehensible.* Is the language used during the task largely accurate? Do learners successfully complete the task with a minimum of error and mis-comprehension? How do learners cope with errors and unknown language items during the task? What support reduces the chances of error? Which support works best?

## Quantity principles (Amount)

5 *Repetition: The more repetitions, the stronger the learning.* Does the task involve plenty of repetition? Does a corpus analysis of the activity show lots of opportunities for learning? What kinds of repetition occur during the task and across later uses of the task? How much repetition is needed to get substantial learning from this task? How can repetition be increased? What spacing of repetition works best? Does redoing the same task several days later increase learning? What patterns of improvement occur during repeated use of the task? Is some intervention needed to bring about improvement during repeated use of the task? Is repetition and the kind of repetition directly related to learning? Are learners willing to do repeated tasks? What kinds of changes are needed to keep a repeated task interesting? What effect does a narrow content focus have on repetition and the difficulty of the task? What are the effects of repetition on accuracy, complexity, and fluency? What changes to the task are needed to get a wider range of learning from the task?
6 *Time-on-task: The greater and longer the attention, the stronger the learning.* Does the task involve lots of attention to what needs to be learned? Is there a direct relationship between time-on-task and learning? How much time needs

to be spent on the task to result in substantial learning? What factors in the design of the task affect the time spent on the task? What other factors affect the time spent on the task? What factors take time away from the goals of the task? How can we deal with these factors? Do observers learn as well as active participants?

## Quality principles (Connections)

Elaboration and analysis increase and strengthen connections between the item to be learned and other knowledge making it easier to access the item.

7 *Elaboration: This includes enriching the encoding of an item through variation.* What are the different types of quality of attention? What kinds of quality most affect learning? How can we investigate the quality of the time spent on the task? What kinds of varied repetition occur during the task? How is this repetition best classified and counted? What are the most useful scales to reveal the extent of variation of vocabulary in language use across the four skills? (Joe, 1998). Are separate scales needed for word form, word meaning, and word use? Is the frequency of various kinds and levels of variation directly related to learning? What kinds of feedback most affect learning? Does this activity strengthen knowledge of previously met words?

8 *Analysis: This involves relating the familiar parts to the unfamiliar whole.* Language analysis works at all levels of language – the components of sounds, the sounds that make up words, sound-spelling correspondences, spelling patterns and rules, word parts, parts of multiword units, parts of speech, grammatical constructions, topic type components, rhetorical analysis, and discourse analysis. Do several members of the same word family occur among the target vocabulary in the activity? Do learners see the connection between the word family members? What kinds of language analysis occur in the task? Is feedback involving grammatical analysis more effective than correction? Does language analysis result in improvement in language use? Does language analysis occur during incidental learning?

# PART 1
# Listening

# 5
# EXTENSIVE LISTENING AND VIEWING

### What is extensive listening and viewing?

Some researchers distinguish extensive listening from extensive viewing. Viewing involves watching video while listening. In this book, we will treat them as one technique, and sometimes use the term *extensive listening* to refer to both. Extensive listening and viewing includes listening to recorded talks such as TED Talks and podcasts, listening to movies, documentaries, drama series and YouTube clips, listening to recorded books, getting involved in conversation, participating in seminars and lectures, and listening to songs. It also includes listening-while-reading and the shared book activity. Like most meaning-focused input and meaning-focused output tasks, extensive listening and viewing does not necessarily involve being tested on what is listened to or viewed, for example, with comprehension questions or information transfer tasks. It simply involves lots of comprehensible listening, in other words, listening at the right level.

Just as there is a wide range of different kinds of written texts, there is a very wide range of different types of spoken texts that can be part of an extensive listening and viewing programme. Although there are many types of spoken texts, extensive listening and viewing simply involve listening and comprehending.

Extensive listening and viewing fits into the meaning-focused input and fluency development strands of a course. It should take up around half of the time in the meaning-focused input strand and one-quarter of the time in the fluency development strand. It involves listening to large quantities of material with a focus on comprehension, so the material must be at the right level for the learner. Because of this, most extensive listening and viewing tasks should be experience

DOI: 10.4324/9781003496151-7

tasks. It is a technique that involves incidental learning, and this is likely to be less effective than deliberate learning. However, extensive listening and viewing provides opportunities for many different things to be learned – the listening skill, pronunciation, vocabulary, multiword units, grammar, as well as the content matter of what is listened to. If large quantities of listening are done, then there can be substantial learning.

Extensive listening requires large amounts of interesting input at the right level for the listener. What is the right level will change depending on whether the listening is at the level of meaning-focused input, where around 2% of the running words are unfamiliar, or at the level of fluency development, where there should be no unfamiliar words. Extensive listening and viewing should involve a wide range of types of listening, including listening to monologue such as weather reports and the news, podcasts and live lectures, listening as a part of interactive dialogue involving the listener, listening to songs, and viewing such as watching movies, documentaries, television or streamed series. Learning from the listening will be enhanced if the listening or viewing is related to other activities such as reporting on the listening, or listening to what has been read, or listening as part of project work.

## What are the learning goals of extensive listening and viewing?

Table 5.1 presents the learning goals of extensive listening. From a language perspective, learning in the meaning-focused strands of meaning-focused input, meaning-focused output, and fluency development is largely incidental learning, because the main focus of the activities in these strands should be on understanding and producing messages. Furthermore, the most likely incidental learning goal in the four skills of listening, speaking, reading, and writing will be on the skills of comprehending and producing messages. In Table 5.1, the most important learning goal is written in italics – listening and viewing with comprehension at a reasonable speed.

TABLE 5.1 The learning goals of extensive listening and viewing

| Goals | Specific focuses |
| --- | --- |
| Language | Learning new vocabulary and grammatical features |
|  | Strengthening and enriching partly known vocabulary and grammar |
| Ideas | Gaining information and enjoyment from listening and viewing |
| Skills | *Listening and viewing with comprehension at a reasonable speed* |
| Text | Developing familiarity with a range of listening genres |

*Note*: *Italics* indicates the major goal.

The major learning goal of extensive listening and viewing is development of the listening skill through large amounts of comprehensible listening and viewing. For learners at the beginning and intermediate levels with vocabulary sizes of less than 5,000-word families, specially prepared or carefully chosen listening material is needed. In most unsimplified material the number of unfamiliar words is too large, and the density of unfamiliar words is too high for comprehensible listening at a reasonable speed of around 150 words per minute.

The kind of learning involved in extensive listening is largely incidental learning, where the learner is focused on listening and following what is happening. The development of the listening skill comes from doing lots of listening at the right level.

The fluency development aspect of the listening skill can be dealt with in two ways in an extensive listening programme. One way is through listening to or viewing material which is well within the learners' language knowledge – easy listening. The other way, which at present is the most feasible, is listening to material which has been read or listened to before, with the aim of better comprehension. This repeated listening can be supported by using speed-controlled materials, and by intensive reading-based study of scripts, following the progression of intensive study, listening-while-reading, listening for meaning-focused input, and finally listening for fluency development.

A secondary goal of extensive listening and viewing is vocabulary learning. Vocabulary learning occurs through guessing from context clues, through subtitles and captions, and through repeated incidental meetings with words in varied contexts. For learners of English as a foreign language, the amount of incidental vocabulary and grammar learning is likely to be small, simply because it is difficult to get large amounts of listening input at the right level.

Table 5.1 includes an ideas goal, gaining information and enjoyment from listening and viewing. Extensive reading has a similar goal. Learners need to develop the language and skills needed for listening and viewing, but also need to gain pleasure from listening and viewing, so that they keep doing it for its own sake as well as a way of learning the language. This idea lies behind learners choosing what they view and listen to.

### How does extensive listening and viewing help learning?

In this section of each chapter, we look at how the eight principles of learning described in Chapter 4 affect learning through each particular technique. That is, having looked at the learning goals of extensive listening and viewing, we now look at how these goals can be achieved. The most important factor affecting how extensive listening and viewing helps learning is the large quantity of varied listening input at the right level for each learner. This large quantity of practice improves the listening skill and provides opportunity for frequent meetings with spoken vocabulary, multiword units, and grammatical features. By being at the right level, the learners are not overloaded with unfamiliar vocabulary and overly complex grammatical constructions.

In essence, extensive listening and viewing helps develop the listening skill through highly transferable quantity of practice. The practice is highly transferable because it is like the listening that learners may need to do in their normal use of English. Extensive listening and viewing helps vocabulary learning through the quality feature of varied meetings, although compared to vocabulary learning through extensive reading, the effect is small, largely because of the transitory nature of the spoken input.

Extensive listening applies the principles of motivation, focus of attention, quantity of attention, and quality of attention in the following ways.

*Motivation:* If the learner has choice in the input used for extensive listening and viewing, this can increase engagement with the activity (Principle 1 Motivation). The vocabulary and grammatical demands of material for extensive listening and viewing should be controlled in order to be at the right level for the learners so that the listening is comprehensible (Principle 2 Self-efficacy). At present, because of a lack of listening material at various levels, this is difficult to do.

*Focus:* In extensive listening and viewing, the focus of attention is on the content (the message) of what is listened to. In order to access this message, learners need to focus on words and their meanings, multiword units, and grammar. The kind of focus is transfer-appropriate in that it involves normal language use (Principle 3 Focus). If learners are listening at the right level for them, which is a requirement for extensive listening, then their recall and guessing from context of word meanings is likely to be largely accurate (Principle 4 Accuracy).

*Quantity:* If the learners do lots of listening, then they are likely to meet many of the high-frequency words, multiword units, and grammatical constructions several times (Principle 5 Repetition). The quantity of attention given to any particular language item is rather brief, because it is incidental attention. Extensive listening, therefore, does not provide very strong application of Principle 6 (time-on-task) for language items, although it does provide plenty of time-on-task for improving the listening skill.

*Quality:* When learners meet vocabulary and grammatical features again while listening, these are met in varied contexts which provide a reasonable level of elaboration (Principle 7 Elaboration). If learners meet various members of the same word family in their listening, then there may be a small amount of analysis occurring (Principle 8 Analysis). Overall, extensive listening provides good opportunities for learning to occur in that many of the principles of learning have a chance to be well applied. The weaknesses of extensive listening are that the input is transitory and that the learning is largely incidental. The strength of extensive listening is that large quantities of listening provide many opportunities for the cumulative learning of many different language items and subskills.

## What are the requirements of extensive listening and viewing?

We have looked at the goals of extensive listening and viewing and how these goals are likely to be achieved. We now look at how this learning can be supported.

### How can you prepare for extensive listening and viewing?

Ideally, there should be a variety of listening and viewing material at vocabulary-controlled levels from around 100 different word families to 8,000-word families and beyond. Until we have this, then being able to read the script first as a kind of intensive reading, getting on top of vocabulary and grammar issues, is very useful preparation. After that, repeated listening varying the speed of delivery can result in meaning-focused input and eventually fluency development.

### What texts can be used for extensive listening and viewing?

Songs make very good use of the high-frequency words of English, but a vocabulary size of 3,000-word families is needed to get 97% coverage. Songs, however, are short, with an average length of around 300 words, and can be listened to repeatedly. There is a lot of variation in songs in terms of length (tokens), repetitions, number of types, and number of families, but a typical song will contain around 80-word families and on average only eight of these families will be beyond the first 1,000. If elementary learners learned the words of two songs a week, they would increase their vocabulary size by around 20 words per week, which is 800 words over a 40-week school year. The lyrics of most songs are available on the internet.

Movies are typically about an hour and a half to two hours long, with the average movie involving around 9,000–10,000 running words. Movies can differ greatly in vocabulary load, with most requiring knowledge of around 7,000-word families to get 98% coverage (including proper nouns, marginal words, and transparent compounds in the coverage figures), and around 3,000-word families for 95% coverage (Webb & Rodgers, 2009a). With 95% coverage, one running word in every 20 (5%) will be an unfamiliar word. Even in children's movies, such as *Shrek* or *Toy Story*, there may be 300 or more different word families beyond the first 2,000 (Newton & Nation, 2021). This is quite a heavy vocabulary burden, but one that learners might be willing to deal with if their motivation is high, or if they find the movie engaging enough. There are plenty of film scripts available on the internet. Working on understanding a movie is probably best approached as a kind of project work (see Chapter 22).

Episodes of television series provide shorter texts for viewing. Each episode tends to be around a half hour or an hour long. The coverage figures for television episodes are similar to those of movies, requiring at minimum a vocabulary of 3,000 words to get 95% coverage and around 7,000 words to get near 98% coverage (Webb & Rodgers, 2009b).

TED Talks range greatly in length and difficulty, but most are quite short and some are just a few minutes long. Coxhead and Walls (2012), examining talks around six minutes in length, found that around an 8,000–9,000-word vocabulary was needed to get 98% coverage, but with talks this length (less than 1,000 running words long) getting on top of words beyond learners' current levels would not be too big a task. Scripts for TED talks are available, and the speed can be controlled.

### How much time should be given to extensive listening and viewing in a general language course?

Extensive listening and viewing should make up half of the meaning-focused input strand. It should also make up one-quarter of the fluency development strand. In total, this would make up three-sixteenths of the course time, or about three-quarters of an hour a week where course work and homework occupy around four hours a week. This is the same amount of time as extensive reading. Because speaking with others also involves listening, the amount of time given to extensive listening may be a bit more than that. Extensive listening and viewing should be a substantial part of a well-balanced course.

### How can extensive listening and viewing be done well?

In this section of each chapter, we look at the steps involved in using the technique well so that it is likely to meet the learning goals described above.

Extensive listening and viewing can be done as an individual, pair, group, or whole class activity. We will begin by looking at extensive listening at the elementary level of proficiency where learners know only a few hundred words, and then look at listening and viewing at the intermediate and advanced levels. At each of the levels, it is important to use listening material that is within the proficiency level of each learner. It is also useful to control the speed of listening to suit the learners' skill level. In all of the activities described below, it is very helpful for the learners to listen to the same material several times on different occasions to develop fluency in listening.

## Listening to songs

Each week, each learner chooses two songs to study and listen to.

1. Choose the first song and get the lyrics of the song from the internet.
2. Look up the unknown words in the dictionary and make sure you understand the meaning of the song well.
3. Listen to the song several times on several days until you have memorized the song. Singing along with the song will help learning, as will trying to recall the lyrics of the song without reading them.
4. For a few minutes in class, let someone else listen to your song and explain the song to them.
5. Listen to the same song again several times over the following few months.
6. Put the name of the song on your list of songs with the date, so that you and the teacher can see how many songs you have learned.
7. Repeat the steps with another song.
8. Keep recalling the songs you have learned.

Learners can learn the same songs as their friends are learning if they wish.

## Listening-while-reading

Many graded readers have accompanying recorded versions of their written texts. The reading skill can be used to support skill at listening. Listening-while-reading can be done as an individualized activity. Xreading provides listening-while-reading.

1. Each learner chooses a graded reader that is well within their reading proficiency level. The graded reader should also have an accompanying audio-recorded version.
2. The learner begins listening-while-reading, adjusting the speed of the listening to suit their listening skill.
3. If learners' skill at listening is not very good, then the same material should be listened to several times on different occasions, adjusting the listening speed, and eventually listening without reading.

Listening-while-reading results in greater vocabulary learning than listening without reading support (Brown, Waring & Donkaewbua, 2008).

## Prepared viewing

Prepared viewing can be seen as an advanced version of listening-while-reading, in that the written script is used to support viewing. It is probably best suited to upper-intermediate and advanced learners. In prepared viewing, the script is studied before listening. Prepared viewing can be done as a whole class activity, or as an individualized activity. A more detailed description of this activity can be found in Chapter 4 of Newton and Nation (2021).

1  The teacher chooses a short film which has captions, and which also has a written script available. Note: Captions are a written form of the spoken language in the film. Subtitles are a written translation into another language of the spoken language in the film.
2  The teacher analyses the script using VocabProfiler on the Compleat Lexical Tutor web site to find the vocabulary in the film that the learners are unlikely to know.
3  The learners and the teacher work through the script as a form of intensive reading, dealing with unknown vocabulary, necessary background knowledge, and any other points of difficulty.
4  The learners then view and listen to the film, with the script in front of them if necessary and later without the script.

This activity has been described as using a short film. This is because the unknown vocabulary load of movies and television series can be quite heavy. Even if learners have a vocabulary size of around 3,000 words, there are likely to be several hundred unknown words in the movie. However, interest in the movie may be strong enough to allow learners to tolerate this amount of required learning.

### Assisted viewing

Assisted viewing involves the use of captions and then subtitles. It is suited to high-intermediate and advanced learners. For most movies and TV series, learners will need a vocabulary size of around 7,000-word families for really comfortable viewing, depending on the movie. Closed captions which are often used by native-speakers who are hard-of-hearing can assist language learners with listening in the same way that reading-while-listening helps.

If subtitles in the learners' first language are available, these may help with following the story and support the learning of new vocabulary.

### How can I check that extensive listening and viewing is working well?

The major requirement of the meaning-focused strands is quantity of language use at the right level for the learners. So, the first thing to monitor for extensive listening and viewing is whether the learners are doing large quantities of meaning-focused listening. Learners should have some way of noting the extensive listening and viewing that they are doing so that the teacher can check. When extensive listening and viewing is done in class, the teacher needs to check that each learner is working at the right level, which means that they adequately comprehend what they are listening to. This can be as simple as watching to see if they are enjoying what they are listening to, or asking if they understand, and may involve occasional checking of comprehension.

### Are there digital applications of this technique?

The major challenge in extensive listening and viewing is finding material at the right level. It is now relatively straightforward to produce graded reading material because we have well-developed word lists and there is technology to analyse and adapt the vocabulary of written texts. The next technological frontier for language learning is to develop programmes that can be used to adapt the spoken form of spoken text within a controlled vocabulary. At present, text selection is the major way of finding texts at the right level and this is of very limited value in that there are many interesting spoken texts, including movies and short clips, that require learners to have at least a 3,000-word family vocabulary, and typically a larger vocabulary, for comprehensible input. Most of the technology already exists, but it needs to be brought together and adapted for the preparation of controlled listening input for language learning.

The technology of speech to writing and writing to speech is now well developed and so it is relatively easy to find reading support for listening and viewing. The electronic graded reader web site, Xreading, provides text to speech support for graded reading.

The internet has provided a wealth of material for extensive listening and viewing, and now it is possible to control the speed of listening without distorting the sound. This listening material can be used on cell phones, tablets, and desk-top computers making it accessible for many learners.

There is now a growing body of research on *language learning in the wild* which looks at the incidental learning of foreign languages out of class time, largely through songs, movies, television, and gaming on the internet.

### Revisiting and linking to other activities

Listening-while-reading is a very useful version of extensive listening for learners whose reading skill is better than their listening skill. In listening-while-reading, learners simply follow a recording, or the teacher reading aloud, while reading the written version of the same input. This can be done with graded readers, film scripts, songs, and recorded talks with scripts such as TED Talks.

Listening is a useful way or revisiting reading texts from previous lessons. The delayed sequence of read, read-and-listen, listen, and listen under time pressure can help maintain interest.

## What does research say about the effectiveness of extensive listening and viewing?

In a qualitative study of successful language learners, Tsang (2023) found that the successful learners enjoyed dealing with input, either spoken or written but not usually both, and learned without really intending to learn. Listening and viewing tended to be viewed more positively than reading. The learners felt that learning through one skill not only benefitted productive use in that skill but also benefitted other skills. That is, listening helped writing and reading helped speaking.

Vocabulary learning can occur from viewing, although the gains are small (Peters & Webb, 2018). Research supports the use of captions and subtitles in movies to help vocabulary learning (Montero-Perez, Den Noortgate & Desmet, 2013; Peters, Heynen & Puimège, 2016). The factors described in the principles in Chapter 4 affect vocabulary learning from viewing, because the principles apply to both incidental and deliberate learning.

The findings of research by Boers, Warren, Grimshaw, and Siyanova-Chanturia (2017) suggest that learners doing activities like listening-while-reading and listening with captions need to eventually move to listening only, to ensure that the spoken form is getting the attention it needs. The principle that we learn what we focus on works here. To improve listening, our focus needs to be on listening.

## Research questions

Of the four skills of listening, speaking, reading, and writing, listening is the least researched. There is plenty of research about the vocabulary coverage of listening texts and on vocabulary learning from listening, but we lack research on adapting listening texts to learners' proficiency levels and on improving the listening skill.

The most important research question in extensive listening is, can we develop computer programmes to adapt listening and viewing material so that the vocabulary and grammar can be controlled in the same way that we can control the material for extensive reading.

### *Motivation principles (Engagement)*

For learning to occur there needs to be a willingness to focus on what needs to be learned, and to give it quantity and quality of attention.

1. *Motivation: The degree of engagement with the task affects the likelihood of learning occurring.* Does being able to choose what to listen to or view increase learners' willingness to do extensive listening? Is pair listening more motivating than listening alone? Do obvious signs of progress, such as keeping records of the amount listened to or periodic tests, increase the willingness to do extensive listening? When learners experience success in extensive listening, does this increase their willingness to do more?
2. *Self-efficacy: Our confidence in our own skills of learning affects our success in learning.* The successful completion of a task is an indication that the task is likely to contribute to self-efficacy. When researching a task, it is worth looking closely at the difficulties learners encounter when doing the task and the degree of ease with which they overcome the difficulties. The difficulty of a task depends on the learners' proficiency and the language control and the demands of the task. Useful research questions include: What are the difficulties that learners experience during extensive listening? What support makes extensive listening easier? How effective is this support? When we look at language control in extensive listening, useful questions include: How feasible is simplification through the editing of podcasts and videos? Is it better to make changes to videos and podcasts obvious to the listener? How feasible is the procedure of (1) intensive reading of the written script, (2) listen and read, and (3) listen? Is it too time-consuming? Is it demotivating?

## *Focus principles (Usefulness)*

Learning requires giving attention to what needs to be learned.

3. *Focus: We learn what we focus on, and in addition, our learning is more useful if it closely resembles the use that we need to make of what we learn (transfer-appropriate).* Is listening-while-reading more effective and efficient than just listening? What adjustments are needed to make listening-while-reading more effective for improving listening? Where do learners direct their attention during listening-while-reading? Does extensive listening increase listening fluency? Does improvement in extensive listening transfer to different listening tasks, such as dictation or listening followed by comprehension questions?
4. *Accuracy: Our learning is more efficient if the information we are focusing on is complete, accurate, and comprehensible.* How do learners cope with unknown words during extensive listening? What density of unknown words is manageable during extensive listening? Is viewing easier than listening? Does viewing distract attention from language features? Is listening-while-reading better than reading-before-listening in increasing listening accuracy?

## Quantity principles (Amount)

5  *Repetition: The more repetitions, the stronger the learning.* How effective is repeated listening? What is the best amount of delay between repeated listening tasks? Are learners willing to do spaced repeated verbatim listening tasks? Does narrow listening increase vocabulary frequency and reduce vocabulary load?
6  *Time-on-task: The greater and longer the attention, the stronger the learning.* Is there a direct relationship between the amount of listening and viewing done and improvement in listening and viewing proficiency? How much extensive listening do learners need to do to learn the high- and mid-frequency words? (see Nation, 2014b).

## Quality principles (Connections)

Elaboration and analysis increase and strengthen connections between the item to be learned and other knowledge making it easier to access the item.

7  *Elaboration: This includes enriching the encoding of an item through variation.* What are the most useful scales to reveal the extent of variation of vocabulary in listening material? (Joe, 1998). Are separate scales needed for word form, word meaning, and word use? Is the frequency of various kinds and levels of variation directly related to learning?
8  *Analysis: This involves relating the familiar parts to the unfamiliar whole.* Does meeting members of word families during listening increase general awareness of word parts? Do phonological changes involved in word building (advertise-advertisement; impose-imposition) make family members less recognizable while listening? Does the deliberate learning of word parts and doing word part analysis have strong effects on the comprehension of family members during listening?

The most urgent research need for extensive listening and viewing is developing technology to make vocabulary-controlled listening and viewing material, so that learners at all levels can listen and view monologue and interactional material at the right level for them.

# 6
# DICTATION

## What is dictation?

In its most typical form, dictation is a four-step procedure. It involves listening to a text around 100–150 words long, then listening to it again phrase by phrase with pauses between each phrase and with the learners attempting to write each phrase, and then listening to whole text again to check for errors and omissions. The dictation is then marked either by the teacher, or by the learners with the correct written text for comparison. The text used for dictation should not contain unknown vocabulary.

Because of its main focus on the formal accuracy of listening, dictation is part of the language-focused learning strand of a course. It is a guided technique where the major learning focus is on accurate listening. The complication with dictation as a listening technique and as a testing technique is that it also relies on writing. Some researchers have suggested that spelling errors should be ignored when marking dictation. Because dictation involves using known material and repetition through the same material occurring at each of the four steps, it can support the incidental strengthening and enrichment of language features, particularly vocabulary, multiword units, and grammar. Dictation involves listening to connected text in two steps of the activity, but its main focus is on connecting spoken and written forms, particularly at the phrase level.

Dictation is like a listening-based form of intensive reading. It involves a focus on a relatively short text with the goal of hearing and understanding it with a high degree of accuracy, and getting feedback and help on points of difficulty.

**TABLE 6.1** The learning goals of dictation

| Goals | Specific focuses |
| --- | --- |
| Language | Strengthening and enriching partly known vocabulary and grammar |
|  | Deliberately focusing on multiword units |
| Ideas |  |
| Skills | *Accurately connecting spoken and written language* |
| Text |  |

*Note:* The major goal is in *italics*.

## What are the learning goals of dictation?

Table 6.1 lists the learning goals of dictation.

The major learning goal of dictation is a language accuracy goal, that is, helping learners accurately recognize the spoken forms of words and phrases. The proof of correct recognition is the accurate production of the written form.

## How does dictation help learning?

In essence, dictation helps the listening skill through deliberate attention to the lexical and grammatical accuracy of what is listened to.

Dictation requires learners to listen to a text, write it, and read it to check its correctness. If it is done properly with phrases of around 5–7 words long, it requires comprehension of the text. In languages such as Indonesian and Maori, where there is a very regular relationship between sound and spelling, a simple dictation could be done accurately by an English speaker without comprehending what is being said. When doing dictation with learners who are very familiar with the script, the phrases dictated would need to be around seven or eight words long so that comprehension is needed to be able to recognize and temporarily retain what is said.

*Motivation:* The motivation in dictation is a puzzle-like accuracy motivation, namely "Can you get it right?" If the dictation text has been well-chosen, then learners should get it correct, meeting the self-efficacy aspect of motivation.

*Focus:* The focus of attention is on the correct spoken and written forms of the words and multiword units, and if the speed of delivery of the whole text and the dictated phrases is at roughly normal speed, then there will be opportunities for some transfer-appropriate learning. Dictation also requires attention to grammatical features, and the corrective feedback that occurs in the final step of dictation can help draw deliberate attention to features such as inflected forms, agreement, the use of function words, and word order.

*Quantity:* Because dictation should contain words that are already known to some degree and can use text already met in previous lessons, it provides varied repetition of partly known vocabulary and multiword units. Because a dictation involves the four steps of listening to the whole text, listening to and writing the phrases, checking the writing while listening to the whole text again, and finally marking the writing, there are at least four meetings with each word or multiword unit. If Sawyer and Silver's (1961) recommendation is followed of doing the same dictation again over several days, then the repetition is greatly increased. Dictation thus involves plenty of quantity of attention through repetition.

Nation (1991a) argues that holding a spoken phrase in memory before writing it helps in the learning of multiword units. This holding in memory is a quantity-based feature in that it involves prolonged attention and repetition through the use of the phonological loop.

*Quality:* Dictation provides quality of attention through variation, the variation coming from the different modalities of listening, writing, and reading. The activity involves deliberate attention rather than incidental attention.

## The requirements of dictation

### How can you prepare for dictation?

In the writing step of dictation, the division of the text into phrases should try to make each phrase a meaningful unit, and the length of the phrases should be long enough to encourage the learner to treat each phrase as a meaningful unit rather than a series of isolated words.

It is worth taking some care when dividing the text into phrases for the dictation. Ideally, all the phrases should be around five to seven words long, but sometimes it is necessary to use an occasional shorter phrase or a slightly longer one to fit the grammar of the text, as each phrase should be a coherent grammatical unit.

### What texts can be used for dictation?

The texts used for dictation should contain largely familiar vocabulary, grammar, and content. This is to reduce the opportunity for error and to provide the opportunity to enrich and strengthen partly familiar language items. Dictation is an excellent technique to use as a way of revisiting material that has already been covered in earlier lessons or in earlier parts of the coursebook.

### How much time should be given to dictation in a general language course?

Dictation is part of the language-focused learning strand of a course and needs to share time in this strand with a range of other activities, such as learning spelling and pronunciation, intensive reading, learning from vocabulary flashcards, getting feedback on writing, developing language learning strategies, and understanding the principles of learning. Using the dictation technique about once every two weeks is a reasonable amount of time to spend on it.

## How can dictation be done well?

Dictation aims at increasing the skill of listening involving known language items. It provides the opportunity to listen to normal spoken language with the chance to get feedback on the accuracy of the listening.

1. The teacher should choose a coherent dictation passage around 100–150 words long that does not contain unfamiliar vocabulary. The passage can be part of an intensive reading text used in a previous lesson or some other text that is largely familiar. If the text contains unfamiliar proper names, these could be written on the whiteboard before the dictation is given.
2. The teacher goes through the text dividing it into coherent phrases, with each phrase being around five to seven words long. The teacher can use slash marks to divide up the text, as in the following example.

    The Inuit live in Canada,/ Greenland and the north of America.// They were the first people/ to live in these countries,/ arriving there about 5,000 years ago.// They live in a land/ of ice and snow,/ a land without trees.// For nine long months of the year/ it is cold, dark winter,/ while summer is only three short months.// Today, many Inuit live modern lives/ in towns and cities,/ but not so long ago/ the people lived the way/ their parents and their parents' parents/ had lived for thousands of years.//
3. When doing the dictation, for the first listening, the whole text and the phrases should be read at a normal speaking speed (around 150 words per minute) rather than at a slow speed with over-deliberate pronunciation. This is to practice normal listening and to help learners become familiar with the typical features of connected speech. This step provides an opportunity to comprehend the whole text. At this step, the learners could ask questions about parts they did not comprehend, because the goal is accuracy.
4. The next step is to read each phrase while the learners write it. Each phrase should be said once and should be spoken at normal speaking speed without over-deliberate pronunciation. The teacher should pause after each phrase in order to give the learners plenty of time to write it. Some punctuation can be dictated, namely commas and full stops.
5. After all the phrases have been written, the teacher says, "Now get ready to check your work". The teacher reads the whole text again at normal speaking speed and with no pauses after each phrase, so that the learners can check what they have written and make any final corrections.

6 The dictation is now marked, and the teacher and learners can discuss errors and gain further spoken feedback. The feedback on accuracy in the final step of dictation is a very important part of learning from dictation, and there should be enough time to focus on points of difficulty and to learn from them. There are many ways of marking dictation and giving feedback and the teacher should choose one that makes it easy for the teacher to do dictation often without a heavy marking burden. The teacher can collect the dictations and mark them as a way of the teacher getting some feedback on how well the learners are doing. Alternatively, the teacher can provide an answer sheet or refer the learners to the appropriate part of the coursebook and each learner can use this to mark their dictation or their classmate's dictation. Later in this chapter, there are some other suggestions for marking dictation.
7 Redoing the dictation a few days later is an excellent way of applying the results of this corrective feedback. The learners can be challenged to get it 100% correct.

*How can I check that a dictation activity is working well?*

A dictation activity is working well if learners have a high accuracy score on the dictation. If everyone gains a perfect score, the dictation may be too easy. Some teachers get learners to use a different coloured pen at the checking stage (the third reading of the dictation) to see if there are changes made then. Such changes, if correct, would show learning through repetition of the dictation.

### Revisiting and linking to other activities

Dictation is an excellent technique for revisiting material in a coursebook, because it involves minimal preparation, and can involve exactly the same steps each time, making it a technique that learners can quickly become familiar with. Dictation can be used to revisit reading texts. In general, dictation does not work well with texts involving dialogue because punctuation plays an important role in the written versions of those texts, and except for some commas, full stops, it is probably best to avoid dictating punctuation marks. Victor Borge's phonetic punctuation is a comedy routine that is worth tracking down on YouTube to see the lighter side of dictation.

Dictation is a useful way of providing learners with a written text (such as a song or a set of instructions) that can then be used for other activities.

### What are the variants of dictation?

There are many variants of dictation. These include different ways of carrying out the various steps in dictation, and more distant variants using different language skills.

### Variants of the steps of dictation

Dictation is an easily prepared activity that can become a part of the regular classroom routine. The following variations can add variety to this routine and can refocus the learning goal of the dictation activity.

### Running dictation

A short dictation text typed in a large font is posted on the wall outside the classroom. Learners work in pairs or small groups. One learner is the writer and the other is the runner who goes to the dictation text, memorizes a short sentence, returns to the writer, and retells it. If the learners are working in groups, the activity takes the form of a relay in which the first runner reads the first sentence of the short text and then runs to another learner and tells them what they have read. The second learner then runs to a third learner and does the same. The third learner in turn tells the writer what they have heard. This variation makes the learners hold the phrase in their memory for a longer time than usual, thus emphasizing the multiword unit learning goal of dictation.

If the emphasis is on speaking and listening and not reading and writing, the teacher can sit outside the classroom and say the sentences to the learners. Instead of writing, the sentences can be instructions to draw things spoken by the teacher to the runners.

e.g. For picture one, draw a man carrying five books and a bag of rice.
For picture two, draw two girls kicking a ball and a dog chasing a duck.

### Dictation of long phrases

During the writing step of the dictation, instead of reading short phrases once, the teacher can read long phrases or sentences several times. Each group can be about ten or more words long.

### Guided dictation

Nouns, verbs, adjectives, and adverbs are written on the blackboard in the same order as they are in the text. Thus, when the learners listen to the text, they can give their attention to the other difficult words. If the words are written in sentence groups as they are in the text, whole sentences instead of phrases can be read at once during the dictation. The words on the blackboard help the learners remember the complete sentences. Here is an example of the words on the blackboard based on the text in brackets and italics:

person… die… Bali… family… friend… usually… sad
(When a person dies in Bali, the family and friends are not usually sad.)

death… beginning… life.
(For them death is the beginning of another life.)
Dead… person… come… world… another… shape
(The dead person will come back in the world in another shape)
If necessary, the teacher can read each sentence more than once.

*Dictation for a mixed proficiency class*

If the class has some learners who are good at dictation and others who are not very good, the teacher can read the text in a special way. She reads the dictation through once without stopping. Then when she reads a phrase for the learners to write, she reads the phrase quite quickly so that the proficient learners can write it and then she waits a few seconds and reads the phrase again more slowly for the other learners. During the second reading, the proficient learners just check their work. The teacher goes through the dictation, reading each phrase twice in this way.

*Peer dictation*

The learners have a copy of the dictation text in front of them. They work in small groups, with one person in the group reading the dictation for the others to write. It may be turned into a competition in the following way. The learners work in pairs. One learner reads a dictation while the other learner writes. They have only a limited time to do the dictation, because as soon as one pair of learners has finished the dictation, they say "Stop!" and the rest of the class must stop work. The learner who is writing can ask the other to repeat words and phrases, and to spell them aloud. This is an example of superior-inferior group work (Chapter 3).

*Completion dictation*

This variation of dictation is particularly suited to learners who struggle with dictation, particularly because of difficulty in writing. In this guided technique, part of the writing is already done for the learners, in that they do not have to write everything initially. The learners are given several printed copies of the text. One copy has a few words missing, the next copy has more words missing, and so on. The learners listen to the text being read by the teacher phrase by phrase and fill in the words missing on their first copy. Then the teacher reads the text again and the learners fill in the missing words on the next copy which has more words missing than the first copy. This continues until the learners are writing the whole dictation. Before the learners fill the words in the second and later copies, they fold their piece of paper so that they cannot see the texts that they have already filled in. Here is an example.

1  When _____ person dies _____ Bali, _____ family and friends _____ not usually sad. For them, death _____ _____ beginning of _____ life. _____ dead person will come back _____ _____ world _____ another shape. Before this happens, _____ old body must go.
2  When _____ person dies _____ Bali, _____ family _____ friends _____ _____ usually sad. _____ them, death _____ _____ beginning _____ _____ life. _____ dead person _____ come back _____ _____ world _____ another shape. _____ this happens, _____ old body _____ go.
3  _____ _____ person _____ _____ Bali, _____ family _____ friends _____ _____ _____ sad. _____ _____, death _____ _____ beginning _____ _____ life. _____ dead person _____ _____ _____ _____ _____ world _____ _____ shape. _____ this _____, _____ old body _____ _____.

More and more words are taken out until the learners are writing every word in the text.

*Perfect dictation*

After the dictations have been marked, it is usually good for the learners to hear the dictation again while they look at their marked work so they can pay attention to the parts where they made mistakes. Sawyer and Silver (1961) suggest that after the dictation has been marked and returned to the learners, it should be dictated again so that they do not make the same mistakes they did during the first time. The dictation is then marked again, either by the learners or by the teacher. It is given again on another day, so that by the time the dictation has been given for the third time, the learners almost know the dictation by heart and are able to write it perfectly. Thus, the first marking is only the first step in the teaching, and the learners will eventually produce a perfect copy.

*Sentence dictation*

The teacher says sentences and the learners write them. Tucker (1972) suggests that after each sentence has been given as dictation it should be corrected before the next sentence is given as dictation. In this way the learners see their mistakes immediately and can improve during the exercise. The correction can be done by the teacher or a learner writing the sentence on the blackboard and with the learners checking their own work.

*Unexploded dictation*

The teacher records a text at normal speaking speed and without the pauses that would normally be in a dictation. The learners load the dictation on to their cell phone and then have to each make their own transcription of the text, pausing and replaying the text to keep listening to the text until they can make an accurate transcription. There is now cheap software (http://www.ronimusic.com/leftframe.htm) which allows recordings to be slowed down without changing the pitch. Learners can thus listen to texts that would normally be at too fast a speed for them.

*Marking using the pyramid procedure*

The pyramid procedure (Jordan, 1990) is a particularly efficient way of marking dictations. The pyramid procedure involves doing substantially the same task several times, first individually, then in pairs, then in small groups, and then as a whole class. When applied to dictation, this involves each learner checking their own dictation for errors and correcting them. Then learners work in pairs to compare their dictations to see where they agree and disagree. Where the dictations are not the same, they try to agree on the correct form. Then in groups of four, they go through the same comparison procedure. Then the whole class works together with the learners questioning the teacher on problematic parts of the dictation. After this, the learners are shown the correct written text.

*Marking with immediate feedback*

When doing the dictation, one learner can write the dictation on the whiteboard, while the others write in their books. As the learner writes, the teacher can make quick corrections to the learner's work on the whiteboard, so that the whiteboard contains an accurate version of the dictation. The learners can then look at the whiteboard to correct their dictations. This technique is called programmed dictation, because it gives immediate feedback to the learners.

*Variants of dictation involving other language skills*

Figure 6.1 shows how dictation is related to several other techniques. The main difference between the four techniques is the medium of input and output. Dictation has listening input and written output. Delayed repetition has listening input and spoken output. Read-and-look-up has reading input and spoken output, and delayed copying has reading input and written output. They all involve holding language material briefly in memory before producing it. Let us now look at the three techniques other than dictation.

## 80 Listening

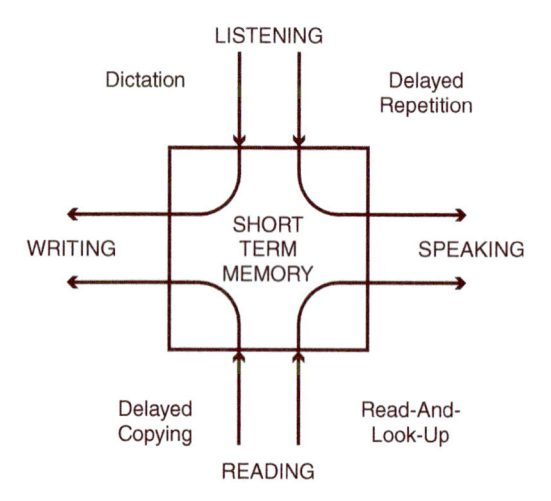

```
                    LISTENING
      Dictation              Delayed
                             Repetition
                  ┌─────────┐
                  │  SHORT  │
         WRITING  │  TERM   │  SPEAKING
                  │ MEMORY  │
                  └─────────┘
       Delayed               Read-And-
       Copying               Look-Up
                     READING
```

**FIGURE 6.1** Variants of dictation.

Michael West (1955) devised this technique as a way of helping learners learn from written dialogues and to help them put spoken expression into the dialogues. West regarded the physical aspects of Read-and-look-up as being very important for using the technique properly. The learners work in pairs facing each other. One is the reader; the other is the listener. The reader holds the piece of paper or the book containing the dialogue at about chest level and slightly to the left. This enables the reader to look at the piece of paper and then to look at the listener, moving only their eyes and not having to move their head at all. The reader looks at the piece of paper and tries to remember as long a phrase as possible. The reader can look at the paper for as long as is necessary. Then, when ready, they look at the listener and say the phrase.

While they look at the paper, they do not speak. While they speak, they do not look at the paper. These rules force the reader to rely on memory. At first the technique is a little difficult to use, because the reader has to discover what length of phrase is most comfortable and has to master the rules of the technique. It can also be practised at home in front of a mirror. West sees value in the technique because the learner

> has to carry the words of a whole phrase, or perhaps a whole sentence, in his mind. The connection is not from book to mouth, but from book to brain, and then from brain to mouth. That interval of memory constitutes half the learning process…. Of all methods of learning a language, Read-and-Look-up is, in our opinion, the most valuable.
>
> *(West, 1955, p. 12)*

*Delayed copying*

This technique involves copying from a reading text (Hill, 1969). An essential feature of the technique is that the learners try to hold as large a phrase as possible in their memory before writing it. So, instead of copying word for word, the learners read a phrase, look away from the text, and then write it. Unlike dictation, this technique is ideally suited for individual practice.

*Delayed repetition*

This technique has sometimes been used as a language proficiency test. This is because the length of the phrase that a learner can hold in memory has been regarded as an indicator of language proficiency (Harris, 1970; Lado, 1965). Instead of being an individual test, it can be used as an exercise either with the whole class or in pairs. When it is used as a whole class activity, the teacher says a phrase, counts to three and then gets the class to repeat it. The length of the phrase is gradually increased and the pause between listening and speaking can also be increased.

These three techniques can usefully be regarded as variations of dictation, each making use of the same aspect of memory but using different media. There are further variations that can be applied to them. One that can be easily applied to all of them is to provide some written support in the form of the main content words so that a much longer phrase can be held in memory. For example, the words *waves green up where die* are always available for the learner to look at while remembering and producing *Sea waves are green and wet, but up from where they die*. With dictation and delayed copying, the clue words can be on the sheets with spaces between them for the learners to fill in.

Lado (1965, pp. 128–129) looked at the role of memory span as a means of measuring second language proficiency, and concluded:

1 Memory span is shorter in a foreign language than in the native language.
2 Memory span in a foreign language increases with mastery of the language.
3 The difference between the native and the foreign language memory span is greater when the material in the foreign language contains the pronunciation and grammatical contrasts between the languages.
4 The relation of memory span to foreign language learning is greater for contextual material than for numbers.

Harris (1970) developed a group-administered memory span test. He found that "the difficulty of the test sentences appeared to be determined very largely by their length and syntactical complexity" (p. 203). Syntactical complexity was determined by the presence of subordinate clauses. Performance on the memory span test "correlated quite highly (from .73 to .79) with performance on standardized listening and grammar tests of English as a foreign language" (p. 203).

Although the experiments mentioned above have given valuable information on the relationship between memory span and foreign language learning, three important questions remain to be answered. (1) Does memory span practice (as in dictation and related activities) increase memory span? (2) Does this increase in memory span result in improvement in foreign language proficiency as measured by a variety of tests? (3) What factors in the techniques involving memory span increase proficiency?

## Dicto-comp and related activities

Dictation and its related activities work mainly at the phrase and clause level. There is a range of related techniques which work with much larger units of language. The dicto-comp (Ilson, 1962; Riley, 1972), also known as dicto-gloss (Wajnryb, 1989), is the best-known example of these. In the dicto-comp, the learners listen as the teacher reads a text to them. The teacher may read it several times. Then, the learners write what they can remember without any further help. The main difference between dictation and the dicto-comp is that in dictation the learners have to remember a phrase of several words as accurately as possible. In the dicto-comp the learners have to remember the ideas in a text of more than a hundred words long and express them in the words of the original or in their own words. The dicto-comp, whose name comes from *dictation* and *composition*, is an experience technique, and is a kind of guided writing. It reduces the cognitive load of a task (in this case, a writing task) by preparing the learners well before they do the task. In dicto-comp and its related techniques, the preparation provides the learners with ideas, language items, and text organization so that they can focus on the skill aspect, which is writing in the case of the dicto-comp. In the dicto-gloss, learners work together in groups to reconstruct the text. The group discussion while reconstructing the text is seen as the major source of learning during the activity, because the discussion focuses on language features.

## Related techniques

Figure 6.2 shows how the dicto-comp is related to other techniques. Note the parallels between Figures 6.2 and 6.1. The big difference is that the activities in Figure 6.2 involve having to recall the whole text rather than a series of phrases.

### Oral reproduction

In this activity the learners listen to the teacher or a classmate tell a story, several times if necessary, and then they retell it to a partner. Often this activity is part of

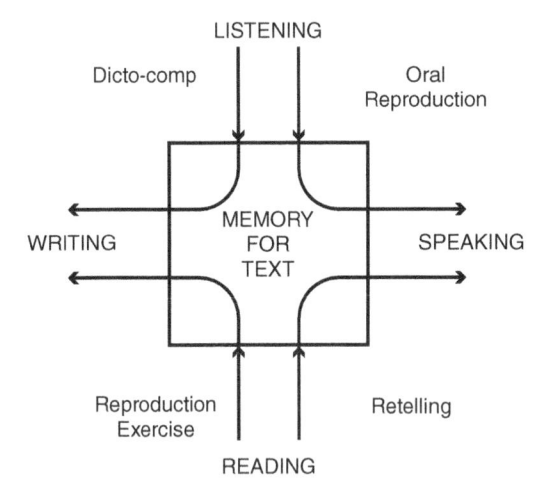

**FIGURE 6.2** Variants of dicto-comp.

a chain of retelling with new listeners, who did not hear the first telling and other retellings, coming into the classroom to listen and retell. It is also possible to do it as a group activity, like dicto-gloss, with learners working together to make the retelling as detailed and accurate as possible.

*Retelling*

The input to this activity is reading. After the reader has reached a good understanding of the written text, it is put away and the reader retells the information to a listener. This can be usefully combined with the 4/3/2 technique (Maurice, 1983), where the same information is told by the same person three times. Each time, however, it is told to someone who has not heard it before and with less time (four minutes, then three minutes, then two minutes) to retell it. This results in increasing fluency in the retellings (see Chapter 12 in this book).

*Reproduction exercise*

This exercise involves reading input and written output. The learners read a text and then have to produce their own written version of it without looking back at the original. The learning benefits of this exercise can be increased, if the learners are required to fill in an information transfer diagram after reading the text. The diagram can be based on the information in the text using a topic type analysis (Nation & Macalister, 2021). The diagram can then be the support for the writing.

Thus, a diagram for a text of the characteristics topic type (Johns & Davies, 1983), such as a description of contact lenses or the baobab tree, could look like this.

| Item: | General category: |
|---|---|
| Characteristics | Evidence for the characteristics |
| Other information | |

Elkins, Kalivoda, and Morain (1972) in an interesting article called "The fusion of the four skills" describe a chain procedure where information is read, then spoken, and then written. This procedure is simply the activities of retelling and dicto-comp chained together and repeated. Elkins et al. intend that there should be a different person at each part of the chain, but as a variation, there are advantages for the development of fluency if the chain is a circle of three people who have to process the same information several times in a different medium.

The four techniques – dicto-comp, oral reproduction, retelling, and the reproduction exercise – are all capable of being adapted to suit the proficiency level of the learners. The main factors in the adaptation, besides the content and language difficulty of the text, are (1) the number of repetitions, speed, or time that the learners have to comprehend and retain the input, (2) the length of the delay between the input and the production of the output, and (3) the degree of detail and resemblance of the input expected in the output. These factors can all be played one against the other. So, in the dicto-comp, the text may be spoken quite quickly but with several repetitions. Alternatively, the text may be spoken quite slowly and with several repetitions, but the learners are expected to write something that quite closely resembles the original.

### Are there digital applications of dictation?

There are several websites that provide activities that are like dictation, but several of them are not very satisfactory because they do not use systematic vocabulary control and do not follow a traditional approach to dictation in that they involve very deliberate slow speech rather than speech near a normal speed. It would be fairly straightforward to make a good dictation website where teachers could upload their own texts marked for pauses, and the website would then go through the steps for dictation including providing feedback on the learners' production. The better websites involving dictation usually include speed controls.

The unexploded dictation technique is well suited to recent technology because replay is now much easier to manage. When the technique was used with manually operated tape recorders, it resulted in a lot of wear and tear on the manual rewind and playback controls.

## What does research say about the effectiveness of dictation?

Dictation is largely unresearched. There is research on memory span, repetition, and corrective feedback that can be applied to dictation, but there is no direct research focusing on dictation as a language learning technique.

### Memory span

Dictation involves working memory and the typical rule for working memory follows Miller's (1956) 7 plus or minus rule, in that we can hold around seven chunks of information in the phonological loop in working memory. The easiest way to think of this is with a phone number. We may be able to hold a seven-digit phone number in our memory, but if we want to hold a longer number, we may have to chunk some of its parts. That is, we may need to treat two or three of the numbers as a single memorable chunk. The critical factor here is what qualifies as a chunk. A chunk is a single piece of information, but what is a single piece of information depends on the knowledge of the person dealing with the information. A well-known phrase may be a single piece of information, but if a particular phrase is not well known, then each word in the phrase may be a different piece of information.

Dictation encourages the chunking of information, and so when the teacher divides up the text into pieces, it is very helpful if each piece makes a coherent unit. As learners' proficiency develops, the length of the pieces of the dictation text can become a little longer. Oller and Streiff (1975) saw the value of dictation as a useful test of language proficiency because it tapped into knowledge of the language system, what they called "grammar-based expectancies".

### Repetition

Dictation involves verbatim repetition with variation in medium from listening, to writing, to reading. Because dictation should involve known or partly known vocabulary, the repetition is more likely to affect the learning of multiword units rather than individual words. The role of dictation in learning multiword units is unresearched, as are most aspects of the use of dictation as a technique.

### Corrective feedback

The type of feedback given to dictation is comprehensive feedback where each error is noted. This is because dictation texts are typically short, around 100–150 words, and there would be few errors to comment on with selective targeted feedback. Where teachers mark dictation, the feedback is typically indirect with the place of the error indicated, but without the correct form being provided. This is because the learners should be able to find the correct form by themselves, or at least with reference to the original text. Where learners mark their own work, either individually or in pairs, the type of feedback is direct, with the correct form being provided.

To maximize the effect of corrective feedback, it would be useful for learners to listen to the whole dictation text again after getting and processing the feedback. The research on written corrective feedback (Bitchener, 2021) suggests that direct feedback accompanied by relevant metalinguistic information, such as indication of part of speech or a simple grammar rule, is usually most effective, although the research on this is not always in agreement and has largely focused on the production of output rather than the processing of input as in dictation.

An issue with corrective feedback on dictation is that learners are more likely to be interested in correcting the dictation rather than focusing on learning about the particular language feature involved in the error. The use of metalinguistic information is a way of keeping the focus on the language feature. Here are some examples of metalinguistic information that might be used in the feedback part of dictation, especially in spoken feedback when the class is discussing the final step.

> The noun is singular and countable, so needs an article.
> The noun has been mentioned before, so needs *the*.
> It refers to more than one, so the plural is needed.
> The subject and verb must agree.
> The sentence needs a finite verb.

If the teacher occasionally marks dictation, then cues such as A for article usage, T for tense, can be used as in written feedback on writing (see Appendix 1).

## Research questions

### *Motivation principles (Engagement)*

For learning to occur there needs to be a willingness to focus on what needs to be learned, and to give it quantity and quality of attention.

1 *Motivation: The degree of engagement with the task affects the likelihood of learning occurring.* Do learners enjoy doing dictation? Do learners see value in doing dictation?
2 *Self-efficacy: Our confidence in our own skills of learning affects our success in learning.* What ensures high success rates in doing dictation?

## Focus principles (Usefulness)

Learning requires giving attention to what needs to be learned.

3 *Focus: We learn what we focus on, and in addition, our learning is more useful if it closely resembles the use that we need to make of what we learn (transfer-appropriate).* What improvement in dictation occurs as a result of doing a series of dictation activities? What improvement in listening skills occurs as a result of doing a series of dictation activities? What learning from dictation activities transfers outside dictation to the comprehension of listening texts? To what degree does writing skill enhance or interfere with success at dictation?

4 *Accuracy: Our learning is more efficient if the information we are focusing on is complete, accurate, and comprehensible.* Do pre-dictation activities (Brown & Barnard, 1975) result in greater accuracy in dictation? Do pre-dictation activities result in learning, or do they simply prime for what is coming? What versions of dictation (traditional, dictation for a mixed class, small group dictation, unexploded dictation) result in accuracy for the greatest number of learners in a mixed-proficiency class? How well do learners handle words in dictation which are regularly spelled but unknown? When the teacher reads the phrases for the learners to write, should they be read slowly and clearly or should they be read at normal speaking speed?

## Quantity principles (Amount)

5 *Repetition: The more repetitions, the stronger the learning.* How much dictation needs to be done to bring about improvement in dictation and listening skills? Is verbatim repeated dictation more effective than varied dictation? Does repeating the same dictation several days later result in extra learning? What is the best way to mark dictation?

6 *Time-on-task: The greater and longer the attention, the stronger the learning.* Is the four-step traditional dictation sequence the most effective sequence for learning from dictation?

## Quality principles (Connections)

Elaboration and analysis increase and strengthen connections between the item to be learned and other knowledge, making it easier to access the item.

7 *Elaboration: This includes enriching the encoding of an item through variation.* What kind of feedback on dictation helps learning the most?

8 *Analysis: This involves relating the familiar parts to the unfamiliar whole.* Is feedback on dictation that involves grammatical analysis more effective than simple correction?

Any research on dictation would be greatly welcome. The most useful would be on what learning occurs from doing dictation.

# 7
# EASY LISTENING

## What is easy listening?

Easy listening is a fluency development activity and can take several forms. It can involve Quicklistens (Millet, 2014), listening to stories (an activity which involves graded readers) (Nation, 2024), shared reading where the teacher and learners interact about a reading text (Senechal & Cornell, 1993), and repeated listening where the same text is listened to several times. As we saw in Chapter 1 on the four strands, a fluency technique needs to meet five criteria. These criteria in order of importance are the activity involves easy material, the language use is largely accurate, there is pressure to go faster, the focus is on conveying meaning, and there is a large quantity of practice. Table 7.1 shows how these criteria apply to easy listening.

Easy listening does not fit the fluency criteria as comfortably as fluency activities in the other skills, largely because the pressure to go faster needs to be individually controlled, and this is not so easy with activities such as Quicklistens and shared reading which are usually done as whole class activities. Quicklistens can be recorded and learners can playback individually and can control the speed on playback devices. This does not work for shared reading. Moreover, because listening is typically slower than reading, listening texts tend to be shorter than reading texts, reducing quantity of input. Teachers can provide more easy listening through the regular use of the L2 in classroom management.

## What are the learning goals of easy listening?

Easy listening is a fluency development activity, and thus depends on using very easy material.

DOI: 10.4324/9781003496151-9

**TABLE 7.1** How easy listening meets the five fluency criteria

| Criteria | Features of easy listening |
| --- | --- |
| Easy material | The listening texts are written within a strictly controlled vocabulary or are repeated |
| Good comprehension | The texts are easy, and any comprehension questions are not tricky |
| Pressure to go faster | The speed of the spoken input is matched to the learners' proficiency |
| Meaning-focused | The focus is on understanding the input. Quicklistens involve comprehension questions, and shared reading involves interaction about content |
| Quantity of practice | Easy listening should be a regularly scheduled activity |

**TABLE 7.2** The goals of easy listening

| Goals | Specific focuses |
| --- | --- |
| Language | Strengthening and enriching partly known vocabulary and grammar<br>Pushing learners to work with a larger unit of processing than single words |
| Ideas | |
| Skills | *Listening with fluency* |
| Text | |

*Note*: The major goal is in *italics*.

As Table 7.2 shows, the major learning goal of easy listening is to increase listening fluency so that learners are listening at a speed of around 150 words per minute. A secondary goal of easy listening is to strengthen knowledge of words and grammatical constructions that are already known or partly known.

### How does easy listening help learning?

Easy listening helps develop fluency through quantity of practice with easy material. Because the material is easy, the learners can process the material quickly without the distraction of unfamiliar items.

*Motivation:* Because listening fluency materials are easy, learners should experience success (self-efficacy). Seeing progress in a listening fluency course is more difficult than in a speed reading course, because there is no graph showing the speed gains in words per minute. However, if recorded texts are used, then increase in playback speed can be a sign of progress.

*Focus:* In easy listening, the focus is on adequate comprehension of the input (focus). The focus on comprehension is useful, because improvement in skill in use largely involves incidental learning through transfer-appropriate quantity of use.

*Quantity:* Quantity of practice with easy material is the main factor affecting the development of listening fluency. Quantity can come through repeated listening (repetition) and through large quantities of easy listening input (time-on-task).

*Quality:* Large quantities of input provide opportunities for the same words, multiword units, and grammatical constructions to occur in varied contexts, thus enriching knowledge (elaboration).

As with developing reading fluency, listening fluency activities are likely to push the listener to work with a larger unit of language than the word.

## What are the requirements of easy listening?

The major requirement for easy listening is easy material. While it is good to have material at a variety of levels to suit proficiency levels within a class, the main requirement for fluency development is that the material should be easy, and it is not a great concern if it seems too easy for some learners. Nonetheless, having access to various levels of easy material is valuable, because it is highly likely that increases in fluency are partly the result of increases in speed of access to the meanings of particular words. Thus, having easy listening material at a variety of levels helps in providing practice with quickly accessing more words.

### How can you prepare for easy listening?

Teachers should know the vocabulary levels of their learners so that they can choose and prepare material at the right level. The Vocabulary Levels Tests on Paul Nation's resources pages are the most suitable tests for most learners of English as a foreign language. Not all levels of the tests need to be used.

It is worth having plenty of recorded easy listening material. The extensive reading web site *Xreading* has recorded versions of many of the graded readers on its site. There is variety of listening material on the web but this needs to be chosen carefully.

Information transfer activities (Chapter 17) can be used for easy listening with the teacher working from a completed information transfer diagram rather than a text to provide listening input.

### What texts can be used for easy listening?

The graded readers which are used for listening to stories can be chosen from the prize winners of the annual Extensive Reading Foundation competition. These are all excellent books with great content and good language control. They are books that learners would be quite happy to listen to several times during a course.

## How much time should be given to easy listening in a general language course?

Easy listening is a fluency development activity and should take up one-quarter of the fluency development strand. The fluency development strand should occupy one-quarter of the course time, so that means that easy listening should occupy round one-sixteenth of the total course time. Much of the listening involved in 4/3/2, informal conversation, problem-solving speaking, and prepared talks and other activities involving spoken interaction involves input from other learners of roughly the same proficiency level, and some of this could be considered as easy listening and counted as part of fluency development.

## How can easy listening be done well?

### Quicklistens

Sonia Millett (2014) has prepared material called *Quicklistens* which consist of easy questions to accompany recordings of graded readers at the 400, 600, and 700 word levels. Quicklistens involve listening to a section of a graded reader audio recording while writing answers to questions at the same time. The material is aimed at increasing listening fluency, so the comprehension questions provide a useful check that listening speed is also accompanied by good comprehension.

1 Quicklistens work best if they involve listening to parts of the same graded reader so that knowledge about the story and characters is built up over time. So, the first step is to choose an interesting reader, divide it into short sections and prepare questions on each section. Sonia has prepared material that is available on Paul Nation's resources pages.
2 The teacher introduces the graded reader to the class drawing on learners' background knowledge.
3 The teacher previews the questions for the first section.
4 The learners listen to the section or a recording of it and answer the questions as they listen.
5 The teacher quickly goes over the answers.
    Steps 2–5 are repeated in subsequent lessons, with Step 2 being chosen from a range of activities including the teacher and learners recalling what happened previously, practising pronouncing the questions, and predicting what might happen. The activity, however, always involves pre-viewing the questions. Research on Quicklistens shows that the greatest improvement

occurs if learners do listening-while-reading immediately followed by listening while answering the comprehension questions. So, Step 3 above could be replaced by listening-while-reading, followed by looking at the questions. Step 4 would remain as answering the questions while listening so that the focus of the activity is firmly on listening comprehension.

## Listening to stories

The technique of *Listening to stories* is a form of extensive listening that is especially suited to low-intermediate proficiency learners. It is done as a whole-class activity.

1. The teacher chooses a book that is at roughly the right level for the learners and has an engaging story. Typically, it will need to be a graded reader, and it would be wise to choose an award-winning book from the winners of the Extensive Reading Foundation annual graded reader competition, as these are likely to be very well written and interesting.
2. The teacher sits next to the whiteboard and begins to read the story. In the early stages of the reading, the reading is not very fast and each phrase is repeated.
3. When a word or phrase occurs that might cause a problem for the learners, the teacher writes it on the whiteboard. If the word occurs again, the teacher points to the word on the whiteboard. The teacher watches carefully to make sure that the learners are following the story and are interested. It is useful if learners are willing to make small gestures, such as a wave of the hand, if they do not understand a particular phrase or sentence. The aim is to present the story in a way so that all can follow it.
4. After about ten minutes of this, the teacher stops and says, "To be continued".
5. A few days later, the teacher continues reading the story. As the learners become familiar with the story, the teacher can read a bit faster, repeat only some of the phrases, and note down fewer words on the whiteboard. After several sessions of this, the teacher may be able to read at a normal speed with little repetition. Over a period of time, this activity moves from being a guided (language-focused learning) activity to a meaning-focused input activity, and finally to a fluency development activity.
6. After the listening to stories activity has eventually been completed for a particular book, learners may choose to listen to the same story again, this time as an individual activity using a recording.

If the story for this activity is well chosen, this activity becomes one that the learners look forward to and enjoy in much the same way as they enjoy watching a soap opera series on television.

*How can I check that an easy listening activity is working well?*

Easy listening is a fluency development activity, and so the first thing to look for is how quickly learners are doing the listening. If the speed is close to 100–150 words per minute, the activity is working well. Fluency without accuracy is not really fluency, so the second thing to look for is if learners have adequate comprehension of what they are listening to. For fluency activities, 100% accuracy is not likely or even desirable, because time pressure will inevitably result in some performance errors that are not the result of inaccurate knowledge. Quicklistens have comprehension questions to check accuracy. While using listening to stories, the teacher can ask learners occasional questions to check whether they are following the story.

**What are the variants of easy listening?**

The *Shared reading* or *Blown-up book* technique is very commonly used with young native speakers. It involves reading and listening, with the major focus on listening, but with the goal of getting learners interested in reading. The teacher uses a very large copy of a reading book (search for *big books* or *shared reading* on the web). Some publishers produce these specifically for the shared book activity, but they are books intended for native speakers and would be too difficult for many young foreign language learners. However, an enlarged photocopy could work for graded readers. The teacher sits in front of the class, holding the book so that all can see it. The teacher tells the learners the title of the book and asks them what they think it might be about. After a bit of discussion, the teacher starts reading the story. Every so often the teacher engages the learners in talking about the story, what will happen next, what they think of the characters and so on. Big books are usually quite short and so the teacher reads the story to the end, interacting with the learners during the reading. On another day, the same book could be read again. The learners may be asked to choose what book they want to hear again. There are usually regular copies of the book available, so that learners can read the book by themselves later if they wish. The shared book activity is a way of copying the activity of a parent reading to their child, except that the teacher is reading to the whole class. Shared reading is sometimes called interactive reading.

*How can easy listening be used at all levels of proficiency?* Easy listening can be done at all levels depending on the texts that are used. Easy listening can be seen as a part of an extensive listening programme, where two-thirds of the programme is more challenging listening (meaning-focused input) and one-third is easy listening (fluency development). At elementary levels, the listening texts should be the lowest levels of graded readers and should involve plenty of repetition, both when listening to the text (repeating phrases and sentences) and when coming back to the text to listen to it again. Listening-while-reading can be a useful way of beginning easy listening.

At advanced levels, easy listening should involve fast-paced input.

### Are there digital applications of this technique?

Listening-while-reading is especially suited to computer-assisted learning, especially if the rate of delivery is able to be controlled, and if there is easy immediate replay of the previous sentence. Many web sites, such as TED Talks, provide a written script and in some cases captions to accompany videos. The online graded reading programme *Xreading* provides opportunity for listening-while-reading, as well as speed-adjusted listening without sound distortion.

### Revisiting and linking to other activities

Easy listening should include repeated listening. Repeated listening can include immediate repeated listening, where the same text is listened to again just after listening to it, and delayed repeated listening where the same text is listened to again several days or weeks later.

Listening to a previously read reading passage is a good way of returning to old material in a course.

### What does research say about the effectiveness of easy listening?

Chang and Millett (2014, 2016) have looked at the effects of Quicklistens on listening accuracy (comprehension questions) at a speed of around 100 words per minute. The greatest improvement occurred when learners did listening-while-reading followed by listening only on the same text. The listening only follow-up activity ensured that the learners did not rely solely on reading. However, there needed to be large quantities of input (around two hours per week involving one whole graded reader per week) over several weeks to get striking results, but the improvement was substantial. Improvement was directly related to the amount of work done. The learners in their experimental studies initially struggled with the listening-while-reading, but after completing four or five graded readers they reached a higher level of comprehension and then continued to make substantial gains. Their attitude to the activity also became more positive when they experienced the gains that they were making. The learners were working with the Oxford Bookworms Level 1 & 2 graded readers. Chang and Millett (2016) found the listening-while-reading also improved reading rates and comprehension.

There are three important lessons from the Chang and Millett studies.

1 Quantity of practice is needed to make meaningful gains in language use.
2 One skill can support the use of another (reading can support listening), but ultimately quantity of unsupported practice is needed in the target skill.
3 The case studies in their research show that there is an initial low-proficiency barrier to overcome before learners can make substantial growth in the listening skill. Learners need strong encouragement to overcome this barrier.

Easy listening as a fluency development activity is still under-researched. The small amount of case study research has revealed very interesting findings, and we need more of this to guide our use of the technique.

## Research questions

### Motivation principles (Engagement)

For learning to occur, there needs to be a willingness to focus on what needs to be learned, and to give it quantity and quality of attention.

1 *Motivation: The degree of engagement with the task affects the likelihood of learning occurring.* What motivators can be used to push learners to do the amount of practice needed to overcome the initial low-proficiency barrier in listening-while-reading?
2 *Self-efficacy: Our confidence in our own skills of learning affects our success in learning.* Does easy listening have positive effects on learners' willingness to do more listening?

### Focus principles (Usefulness)

Learning requires giving attention to what needs to be learned.

3 *Focus: We learn what we focus on, and in addition, our learning is more useful if it closely resembles the use that we need to make of what we learn (transfer-appropriate).* What role can speed adjustment of input play in listening fluency development? Does improvement in easy listening transfer to more challenging listening?
4 *Accuracy: Our learning is more efficient if the information we are focusing on is complete, accurate, and comprehensible.* Are comprehension questions necessary to get learners involved in easy listening? Do learners prefer to have comprehension questions? Do comprehension questions affect what learners do during easy listening? Is easy listening more effective if learners

can control the input during easy listening, for example, to change the speed, to immediately replay parts of the input, to listen several times? Is vocabulary control the major factor affecting difficulty in easy listening?

## Quantity principles (Amount)

5 *Repetition: The more repetitions, the stronger the learning.* Does repeated listening have different effects from easy listening?
6 *Time-on-task: The greater and longer the attention, the stronger the learning.* Is the amount of easy listening directly related to improvement in listening fluency? How much easy listening is needed to get substantial improvement in listening fluency?

## Quality principles (Connections)

Elaboration and analysis increase and strengthen connections between the item to be learned and other knowledge making it easier to access the item.

7 *Elaboration: This includes enriching the encoding of an item through variation.* Does easy listening result in greater knowledge of multiword units? Does easy listening strengthen vocabulary knowledge of previously known words?
8 *Analysis: This involves relating the familiar parts to the unfamiliar whole.* Can listeners cope with previously unfamiliar family members during easy listening?

The most useful research on easy listening would be the same as that for extensive listening and viewing, namely developing the technology to make vocabulary-controlled listening material. Beyond that, research should focus on the effect of easy listening on fluency development.

# PART 2
# Speaking

# 8
# INFORMAL CONVERSATION

### What is informal conversation?

Informal conversation involves two or more people talking to each other with an emphasis on the interactional rather than transactional aspects of conversation (Brown, 1978). That is, informal conversation is not carried out to convey important information but to maintain friendly contact through interaction. At elementary levels, informal conversation involves memorized dialogues, but as proficiency develops, the conversation becomes more unpredictable.

### What are the learning goals of informal conversation?

Table 8.1 presents the learning goals of informal conversation.

The major learning goal of informal conversation involves learning the language and skills needed to talk with others in a friendly co-operative way. At the same time, informal conversation involves learning the vocabulary and multi-word expressions typically used in social interaction. The skills of interaction include speaking with a reasonable level of fluency, being able to deal with conversational difficulties and misunderstandings, and being able to start, maintain, or end the conversation. Biber and Conrad's (2009) research on text types suggests that the spoken language/written language distinction is the one most marked by vocabulary and grammatical differences.

### How does informal conversation help learning?

Much learning during informal conversation will be incidental, but early in a course there should also be a substantial amount of deliberate rote learning of

DOI: 10.4324/9781003496151-11

**TABLE 8.1** The goals of informal conversation

| Goals | Specific focuses |
|---|---|
| Language | Learning new vocabulary and grammatical features for productive use |
|  | Strengthening and enriching partly known vocabulary and grammar with a focus on accuracy in spoken production |
| Ideas |  |
| Skills | *Learning the interactional language and skills of conversation* |
| Text | Learning how to start, maintain, and end a conversation |

*Note*: The major goal is in *italics*.

multiword units, phrases, and sentences. These should be learned to a good level of fluency. There will also be the opportunity to learn through negotiation and language-related episodes which temporarily deliberately focus on areas of misunderstanding or lack of understanding in the context of conversation. In essence, informal conversation helps learning the skill of speaking through a large quantity of highly transferable practice.

*Motivation:* Informal conversation is probably what most learners of a language want and expect to learn when they learn a foreign language, so motivation should be high for such learning (motivation). The memorization of useful phrases and sentences is a quick way of becoming fluent even at a very low level of proficiency (Palmer, 1925), and if the phrases and sentences are well chosen, this enhances motivation.

*Focus:* The focus in informal conversation activities should be on highly transferable spoken communication with a high degree of accuracy. The deliberate learning aspects of informal conversation also have an accuracy focus.

*Quantity:* Spaced repetition is the most important factor in learning informal conversation. Dialogues should be practised many times on different occasions, so that they eventually require little effort to produce.

*Quality:* Part of the survival language syllabus is learning how to control input and seek help with language issues. Phrases like "Could you please say that again?", "What does __ mean?", "Please speak more slowly.", and "What is this called?" allow the learner to learn from input and make the input memorable through elaboration.

## What are the requirements of informal conversation?

### *How can you prepare for informal conversation?*

At the elementary and intermediate levels, preparing for informal conversation involves the preparation and memorization of useful sentences and phrases.

Memorization involves the principles of learning described in Chapter 4, with repetition being the critical factor involving plenty of spaced retrieval.

Preparation for informal conversation should involve some deliberate attention to prosody. This should involve giving attention to stress and intonation, rhythm (stress-based timing), learning about and practising deletion (got to -> gotta, let go -> leggo), and insertion (far away -> faraway; two apples -> two wapples). The simplest way to go about this is to practice forms like *gunna* (going to), *wonna* (want to), *howayou* (how are you?).

A very useful way of practising sentence stress and intonation is to take a short sentence and then gradually add more words to it (Bauer, 2023). For example, Where are you going? Where are you going with that? Where are you going with that on your back?

### *What topics can be used for informal conversation?*

Informal conversation can cover a range of daily topics. For older elementary learners, the survival syllabus for foreign travel (Nation & Crabbe, 1991) should be among the very early topics. This covers the main headings of Greetings and being polite, Buying and bargaining, Reading signs, Getting to places, Finding accommodation, Ordering food, Talking about yourself and talking to children, and Controlling and learning language. The survival syllabus has now been translated into several languages and these can be found on Paul Nation's resources pages under Vocabulary Lists. The 1991 article about the survival syllabus is also freely available on the resources pages under Publications.

Most coursebooks have a good coverage of a range of topics for informal conversation and the web site http://www.esldiscussions.com/ has a large number of topics and questions. Appendix 5 of Nation (2024) *What should every EFL Teacher Know?* contains 100 easy topics.

### *How much time should be given to informal conversation in a general language course?*

Informal conversation fits into the four strands of a course because it involves both speaking and listening, and deliberate learning, language use, and fluency development. It seems reasonable to give about a third of meaning-focused input and meaning-focused output strands to informal conversation, with the other two-thirds involving problem-solving role play (see Chapter 9) and prepared talks (Chapter 10). Watching movies and television series (viewing) can be considered as contributing to informal conversation in that most movies and fiction television series involve lots of dialogue. In a whole course, informal conversation could take up around one-sixth of the total time, especially if informal conversation is seen as also involving the fluency development strand.

### How can informal conversation be done well?

The critical learning factor in learning to do informal conversation well is quantity of practice, particularly repetition involving spaced retrieval. In the following series of steps, we will focus on using memorized dialogues.

1 An informal conversation activity should begin with learners listening to the dialogue that they are going to practice while they see the script. If the dialogue is recorded, this will allow it to be replayed for several listenings. Between each replay, the teacher can point out features that the learners should give special attention to such as useful phrases, stress and intonation, and the pronunciation of particular words.
2 The learners then practice the conversation in pairs, reading from the script, each taking a different part in the conversation. In these first two steps, the focus is on accuracy.
3 The next steps involve a focus on memorization and fluency. The learners form new pairs, with each sticking with the same part that they previously practised. They then practise the conversation again twice and then form new pairs.
4 The new pairs now take different parts in the conversation (speaker A becoming speaker B and vice versa), and practise it again twice.
5 On at least two other days, the same conversation is practised again, at least twice on each occasion, without using the script if possible. If some help is needed, the first couple of words of each line is put on the whiteboard as cues to help recall.
6 On a later occasion, the learners think about some small content changes that they could make to the conversation and practise it again with the changes.

By the end of Step 6, the learners should be quite fluent in the conversation and can do it without the script or any notes.

### How can I check that an informal conversation activity is working well?

At the elementary level, the first thing to observe is the accuracy of the activity. That is, is the language used correctly? The second thing to look for is the degree of fluency.

At an advanced level, accuracy is still important, but it is worth observing how well the learners are managing the conversation. Are they dealing well with any breakdowns in communication? Are they involving others in the conversation and managing turn-taking well? Are they using reduced spoken forms and conversational phrases well?

## What are the variants of informal conversation?

An important strategy to learn as a part of informal conversation is the strategy called Q->SA+EI which stands for the rule that a question (Q) should be answered by giving a short answer (SA) and then extra information (EI). This strategy is a way to encourage others to keep talking to you, and for you to steer the conversation in the direction you want (Holmes & Brown, 1976; Nation, 1980). The extra information can be a fact, a feeling, or a question. So, for example, if someone asks "How long have you been here?", you can answer "Three months. I had a few difficulties when I first arrived." Here the information is a fact and it will lead the questioner to ask about the difficulties. The extra information could be a feeling "I have really enjoyed being here.", or a question "I wonder if you can help me with a small problem I have?" Compare the effect if the response was simply the short answer, "Three months". This short reply would probably be interpreted as an unwillingness to proceed with the conversation. If a second question also received a short reply, it would border on being impolite. Learners should memorize the formula (Q->SA+EI) and practice giving short answers with extra information of various kinds until they become good at it. Occasionally, the extra information can be more than a single sentence and can involve a long-turn (see Chapter 10) where the speaker talks for several sentences on a well-prepared topic.

This Q->SA+EI strategy is particularly useful in interviews, where the person being interviewed leads the interview by providing certain kinds of extra information. Interview activities are very useful ways of practising informal conversation. A guided interview can start from a list of questions and can involve some preparation and later on some role play.

Giving and understanding directions is a useful conversation activity, especially if the listener interacts with the speaker to check that they have understood correctly and to seek further clarification. Following directions is a superior-inferior group work activity (Chapter 3), where one learner has the information that the other learner wants. It can involve following directions on a map (an activity becoming rarer with GPS on mobile phones, but nevertheless still useful), assembling a LEGO model, completing a plan or diagram, or noting down a recipe or steps in solving a computer-use problem.

It is useful for a teacher to be able to draw on a range of ways to get learners to practise memorized dialogues. This range of ways should include ways of making the activity easier or more challenging. Here are some ways of making the activity easier.

1  The learners can refer to the written conversation while they speak.
2  The learners can have a cue sheet or look at the whiteboard with some of the key words or pictures to prompt their memory, or with the first two or three words of each line.

3  The learners can work in groups of three with two as speakers without the script and the third learner with the script acting as prompt to provide cues when the speakers can't remember what to say. They can take turns at being the prompt, meaning that they will need to practise the dialogue at least three times.

Here are some ways of making the activity more challenging.

1  The dialogue is performed without the script.
2  When a memorized dialogue has been well practised, each learner thinks of a question to include that their partner is not expecting. To ensure that the question is correct, the learner can check the question with a different learner before using it.
3  The learners can be challenged to say the conversation a bit faster than they would normally say it.
4  The activity is done as a role play activity, with learners having to take on various emotions as they perform the dialogue. For example, one pretends that they are very tired, or in a hurry, or very enthusiastic.

Role play activities can provide an opportunity to practice a range of conversational skills in the classroom that will be useful outside the classroom. In a role play, each learner can have a role card which describes who they are and particular goals and limitations that they need to take account of during the role play. Here are some sample role play cards involving a visit to the doctor. Notice how the information on the role cards contains words and phrases (diarrhoea, possible side-effects, develop further complications) that the learners could use. Notice also that the roles contain information that will make the two speakers have to argue with each other.

| Learner A | Learner B |
| --- | --- |
| You have a stomach-ache and diarrhoea. You are on holiday away from home and have not met this doctor before. You think that your illness is not very serious and really do not want to take any medicine because you are afraid of possible side-effects. You do not have medical insurance. | You are the doctor. You have not seen this patient before. You are worried about the patient because they seem dehydrated (you may have to explain what this word means), and a bit confused. You think that they should spend a night in hospital to make sure that they do not develop further complications. |

### *How can informal conversation be used at all levels of proficiency?*

The earliest informal conversation involves memorized pairs of sentences – question and response, or statement and response, and short dialogues to memorize. The memorized dialogues become longer as proficiency develops and can involve small amounts of variation and improvisation. At the intermediate and advanced levels, dialogues no longer need to be memorized, although there can be useful phrases and expressions that are worth deliberately committing to memory. At these levels, the focus can move to skills in managing a conversation, and more time should be given to problem-solving activities (Chapter 9).

### Are there digital applications of this technique?

Informal conversation includes spoken interaction on mobile phones and through apps such as *Skype*, *Zoom*, *Line*, and *WhatsApp* which can involve face-to-face interaction. There are likely to be some factors that make interaction through phones and apps different from in-person interaction, but these factors are likely to have only small effects. The internet has greatly increased the opportunities for a learner doing self-study to practise informal conversation. As the research increases, it will be interesting to see how digital chat of various kinds develops its own unique features and the significance of these features. The rapid growth of artificial intelligence also increases possibilities for practising informal conversation.

### Revisiting and linking to other activities

Because repetition is so important in learning informal conversation, it is worth the teacher keeping a note of the number of occasions that the same dialogue has been practised. It would be worth developing a rule-of-thumb based on experience in monitoring such activities that could guide revisiting. That is, *five occasions – ten repetitions* could be the rule-of-thumb, meaning that the learners should come back to the same dialogue on five different days with a total of ten repetitions (an average of two on each occasion). Experience will show if this rule-of-thumb is easily enough or too much, or not enough with a particular group of learners.

Informal conversation is not easily linked to other material such as reading passages or extensive reading, or even to the more formal prepared talks. It could be useful to link informal conversation to letter writing where the letter writing reports on an informal conversation ("I met Ken the other day and he said …"), but letter writing is rapidly becoming a disappearing art. Biber's (1989) text type analysis showed a strong similarity between informal conversation and friendly letters in the language features used. Email and written internet chat does not seem to be taking on the same forms, although talking on mobile phones and through social platforms is clearly informal conversation and could be used as a way of practising it.

## What does research say about the effectiveness of informal conversation activities?

Vocabulary frequency counts comparing spoken versus written material show marked differences in the frequencies of particular words and in the coverage of texts. A relatively small spoken vocabulary can be used to say a lot. Michael West's (1960) Minimum Adequate Vocabulary for speaking consisted of 1,200-word families. West trialled this vocabulary by re-writing a lot of conversational material within it. Corpora of conversational English typically require a vocabulary size of 6,000 words or less to reach 98% coverage (Adolphs & Schmitt, 2003; Webb & Rodgers, 2009a, 2009b), but as West has shown, a lot can be said with a much smaller vocabulary.

In second language acquisition research, informal conversation activities have largely been investigated as opportunities to learn language through various kinds of language-related episodes (LREs), rather than as opportunities to improve conversation skills. Research in sociolinguistics, however, has focused more on the role of conversation in getting things done and in establishing social relationships.

## Research questions

### *Motivation principles (Engagement)*

For learning to occur there needs to be a willingness to focus on what needs to be learned, and to give it quantity and quality of attention.

1. *Motivation: The degree of engagement with the task affects the likelihood of learning occurring.* Does learning the survival vocabulary have a strong effect on motivation to keep learning? Do learners see informal conversation as their major goal in learning English?
2. *Self-efficacy: Our confidence in our own skills of learning affects our success in learning.* What do learners find difficult about informal conversation?

### *Focus principles (Usefulness)*

Learning requires giving attention to what needs to be learned.

3. *Focus: We learn what we focus on, and in addition, our learning is more useful if it closely resembles the use that we need to make of what we learn (transfer-appropriate).* Are memorized sentences actually used in uncontrolled speaking tasks? How does memorization help spoken language use? How can we measure when memorized use becomes integrated into language knowledge? What are the most useful topics for memorized conversations?

4 *Accuracy: Our learning is more efficient if the information we are focusing on is complete, accurate, and comprehensible.* What interventions most affect accuracy and complexity in informal speaking?

## Quantity principles (Amount)

5 *Repetition: The more repetitions, the stronger the learning.* How much revisiting is needed for memorized conversations?
6 *Time-on-task: The greater and longer the attention, the stronger the learning.* Should an informal speaking group consist of learners of roughly equal proficiency or very different levels of proficiency? What are the effects on participation, correction and negotiation, mutual benefit, and motivation to speak?

## Quality principles (Connections)

Elaboration and analysis increase and strengthen connections between the item to be learned and other knowledge making it easier to access the item.

7 *Elaboration: This includes enriching the encoding of an item through variation.* How can learners be moved from memorized conversations to free conversation?
8 *Analysis: This involves relating the familiar parts to the unfamiliar whole.* What role does listening play in establishing skill in informal conversation?

The most needed research on informal conversation is on the role of memorized conversations in developing proficiency in informal conversation.

# 9
# PROBLEM-SOLVING SPEAKING

### What is problem-solving speaking?

Problem-solving speaking includes pair and small-group activities where learners work together to solve a problem that they have been set. Typically, the problem involves some real-life dilemma where there is not one correct answer, but learners have to use their judgement and negotiate to reach agreement within their group. The major learning goal in problem-solving activities is to develop and practice the language and communication skills needed for transactional spoken interaction. That is, learners practice speaking the foreign language in order to get good at talking with others to get things done.

Problem-solving speaking involves shared tasks where learners can learn from each other (see Chapter 2). From a group work perspective (see Chapter 3), problem-solving speaking involves co-operative tasks where learners have equal access to the same information, although elements of split information can be included in the tasks.

Here is an example of a problem-solving activity.

---

Suggest five or six rules for the use of mobile phones by learners in secondary schools.
Many secondary school children own mobile phones and use them a lot, especially for communicating with their friends on social networks.
Banning the use of the phones may not be an option, because many parents see mobile phones as ways of their children quickly getting help if they need it.
Mobile phones can be very distracting in class. However, phones provide access to the internet and they can be a very useful source of input in some lessons that require gathering information.

---

*(Continued)*

DOI: 10.4324/9781003496151-12

(Continued)

After you have made your list of five or six suggestions, put the items in the list in order. Think carefully about what will guide this ordering. When you have finished doing this, be prepared to give a brief oral report on your list and why you put particular rules in the list.

At least one quarter of the time in a well-balanced language course should be spent doing activities which involve meaning-focused listening and speaking with an eventual fluency development goal. Problem-solving speaking activities are an excellent way of providing some of this kind of activity. It is, therefore, important that a teacher can quickly make, adapt, and organize such activities so that they work well and provide plenty of speaking and listening opportunities for learners working in small groups.

### What are the learning goals of problem-solving speaking?

Because problem-solving speaking fits into the meaning-focused input, meaning-focused output, and fluency development strands, the language learning goals involve incidental learning, that is, learning where the main focus is on something else, namely solving the problem. Table 9.1 describes the incidental learning goals of problem-solving speaking.

The major language learning goal of problem-solving speaking is a skills goal, being able to take part in spoken interaction. Some language learning of pronunciation, vocabulary, multiword units, and grammar may occur through meeting unfamiliar and partly familiar items in context and through negotiation and other language-related episodes.

### How does problem-solving speaking help learning?

This section is organized around the four requirements for learning – motivation, focus on what is to be learned, quantity of attention and quality

**TABLE 9.1** The goals of problem-solving speaking

| *Goals* | *Specific focuses* |
| --- | --- |
| Language | Learning new vocabulary and grammatical features, and improving pronunciation |
|  | Strengthening and enriching partly known vocabulary and grammar |
| Ideas |  |
| Skills | *Practising the skills and language of conversation* |
| Text | Learning how to interrupt, manage turn-taking, support others' speaking, maintain good relationships, and disagree |

*Note*: The major goal is in *italics*.

of attention (Chapter 4). The stronger each of these four requirements are, the more likely learning is to occur. In essence, problem-solving speaking helps learning the skill of speaking through highly transferable quantity of practice. Negotiation and meeting unfamiliar words in context can help vocabulary learning through quantity of deliberate attention to words involving elaboration.

*Motivation:* The motivation of problem-solving speaking tasks is the challenge of doing real-life speaking to solve a problem. Although motivation is likely to be increased if it is an obviously relevant problem, learners can become deeply involved in unlikely tasks such as ranking the top five things to take with you if you are stranded on a desert island, or choosing which of the five people should get a heart transplant.

*Focus:* Problem-solving tasks rely largely on incidental learning because the major focus is on solving the problem. Negotiation of language features such as vocabulary, multiword units, pronunciation, and grammar can add a deliberate focus which will help learning. However, research on vocabulary (Newton, 2013) shows that most vocabulary learning in such tasks is likely to be of unknown or partly known vocabulary that is not negotiated during the activity. Topics need to be carefully chosen and prepared for to ensure accuracy of language use.

*Quantity:* Problem-solving speaking improves skill at speaking through quantity of practice. Skill at speaking involves the ability to draw on language resources of pronunciation, vocabulary, morphology, grammar, and discourse to communicate a spoken message with some degree of fluency under normal time pressure.

Negotiation increases the quantity of attention to language features, and so is more likely to result in learning than noticing which is not negotiated. Even though non-negotiated learning amounts for more vocabulary learning overall, it is less certain to lead to learning. Having a worksheet for the problem-solving task can increase the amount of attention to vocabulary, by encouraging use of the vocabulary and expressions that appear in the information on the worksheet (Joe, Nation & Newton, 1996; Nation, 2022, pp. 188–193). Negotiation and the use of a procedure that involves going over the same material again can increase the repetition of vocabulary and multiword items making them more likely to be learned.

*Quality:* Negotiation puts language features in meta-linguistic contexts and directs deliberate attention to an item. It thus provides a kind of elaboration that helps learning.

Research on vocabulary learning during co-operative tasks suggests that a learner is likely to learn around four or five words during the activity (Newton, 2013).

## What are the requirements of problem-solving speaking?

### How can you prepare for problem-solving speaking?

Problem-solving tasks need to be carefully designed, and while this may at first take some time, with practice it becomes quite easy. The list of topics in Table 9.2 is a useful starting point as each topic has a suggested outcome.

TABLE 9.2  Topics for problem-solving tasks

| | |
|---|---|
| A. THE EARTH | Arrange a timetable |
| Suggest ways of coping with a natural disaster | Decide whether to give up a job in order to continue study |
| Choose ways of dealing with pollution | Locate the assessment for a course |
| Choose animals for the zoo | Arrange the items on the page of a text book |
| Rank ways of using a piece of land | |
| Decide whether a forest should be cleared for a factory | Arrange the parts of a book |
| | Arrange a class's work for the coming week |
| Locate a new road | |
| Arrange the plants in a garden | E. BUSINESS |
| B. THE SELF | Suggest ways of spending an amount of money |
| Suggest ways of losing weight | |
| Suggest solutions to personal problems | Choose which product you should buy |
| Choose a way of dealing with difficulty with a neighbour | Rank cars to buy |
| | Decide whether a shopping mall should be built |
| Rank the items needed for survival | |
| Decide whether to support a losing cause | Decide whether the school should be insured |
| Decide whether to have a dangerous operation | Locate an advertisement in the newspaper |
| | Locate a fast-food business in the town |
| Decide whether someone should be on a life support system | Arrange the floor plan of an office |
| | Arrange the buildings around a town square |
| Decide on a case for abortion | |
| Decide whether nuclear research should continue | F. RELAXATION |
| | Suggest ways of welcoming a new family to the community |
| C. THE HOME | |
| Suggest dangers within the house for a child | Suggest criteria for choosing which TV programmes to watch |
| Choose items from a menu to suit the tastes of the guests | Suggest items to go into a fun park |
| | Choose places for a tourist to visit |
| Rank the improvements that could be made to a house | Choose a hotel to stay in on your holiday |
| | Rank countries to go to for a holiday |
| Decide whether it would be better for both parents to get a job | Decide whether to buy a TV |
| | Decide whether to put on a play |
| Decide whether to have another child | Locate the time for a holiday in the year's events |
| Decide whether to raise a child as a vegetarian | |
| | Locate the venue for a pop festival |
| Locate an addition to a house | Locate a new pub |

*(Continued)*

**TABLE 9.2** (Continued)

| | |
|---|---|
| Arrange the plan of a house | Locate a common room in building |
| Arrange the furniture in a room | Arrange the players in a sports team |
| **D. THE INTELLECT** | Arrange items in a programme of entertainment |
| Suggest ways of helping someone with their study | Arrange guests around a table |
| Suggest items for a teacher evaluation form | Arrange the items in a radio or TV programme |
| Suggest rules for the school programme | **G. PUBLIC LIFE** |
| Choose which book should be published | Suggest ways making people appreciate the police |
| Choose which material to teach | Suggest ways of choosing a leader for a group |
| Choose what should be added to the school | Choose the best candidate |
| Rank learners' answers to a test | Choose the best ways of solving a traffic problem |
| Decide whether schools should be under local control | Rank the options for defending a country |
| Decide whether a child should go to a co-ed or single sex school | Decide whether to privatize public services |
| Arrange the parts of an answer to an exam question | Locate a half-way house or a prison |
| | Arrange the power structure of government |

A worksheet that supports the activity can have a strong effect on the language that is used. The worksheet can provide some background to the problem, the problem itself and the kind of outcome required, and restrictions and limitations that will affect the solution to the problem. Joe, Nation, and Newton (1996) and Nation (2022, pp. 188–193) provide detailed suggestions on how to design such a worksheet and how to plan the activity to maximize vocabulary learning. These guidelines include:

1 Make sure that there is some target vocabulary (about ten words) in the written worksheet for the task and that it occurs in places in the worksheet where it is likely to be used. The worksheet should be around 150 to 300 words long.
2 Design the task so that the written input needs to be used. Have a clear outcome for the task and avoid numbering choices on the worksheet so that learners need to use a description of each choice rather than a number to refer to them.
3 Get each learner actively involved by having jobs or roles, using small groups of learners of roughly equal proficiency within a group, and splitting some of the information so each learner has an essential role to play in the activity.
4 Ensure that the vocabulary is used in ways that encourage learning. This can be done by including some steps to encourage repetition (the pyramid procedure, reporting back, or reflecting on the vocabulary used in the task).

A well-designed worksheet encourages negotiation of the unfamiliar language on the worksheet and provides written input that can be used orally when doing the activity.

*What texts can be used for problem-solving speaking?*

The suggested topics for problem-solving activities in Table 9.2 are arranged under the major headings for West's (1960) classification of his Minimum Adequate Vocabulary for speaking. The items under each heading are organized according to the type of solution – suggest, choose, rank; decide, locate, arrange. Look at the list to become familiar with the six different outcomes.

*How much time should be given to problem-solving speaking in a general language course?*

Problem-solving speaking fits into three strands – the meaning-focused input strand, the meaning-focused output strand, and the fluency development strand. Although the main focus of the activity is on speaking (meaning-focused output), listening (meaning-focused input) is naturally a very important part of the activity. In the meaning-focused output strand, problem-solving speaking shares the speaking part of the strand with informal conversation and prepared talks, suggesting that at most it should occupy around one-quarter of the time in that strand, which is around one-sixteenth of the time in the whole course. If the meaning-focused input aspect of problem-solving speaking is also considered, this would increase the total course time given to problem-solving speaking, but should not double the time, as it is primarily a speaking activity. As problem-solving speaking activities become easier, they can contribute more strongly to fluency development.

## How can problem-solving speaking be done well?

Designing good problem-solving speaking tasks involves choosing a relevant and interesting topic, deciding on an outcome for the task, adding restrictions and requirements, and including a procedure. The task can end with reporting back to the class or some kind of reflection on the task. Here is an example of the worksheet for a problem-solving activity with comments on the parts of the activity.

Here are the steps for making and running the activity.

1 The first step is to choose a topic for the problem-solving task. Table 9.2 contains a large list of possible topics, but it is good to think of topics that recycle material already covered in the course.

| Worksheet for the activity | Comments |
|---|---|
| Decide whether you should take up vaping. | The outcome is a yes/no decision. |
| Vaping is now a very popular activity especially among the younger generation. Research has shown that vaping does help many smokers give up smoking. Research is also beginning to suggest that vaping is harmful for your health, although it is 95% healthier than smoking. | This is background information which contains ideas and vocabulary that is likely to be used by the learners in the activity. |
| You have been a smoker and are trying to quit, for the third time. You are determined to give up smoking, but you feel very uncertain about whether you will be able to quit. | These are requirements and restrictions that make it harder to reach a decision. Their positive effect is to get more discussion and more involved discussion. |
| Vaping will probably cost you less than smoking, but the government is talking about raising the price of electronic cigarettes (e-cigarettes) and making access to e-cigarettes more difficult. | Note that there around ten words and phrases on the worksheet which we hope learners will use in the activity. When observing the activity, the teacher should see if the learners actually use them. These include *vaping, take up, younger generation, research has shown, harmful, trying to quit, access, make access difficult, electronic cigarettes, addictive/ addiction, ingredients* |
| Unfortunately, vaping like smoking is addictive, so replacing smoking with vaping is replacing one addiction with another. | |
| Some ingredients of some e-cigarettes are known to be harmful for your health, but they do not occur in all e-cigarettes. | |

2   The second step is to decide on an outcome for the task. There is a limited number of outcomes that are commonly used in such activities, and providing an outcome makes it much clearer to the learners what they should do and what they need to do to complete the activity. The first group of three outcomes are *suggest*, *choose*, and *rank*. The *suggest* outcome involves coming up with a list of suggestions or just one suggestion. If a list of several suggestions is required, it is good to say how many items there should be on the list. So, the outcome of the activity may be "Suggest three ways of dealing with pollution". The three outcomes of *suggest*, *choose*, and *rank* go together because after suggesting some solutions, learners can then choose the best one, or they can rank them in their favoured order of choice. The *choose* outcome involves selecting an item from a list. The *rank* outcome involves putting items in order according to a given criterion. There is another set of three outcomes, *decide*, *locate*, and *arrange*. The *decide* outcome involves making a yes/no decision. Should a new road be built? Should there be another public holiday? Should hotels be built along the beachfront? The *locate* outcome usually involves the use of a map or a plan, and the learners have to decide where to place a particular building, event, or activity. Where should

the prison be placed in a town? It can also involve placing an item on the timeline. When is the best time in life to do voluntary work overseas helping others? The *arrange* outcome involves putting items in good order so that they can fit into a given plan or satisfy certain requirements. Having just one outcome for a task is probably desirable, but a series of outcomes could be used to increase repetition.

3 The third step is to see what restrictions and requirements could be placed on the task to make it more difficult to solve and thus increase the amount of speaking and interaction involved.

4 We have looked at providing an outcome for a task and adding restrictions and requirements. Another feature that can improve a problem-solving activity is a procedure. A procedure is a series of steps that increase the amount of speaking that learners will need to do to complete the activity, and usually involves some kind of varied repetition of the language used in the activity. Here are the most useful procedures. (1) The pyramid procedure: This procedure can have four steps. It is called the pyramid procedure because it goes down from a small number of people (one) to an increasingly larger number like the shape of a pyramid. Step 1: each learner individually thinks of an answer to the problem. Step 2: the learners work in pairs to reach agreement on an answer. Step 3: the learners work in small groups of three or four people to reach agreement. Step 4: the whole class tries to reach agreement on an answer. In Step 4, if the class is large, one representative from each group of four can take part in the discussion. The pyramid procedure is excellent for language learning because it provides repeated opportunities to say the same things. (2) A sequence of outcomes: This procedure can involve the sequences like suggest, choose, rank where the learners suggest a list of answers, choose the best of them, and then rank them. There are also numerous two step sequences (suggest, choose the best; choose and then rank; suggest and then rank). Other two-step sequences involve decide-locate, and decide-arrange. Using a sequence involves the learners in more work (and therefore more speaking and listening) and provides good opportunities for repetition in different contexts. (3) Expert group-family group: This procedure involves two steps. Step 1: the learners work in expert groups where each group focuses on a different part of the problem and becomes experts about that part. For example, in a ranking activity, each group focuses on two of the eight items to rank so that across four groups all eight items are covered. Step 2: the learners now form family groups where each group contains a mixture of experts, so all parts of the problem are covered. So, for the ranking activity example, each family group of four would contain an expert on items 1 and 2 of the items to rank, an expert on items 3 and 4, an expert on items 5 and 6, and an expert on items 7 and 8. The expert group-family group procedure allows learners to bring a lot of knowledge to the activity from the expert group,

and involves repetition of the same ideas and language in the two steps. (4) Describe, solve, justify: Step 1: before doing the activity, the learners describe and clarify exactly what they have to do and what information they have. Step 2: they do the activity and reach a solution. Step 3: they justify their solution saying why it is the best one and why other possible solutions were not as good. Step 3 can be a report to the whole class or another group. (5) Solve and report: This two-step procedure involves reaching a solution and then reporting on it to the rest of the class. (6) Solve and reflect: This two-step procedure involves doing the activity and then reflecting on the new language items met and used in the activity. This adds a language-focused learning feature to the activity, strengthening language learning. It is very easy to add a procedure to a speaking activity, and the procedures described here do not require the teacher to do a lot of extra preparation. The teacher just needs to become familiar with ways of getting learners to move from one kind of group to another.

5 The topic including background to the topic, the outcome, the requirements and restrictions, and the procedure should be included in a worksheet that all learners can easily see. Around 10–12 words that could be considered target vocabulary for the task should occur in the information on the worksheet.

6 The learners do the problem-solving speaking activity. The members of each group should sit in a small circle so that they have equal access to each other.

7 After completing the task, each group reports to the class on the solution they agreed on.

Here is another example of a worksheet.

---

The number of different kinds of electric cars that are available is rapidly increasing. The problem is not finding a car to buy, but deciding which is the best one to buy. Here are descriptions of five different makes of cars. Choose which one is the best for a family with two young children (aged six and nine).

1 The A. This is the most expensive car. It has a top safety rating (5 out of 5). It can travel up to 350 km on a full charge. It is a bit small inside. It is a bit hard to get parts.
2 The B. This is the smallest of all the cars, but it is also the cheapest. It is very easy to park. It is a very popular car, and it is easy to get parts for it. It has a medium safety rating (4 out of 5).
3 The C. This is a medium-sized car. It has plenty of room inside and for luggage. It has a good safety rating (3 out of 5).
4 The D. This car is fast. It can go from 0 to 100 km per hour in 5.6 seconds. It is expensive and has a very high safety rating (5 out of 5). It is not easy to get parts. A super cool car.
5 The E. This car is a second-hand version of the A. Because it has already been used for three years, its price is very reasonable.

*(Continued)*

(Continued)

The family makes about three long trips per year, otherwise most of the travel is to and from school and to the supermarket. The parents go to work by train and do not need a car for work. The family does not have a lot of money, but they could afford even the most expensive one listed above. If they bought the most expensive one, they would have cut back on other spending.

## *How can I check that a problem-solving speaking activity is working well?*

Problem-solving speaking activities involve co-operating group work. The first thing to look for is whether learners are using the foreign language and are all participating in the activity. An interesting aspect of participation is that some learners may not be saying a lot during an activity, but if they are mentally involved and are following what is being said, they may still be learning by observing others. Some research (deHaan, Reed & Kuwada, 2010) has suggested that being an observer provides better opportunities to learn than being an active participator. Nonetheless, problem-solving speaking aims to develop speaking skills, so some active participation is needed. The second thing to look for is the quality of the language used. Are learners using the language accurately and effectively? The third thing to look for is if the learners are negotiating aspects of the language with each other. Are they seeking clarification? Are they confirming understanding? Are they dealing with lack of understanding? Are they requesting or providing explanations of language items? The fourth thing to look for is whether the activity is moving forward following the steps that need to be followed. If not, the activity may need to be redesigned for future use.

## What are the variants of problem-solving speaking?

In split information tasks (see Chapter 3; Nation, 1977), each learner in a pair or group has a different piece of information which is essential to the completion of the task. Completing split information tasks could be considered a kind of problem-solving speaking. However, split information tasks tend to encourage a focus on the form rather than the meaning of unfamiliar words (Newton, 2013). Split information tasks include the Strip story (Gibson, 1975), and Same or different picture comparison tasks (Nation, 2024, Appendix 3).

Nation and Hamilton-Jenkins (2000) describe problem-solving tasks that are based on a single word or a multiword unit from an accompanying reading text. Here is an example, focusing on the word *refugee*.

> Below is a list of common reasons why people become refugees. Rank them from the most common reason to the least common.

__ They become refugees because there is a war in their country
__ They become refugees because there are no enough jobs in their country
__ They become refugees because their religion is not accepted in their country
__ They become refugees because they are opposed to the government in their country
__ They become refugees because there is a shortage of food in their country

Such activities can focus on the meaning of the word as in the example above, or on the use of the word.

## How can problem-solving speaking be used at all levels of proficiency?

Even low-proficiency learners can do problem-solving speaking activities. There are three main ways of making sure that the learners will be able to do the activities. One way is preparing the learners for the activities, that is, turning them into experience tasks (Chapter 2). Another way involves designing activities which are already at the right level for the learners. A guided element could be added to the activities by providing support for the learners during the activity.

*Preparing learners for speaking activities:* Linked skills: If a problem-solving speaking activity is the third step in a linked skills series (Chapter 21), then the speaking activity will be easy to do because the learners have already gained plenty of input, ideas, and language from the first two activities in the series.

Expert group-family group: The expert group-family group procedure allows learners to work together in the expert groups to become very familiar with the ideas and language needed to do part of the activity. In this preparation in the expert groups, the use of the first language may be very helpful at least in some of the preparation. If the teacher thinks about the difficulties involved in the family group part of the activity, then these difficulties can be the focus in the expert group preparation.

Individual preparation: If learners are given the handout for a speaking activity a day or two before they do the activity, then they can prepare for the activity individually. This preparation can involve finding useful words and phrases, as well as gaining a good understanding of the ideas needed in the activity.

Pre-teaching: Before the learners do the speaking activity, the teacher can guide them in the learning of useful words, phrases, and sentences. These can include things like the following.

I think that you are right.
Okay, but ….
I think that …
I mean …

*Designing activities at the right level for the learners:* The teacher can design the activity so that the language needed to do the activity is already largely within the learners' knowledge.

*Providing support for the learners during the speaking activity:* The written handout that the teacher provides for a speaking activity can have a very strong effect on the difficulty of the activity and what is learnt during the activity. A good written handout contains several sentences of information about the background to the activity and any requirements and restrictions that must be met when trying to reach a solution. The learners should be able to use the material on the handout as a source of ideas and language that they can use during the speaking activity. Here is an example. Notice how each of the items to be ranked is followed by a brief description of this usefulness. Learners can use this description in their speaking when they argue why one item should be ranked higher than another. Notice also that the background information also contains some useful ideas and language that the learners can repeat in their discussion.

---

You live by yourself in a farming area where there is danger from flooding, and the risk of floods gets higher each year. Your home is part of a small rural community, and you are well known in that area.

You will have some warning if a flood is likely to occur, but you have to be prepared to leave your house quickly within a few minutes. What five things will you take with you? Rank them in order of value to you. You can add two or three items to the following list, but your final list must only contain five ranked items.

Family photographs (some of these are very old and there is no other copy of them)

Clothing (it is quite cold when it rains so you may want some extra warm, dry clothing)

Art works (you have three or four original paintings that you really like. They are not especially valuable in monetary terms)

Your wallet (this contains some money, credit cards, and your driver's licence)

Your laptop computer (this contains files from work, and a book you are writing)

A knitted blanket (your grandmother made one for each of her grandchildren before she died)

Bottles of water (during a flood the water supply may become contaminated)

Some food (you may have to leave your home at night and shops will not be open)

---

## Are there digital applications of this technique?

Loewen and Wolff (2016) compared face-to-face oral communication, synchronous oral computer-mediated communication, and synchronous written computer-mediated communication for negotiation of meaning, recasts, and language-related episodes. The two oral communication modes turned out to be similar, though the low numbers of comprehension checks (the speaker checking that what they just said has been understood), language-related episodes, and recasts made comparison difficult. It seems likely that the use of oral computer-mediated communication is likely to be as good as face-to-face communication for learning from interaction. Written computer-mediated communication resulted in many fewer confirmation checks. Confirmation checks occur immediately after an utterance and often involve the listener repeating part of the speaker's utterance to confirm what was just said. Overall, written computer-mediated communication had fewer interactional features than oral communication.

Problem-solving activities can be done remotely through computer-mediated interaction, and of course, oral interaction is preferable for developing spoken communication skills.

The internet can be used by the learners to research the current topic for problem-solving speaking a day or two before the activity occurs. This adds an element of split information to the activity and is likely to increase involvement in the activity. For example, if the activity involves ranking holiday destinations, some learners can research a particular destination so that they become experts on that destination.

### Revisiting and linking to other activities

If problem-solving activities are based on topics and texts already covered in the course, then this will make the task easier and will provide much-needed repetition of language features. A follow-up to problem-solving speaking could involve a written report on the solution reached by the group with some justifications. To make this written task easier, a set format for the report could be provided.

The teacher should consider whether it is worth repeating the same activity again a week or two after the learners first did it. In order to keep the activity interesting, it may be useful to make a few small changes to it, but the idea of repeating an activity is to help the learners become more fluent at doing it so that in the repetition of the activity, they are speaking at a higher level of accuracy and fluency, and with more confidence.

Problem-solving activities can require the learners to do some research on a topic before doing the speaking activity. For example, if the problem-solving activity is done in groups of four, each of the four learners in a group chooses a different holiday destination and gathers some information about it. The information-gathering can be guided by some questions.

---

You and your friends are planning an overseas holiday for two weeks. Choose a holiday destination and go online gather some information about it. The destination you choose should be different from the destinations chosen by the other people in your group. The following questions may help you in gathering information.
Is it expensive to get there?
Is it expensive to stay there?

---

*(Continued)*

(Continued)

What are the things to do there that you all will enjoy?
Will you and your friends be able to eat the local food? What are some of the best dishes?
When the activity begins, take turns to describe your holiday destination and then work with the other members of the group to choose one destination that you all agree on. You do not have to choose the destination that you researched.
After you have reached agreement, work together to prepare a brief written report around 200 words long which says what destination you all chose, and the reasons for that choice.

---

The information-gathering adds a split information element to the activity and ensures that each learner has to speak. The research, presentation, discussion, and reporting back provides opportunity for repetition of useful vocabulary and expressions to occur.

## What does research say about the effectiveness of problem-solving speaking?

Research on peer interaction (Sato & Ballinger, 2016) has shown that learners enjoy working with each other, provide useful and comprehensible feedback, and make use of interaction features that support language learning.

There has been a great deal of research on negotiation, recasts, and language-related episodes and their role in learning from spoken interaction, with the common finding that negotiation (confirmation checks, clarification requests, and comprehension checks), recasts, and language-related episodes help the learning of pronunciation, vocabulary, multiword units, and grammar (McDonough & Sunitham, 2009; Nation, 2022). Newton's (2013) study puts this research in a wider context comparing vocabulary learning from negotiation and learning from meeting in context with no overt attention given to the words. In Newton's study, where a word was negotiated, there was about a 70% chance that it would be retained on the immediate post-test. Where a word was simply met in context but with no negotiation, there was just over a 50% chance that it would be retained. So, negotiation clearly helps learning. However, in the immediate post-test, over 80% of the words answered correctly (but not answered correctly in the pre-test) were not negotiated, while less than 20% were negotiated. Thus, although negotiation helps learning, it accounts for a minority of the learning. Most learning occurs simply through meeting in context. So, when a teacher sees negotiation taking place, the teacher can feel happy that learning is likely to occur. However, the teacher also needs to realize that even without negotiation, a substantial amount of learning is likely to occur from simply meeting the words in context.

McDonough and Sunitham (2009) found that around 76% of their learners' language-related episodes involved vocabulary, and the majority of their negotiations (70%) were successful. So, learners can be useful sources of learning for each other.

## Research questions

### Motivation principles (Engagement)

For learning to occur there needs to be a willingness to focus on what needs to be learned, and to give it quantity and quality of attention.

1 *Motivation: The degree of engagement with the task affects the likelihood of learning occurring.* Does the problem to solve motivate learners to do problem-solving tasks? Do problems need to have real-life relevance to motivate learners?
2 *Self-efficacy: Our confidence in our own skills of learning affects our success in learning.* How much does the group work element of problem-solving tasks support learners' willingness to participate?

### Focus principles (Usefulness)

Learning requires giving attention to what needs to be learned.

3 *Focus: We learn what we focus on, and in addition, our learning is more useful if it closely resembles the use that we need to make of what we learn (transfer-appropriate).* What are the features of good worksheet design? What is the evidence that worksheet design directly affects language use in the activity?
4 *Accuracy: Our learning is more efficient if the information we are focusing on is complete, accurate, and comprehensible.* Do problem-solving tasks involve many language-related episodes? Do these support language learning?

### Quantity principles (Amount)

5 *Repetition: The more repetitions, the stronger the learning.* Do procedures result in repetition? What procedures have the greatest effect on repetition? Is the repetition varied or verbatim? Does the repetition involve target utterances? That is, is it repetition of what needs to be learned?
6 *Time-on-task: The greater and longer the attention, the stronger the learning.* What is the effect of including individual jobs (encouraging others to speak, summarizing, disagreeing, keeping everyone on task) on the spread of participation and quantity of speaking? Do the observers learn as well as the participators?

### Quality principles (Connections)

Elaboration and analysis increase and strengthen connections between the item to be learned and other knowledge making it easier to access the item.

7 *Elaboration: This includes enriching the encoding of an item through variation.* How varied are the forms and contexts of the topic-related vocabulary in a problem-solving task?
8 *Analysis: This involves relating the familiar parts to the unfamiliar whole.*

The most useful research on problem-solving speaking would be on the effect of procedures on increasing spoken participation and repetition. It is easy to include procedures, such as the pyramid procedure, reporting back, and a series of outcomes, in spoken activities but there is no research on their effects.

# 10
# PREPARED TALKS

**What are prepared talks?**

Prepared talks are monologues or long speaking turns that the speaker has prepared for and has practised. A *long-turn* involves speaking on a topic for at least a few minutes and up to an hour or more. Long-turns include presentations using multimedia, lectures, podcasts, and presenting a report. As a part of a conversation, a long-turn may involve one of the speakers going into some detail on a topic, giving a narrative account of some happening, or telling a joke. The preparation involves some language-focused learning, but eventually prepared talks involve meaning-focused output and spoken fluency development. In prepared talks, the learner chooses or is given a topic and prepares a written version of a talk, which is checked for accuracy, and then the learner practises presenting the talk until it can be delivered fluently without having to read it aloud. Prepared talks can be used at all stages of proficiency and can range from relatively short descriptions of aspects of a learner's background to long formal conference talks. Prepared talks begin as guided tasks and then become experience tasks and finally independent tasks.

**What are the learning goals of prepared talks?**

Prepared talks involve the memorization of useful words, multiword units, phrases, clauses, and sentences. They also help turning receptive knowledge of language items into productive knowledge. Table 10.1 presents the learning goals of prepared talks.

**TABLE 10.1** The goals of prepared talks

| Goals | Specific focuses |
|---|---|
| Language | Learning new topic-related vocabulary and grammatical features |
|  | Strengthening and enriching partly known vocabulary and grammar |
| Ideas | Learning how to gather and organize ideas |
| Skills | *Producing a long-turn with fluency* |
| Text | Learning how to plan and manage a formal long-turn in order to convey a coherent argument or message |

*Note*: The major goal is in *italics*.

The major learning goal of prepared talks is a skills goal, producing an accurate spoken monologue or long-turn with fluency. Because of the preparation involved, it allows the deliberate learning of words and phrases, and getting the grammar correct.

### How do prepared talks help learning?

In essence, prepared talks help learning the skill of formal speaking through accuracy of use, and repeated opportunities to practice (quantity) until a high degree of fluency is reached. The learning is highly transferable because it is exactly like what needs to be done when preparing for and delivering a formal talk outside the classroom. Prepared talks also help the learning of language features through repeated deliberate attention during preparation for the talk.

Prepared talks apply the principles of motivation, focus of attention, quantity of attention and quality of attention in the following ways.

*Motivation:* The topics for prepared talks should be chosen so that they are clearly relevant to the learners' needs. They should be topics where the learners bring a lot of background knowledge and personal experience. The learners should be aware that there will be careful feedback on the initial writing so that subsequent oral practice will involve the correct use of the language.

*Focus:* The prepared talks technique represents the use of long-turns in monologue and dialogue, so it is transfer-appropriate. It focuses on accurate, fluent spoken production. The feedback received during the written preparation of the talk ensures accurate use. The repeated practice develops fluency.

*Quantity:* Prepared talks involve varied, repeated retrieval of the language involved in the talk. This repetition will help establish the vocabulary, multiword units, and grammatical features used in the talk. Some of the vocabulary and multiword units in the talk may initially be unfamiliar to the learner.

*Quality:* The writing of the talk and the spoken deliveries to a variety of different group sizes using cue sheets provide a good degree of elaboration. If later talks in the sequence allow listeners to ask questions, this can provide further elaboration. The talk should not contain unanalysed multiword units or grammatical features. Any such items should be analysed, with the help of the teacher if necessary.

## What are the requirements of prepared talks?

### How can you prepare for prepared talks?

Prepared talks will have the greatest value for learners if they involve topics that the learners are likely to deal with outside the classroom. The survival vocabulary for foreign travel (Nation & Crabbe, 1991) involved considerable needs analysis investigation to make sure that learners would have plenty of opportunity to use what they learn. Helping learners choose topics for prepared talks should at least tap into their interests and ideally meet their needs. Learners at school may not have obvious needs for extended uses of English, but these should be looked for and if none are found then their hobbies and interests, such as gaming, sport, or self-defence, could be a source of topics.

Prepared talks need to be written, checked for accuracy, and practised until a good degree of fluency is reached. This can be done in a kind of pyramid procedure, with learners preparing and practising individually, then in pairs, then in groups and finally with the whole class as an audience.

### What texts can be used for prepared talks?

In the early stages of language learning, it is worthwhile for each learner to prepare their own descriptions of themselves, their family, their home town, their country, their hobbies and interests, their job, where they are staying in the foreign country, where they have been in the foreign country and anything else that could be a long-turn in a conversation. The survival vocabulary (Nation & Crabbe, 1991: see also Paul Nation's resources pages) can be a starting point for early prepared talks. Prepared talks can also be jokes or stories, descriptions of movies, book reports, or future plans. For adults, prepared talks can be descriptions of aspects of learners' jobs, their hobbies, or conference papers.

While listening to prepared talks, learners can practice note-taking skills, with the teacher giving some instruction in note-taking.

### How much time should be given to prepared talks in a general language course?

In the spoken half of the meaning-focused output strand, prepared talks share time with informal conversation and group problem-solving speaking activities. The teacher needs to decide what proportion of spoken meaning-focused output should involve conversation, and what proportion should involve monologue. One way would be to give equal time to monologue and dialogues, or give more time to dialogue with about two-thirds of the spoken meaning-focused output time involving conversation. On a 50-50 split, prepared talks would have one-quarter of the meaning-focused output strand which is around one-sixteenth of the time in the whole course. Prepared talks also involve the fluency development strand, where they share time with other speaking activities.

### How can prepared talks be done well?

1  Prepared talks need to be on obviously useful topics, and these may differ from learner to learner. It is worthwhile spending a bit of time with the learners doing needs analysis to choose a useful topic for each learner.
2  When learners are planning their prepared talk before writing it, they can join others in small groups for brainstorming activities to gain ideas about what to include in their talk.
3  Prepared talks need to be accurate, so the learners should prepare a written version of their talk. For long-turns in conversation, this preparation can involve preparing several long-turns on several topics such as talking about yourself, talking about your country, talking about your job or hobbies and interests, and so on.
4  The written version of the talk should be checked by the teacher, with the teacher suggesting some additions to the talk with the aims of improving the talk and stretching the learner's language knowledge. In a large class, this checking could begin with peer checking before the teacher checks a corrected version. The speed of speaking is around 150 words per minute. This can be used as a guide for the length of written version of the talk, with a five-minute talk eventually being around 750 words long (5 times 150).
5  Prepared talks should be practised to a good degree of fluency, so there should be many repetitions of the talk. That is, the preparation for the talk will involve planning the talk, preparing a written version, editing the written version on the basis of feedback, presenting the talk to a single listener, presenting it again to a different listener using only a set of brief notes or a PowerPoint presentation, presenting it to a small group, and then presenting it to the whole class. At each step of this process, improvements can be made. The later deliveries of the talk should not involve reading the script aloud. Later deliveries of the talk can include questions from the listeners. The repetition will ensure that the language features in the talk are well remembered.

### How can I check that a prepared talk activity is working well?

Prepared talks involve preparation over time and so the most important monitoring involves making sure that steps in the activity are being followed and that learners are performing well at each step. Such monitoring needs a checklist for each learner with the items on the checklist corresponding to the steps. Here is a possible checklist.

| Topic |
| --- |
| Data-gathering meeting 1 |
| Data-gathering meeting 2 |
| Data-gathering meeting 3 |
| Practice oral presentation 1 |
| Practice oral presentation 2 |
| Oral presentation |
| Written presentation |

It is important for the teacher to monitor the data-gathering meeting where learners report to peers on the data-gathering, because these ensure that the learners are working on the talk and are not leaving the work until the last moment.

The final oral presentation and the written presentation can be assessed, and the assessment of the written presentation can involve a feedback checklist roughly corresponding to parts of the writing process.

| Focus | Comments |
| --- | --- |
| Choice of topic | |
| Data-gathering | |
| Organization of the data | |
| Quality and accuracy of expression | |
| Formal features | |
| Overall impression & grade | |

Data-gathering deals with the amount and relevance of the data gathered. Formal features deal with the use of headings and subheadings, the formatting of the reference list, and signals to the reader.

## What are the variants of prepared talks?

The *Say it!* activity (see Chapter 3) provides opportunity for a long-turn which is not very long. This is a very useful activity for low-proficiency learners, and can involve a lot of repetition as the small tasks in the activity are done several times by different members of the group.

Long-turns in conversation can be practised in informal conversation (see Chapter 8). The conversation can be prepared for by having a list of common questions that all the pairs can use and add to. The answers to these common questions should involve several sentences. Here some useful common questions:

> Where do you come from? The answer can involve a description of your country and interesting places to visit there. It can also involve what your country is well known for. You could also describe your home town.
>
> How long have you been here? The answer can involve saying when you arrived and when you plan to leave, and the reason for your stay.
>
> Where have you been in this country? The answer can briefly mention several places and involve a longer description of a place you really enjoyed visiting and why you liked it.
>
> What is your favourite food here? The answer can involve mentioning several dishes or fruits, and then spending a bit of time describing one and why you like it.

Using a long-turn to answer a question shows that you are interested in continuing the conversation. A useful way to end such a long-turn would be to ask a question.

Digital story-telling (Huang, 2023) can have positive effects on speaking. Such story-telling is usually done as a group activity, and involves most of the steps of prepared talks.

Interview activities (see Chapter 8) provide a good opportunity for using prepared long-turns, thus allowing the person being interviewed to take control of the interview through the use of a prepared long-turn (Nation, 1980).

There are various activities that require the use of a monologue or long-turn. These include 4/3/2 (Chapter 12), Headlines, Poster presentations, and Linked skills activities (Chapter 21). Headlines involves half of the class being speakers and the other half being listeners. The speakers think of an interesting thing that happened to them and then write a short headline describing it in large letters on a piece of paper. An example could be **Burning Bed Brings Pleasure**. The speakers sit, each with their headline in front of them. The listeners move around individually or in pairs, and when they see an interesting headline, they say "Tell me your story". They listen and then move on to another speaker. Each speaker should have the opportunity to tell their story several times to different listeners.

In Poster presentations, each learner prepares a talk and a poster containing the main points with some pictures, photos, or diagrams to support the presentation. The listeners move around listening to the presentations. Each presenter should have the opportunity to present their talk several times to different listeners. Poster presentations can involve multimedia presentations. Project work (Chapter 22) is an elaborate form of prepared talks, involving much more work and the use of a greater range of language skills.

### How can prepared talks be used at all levels of proficiency?

At the elementary level of proficiency, prepared talks can involve the survival vocabulary for foreign travel (Nation & Crabbe, 1991). After this, the focus can be on memorized conversations including some long-turns of a few sentences. The next step can be monologues such as a daily report on the weather, the presentation of an interesting item in the news, an oral book review of a graded reader, and accounts of recent school or family activities or visits.

At an intermediate level, long-turns in conversation can be quite long. At this level, prepared talks can involve monologues of several minutes that have been carefully prepared for.

At an advanced level, prepared talks can involve academic-style presentations, as in projects (Chapter 22) where the quality of the presentation, in terms of content, organization, and engagement are commented on by the teacher and peers. The presentation can involve digital aids such as PowerPoint.

### How can prepared talks be used in large classes?

From a teacher's perspective, the time-consuming part of prepared talks is giving correction and feedback on the written version of the talk. Because this step is very important in ensuring that prepared talks involve accurate use of the language, teachers need to work out ways of lightening the load of providing feedback. One way is to get the learners to do self-checking, electronic checking, and peer checking to get rid of as many errors as possible before the teacher looks at the work. In addition, particularly for feedback on long-turns in conversation, where the learners may be saying much the same thing, with the permission of individual learners, feedback can be given on a particular written version to the whole class, highlighting or adding useful expressions, noting common errors, and suggesting points to include.

The teacher can stagger the dates on which the written versions are due so that there is not a big load of feedback needed at any one time.

The practice deliveries of the prepared talks can occur in small groups rather than in pairs to keep the noise level lower in large classes.

### Are there digital applications of this technique?

The programme *Grammarly* or a similar app can be used for electronically checking the written version. The spelling and grammar checking facility in Microsoft Word is also a useful way to begin getting rid of errors. While these are unlikely to pick up all the errors, they are a good start.

Recording your written version and then listening critically to yourself may be a helpful next step.

Digital story-telling (Huang, 2023) is a useful version of prepared talks for younger learners and those who wish to use less formal language.

## Revisiting and linking to other activities

Prepared talks involve plenty of repetition of the talk as a part of the normal procedure for the activity. Particularly for advanced learners, it may be possible to directly link the topics of prepared talks to language use outside the classroom. If a learner is preparing for a conference, then the prepared talks activity can be preparation for the conference. If a learner needs to use English in their work or study, then the prepared talks activity can mirror this use.

The teacher may wish to have a direct link between written work and oral presentation of that work. That is, most written work can have the ultimate goal of leading to oral presentation. These oral presentations can also involve note-taking practice for the listeners, questioning of the speaker, and written feedback on the oral presentation.

## What does research say about the effectiveness of prepared talks?

Ellis (2009) looked at three kinds of planning – rehearsal, pre-task planning, and within-task planning. The effects of these three kinds of planning were measured for fluency, complexity, and accuracy of language use, as these are considered to cover the proficiency of a language learner. In many of the studies that Ellis reviewed, the amount of time given to each of the three kinds of planning was much shorter than would be involved in prepared talks. In some studies, planning involved only a minute or a few minutes with the most common planning time being around 10 minutes. In addition, feedback was not necessarily a part of the procedure.

Rehearsal benefits performance of the same task but not similar tasks (Ellis, 2009). The benefits are most obvious for fluency but not so much for complexity and accuracy. If there is relevant feedback between rehearsals, then there are improvements in fluency, complexity, and accuracy (Sheppard, 2006 cited in Ellis, 2009).

Pre-task planning typically resulted in increases in fluency, complexity, and accuracy, with the effects being greater where the learners have used their planning time well. There are many factors that can affect planning, such as amount of time, amount of guidance, task complexity, and learners' attitude to planning. In the prepared talks technique, the amount of time given to pre-task planning and to rehearsal is considerable, and this is likely to result in a high level of performance.

The single study involving within-task planning (Yuan & Ellis, 2003) involved the absence of time pressure on performing the task, so that the speaker can consider what they will say while they do the task. The absence of time pressure had positive effects on complexity and accuracy. Research which has appeared since Ellis's (2009) review has supported the use of preparedness activities (Ellis, 2018; Johnson & Tabari, 2022).

## Research questions

### *Motivation principles (Engagement)*

For learning to occur, there needs to be a willingness to focus on what needs to be learned, and to give it quantity and quality of attention.

1 *Motivation: The degree of engagement with the task affects the likelihood of learning occurring.* How do prepared talks affect motivation to speak?
2 *Self-efficacy: Our confidence in our own skills of learning affects our success in learning.* What is the most difficult step in prepared talks? What support can be provided at this step?

### *Focus principles (Usefulness)*

Learning requires giving attention to what needs to be learned.

3 *Focus: We learn what we focus on, and in addition, our learning is more useful if it closely resembles the use that we need to make of what we learn (transfer-appropriate).* How can we measure the learning occurring from prepared talks? What step occupies the greatest amount of time in prepared talks? Does this focus agree with the learning goals of prepared talks?
4 *Accuracy: Our learning is more efficient if the information we are focusing on is complete, accurate, and comprehensible.* What parts of the preparation most affect the quality of the prepared talk?

### *Quantity principles (Amount)*

5 *Repetition: The more repetitions, the stronger the learning.* Does the same topic-related vocabulary occur in the data-gathering, discussion, writing and oral delivery of prepared talks? What kinds of repetition are involved in prepared talks? Does this repetition help learning?
6 *Time-on-task: The greater and longer the attention, the stronger the learning.* How can digital story-telling be used to maximize language use?

### *Quality principles (Connections)*

Elaboration and analysis increase and strengthen connections between the item to be learned and other knowledge making it easier to access the item.

7 *Elaboration: This includes enriching the encoding of an item through variation.* Does the occurrence of target vocabulary across different language skills

(reading, writing, speaking) have stronger effects on learning than variation of sentence context?
8 *Analysis: This involves relating the familiar parts to the unfamiliar whole.*

Working on a prepared talk is a commonly used technique but there is little, if any, research on the kinds of language use that actually occur during this complex activity.

# 11
# HEARING AND PRONUNCIATION PRACTICE

Hearing and pronunciation practice fits into the language-focused learning strand of a course. It involves guided techniques. Recent work on pronunciation includes consideration of the ethics of pronunciation teaching (Foote, 2017). One major concern is whether native speakers of English should be the model for non-native speakers. This concern has typically resulted in a focus on comprehensibility and intelligibility rather than accuracy, when accuracy is defined in terms of native speaker models.

Although the focus in this chapter is on hearing and pronunciation, the comprehensibility and intelligibility of speech is affected by more than pronunciation alone, and certainly more than the pronunciation of individual sounds. However, this chapter focuses on the pronunciation of individual sounds. Prosody and pronunciation in context are briefly covered in Chapter 8 on informal conversation.

For teachers who cannot read a phonetic transcription and who know little or nothing about individual sounds (segmentals) and prosody (word-stress, intonation, and voice quality), Bauer's (2023) book is an excellent practical introduction to the knowledge needed for hearing and pronunciation practice. If a teacher wants to go beyond providing a model pronunciation for learners and wants to give them detailed guidance in making sounds, especially consonant sounds, then a basic knowledge of articulatory phonetics is needed. This requires some study but is worth the effort.

This chapter covers several simple hearing and pronunciation techniques, including distinguishing sounds, identifying sounds, copying sounds, guided production, and forcing sounds.

## What is hearing practice?

Hearing practice, also called perceptual training, involves listening to sounds in syllables, and includes the two closely related techniques of distinguishing and identifying particular sounds. The easiest activity of the two is distinguishing sounds. It involves hearing two sounds and deciding if they are the same or different. One sound is the target sound that is the learning goal of the activity, and the other is the sound that it is most likely to be confused with. The learners' first language will affect what this second sound is likely to be. For example, the voiced *th* sound (/ð/) could be contrasted with *z* or with *d*. It is easiest to practise hearing the sounds in nonsense syllables such as *tha*, *za*, *da*.

In the distinguishing sounds technique, the teacher says two syllables, for example, *tha tha*, and the learners decide if they are the same or different. The learners signal this by moving one of their hands if they are different, and doing nothing if they are the same.

When this distinguishing activity is easy for a particular sound, the teacher can then move to the identifying sounds activity. In this activity, one sound is said at a time (in a nonsense syllable), either the target sound or the one it is likely to be confused with. When the target sound is said, the learners move their hand. When it is the other sound, they do nothing.

Hearing the target sounds is done for a few minutes, about 20 times in a brief session, and then the activity is done again a few days later and so on, until the learners get good at distinguishing and then identifying the troublesome target sounds.

## What are the goals of hearing and pronunciation practice?

Hearing practice using distinguishing and identifying is useful preparation for pronunciation practice, but it is also useful for comprehending spoken language.

As Table 11.1 shows, hearing and pronunciation practice has a single deliberate accuracy goal, which is being able to accurately hear and produce particular sounds. This does not imply that a native speaker model needs to be used.

Hearing and pronunciation practice can be an opportunity for learners to learn something about phonetics. When learning English, they can learn about

**TABLE 11.1** The goals of hearing and pronunciation practice

| Goals | Specific focuses |
|---|---|
| Language | *Accurate reception and production of L2 sounds* |
| Ideas | |
| Skills | |
| Text | |

vowels, consonants, and semi-vowels, voiced and voiceless sounds, stop sounds and continuant (long) sounds, and the ways in which the sounds before and after a particular sound can change it. Bauer (2023) has a very clear description of English phonetics and phonology for English language teachers.

## What are the requirements for hearing and pronunciation practice?

### How can you prepare for hearing and pronunciation practice?

As we shall see below, the most useful preparation involves working out which sounds need attention, and what components of the sounds need attention. The components of English sounds include whether it is voiced or voiceless, the parts of the mouth involved in the sound, and the type of sound it is (vowel/consonant, stop/continuant/semi-vowel).

For hearing practice, it is useful to work out what nonsense syllables to use. Bauer (2023, Chapter 7) provides a list of nonsense syllables.

### What sounds should be used for hearing and pronunciation practice?

A critical part of preparing for this activity is deciding what sounds to focus on. Typically, the sounds will be ones that are not in the learners' first language, or which are pronounced differently or occur in a different position in a syllable in the first language. Some languages have detailed contrastive analyses comparing the sound system with English. However, teachers will quickly become aware what sounds are likely to be difficult for their learners, especially if learners all have the same L1.

### How much time should be given to focusing on individual sounds in a general language course?

Hearing and pronunciation practice as described in this chapter fits firmly into the language-focused learning strand. It shares time in this strand with the deliberate learning of spelling, vocabulary, grammar, discourse, and pragmatics, as well as the study of principles of learning and language learning strategies. The language-focused learning strand should take up around one-quarter of the total course time, and much less than one-quarter of this time (less than one-sixteenth of the total course time) should involve deliberate pronunciation practice. It is worth noting that learning and practising pronunciation can also occur incidentally through the spoken parts of the meaning-focused input, meaning-focused output, and fluency development strands.

## How does hearing and pronunciation practice help learning?

In essence, hearing and pronunciation practice helps improve the accuracy of listening and speaking through a deliberate focus on accuracy through analysis (quality) and through quantity of guided practice. The learning is not easily transferable to normal language use.

*Motivation:* Most learners want to have a clear and intelligible pronunciation, although this goal may slip a bit with particularly challenging sounds. When learning a language which is very different from the first language, such as a native speaker of English learning a tone language like Mandarin or Thai, the challenge of an intelligible pronunciation can be a very daunting challenge.

*Focus:* Giving deliberate attention to hearing and producing sounds, including the features of sounds (voiced – voiceless, long sound – stop, parts of the mouth), provides explicit knowledge and deliberate control of the pronunciation of individual sounds. This is a starting point for more fluent control. The belief is that, as with vocabulary, explicit learning will also support implicit knowledge as well as explicit knowledge. The worry is that explicit learning, as with the learning of grammar, will not readily move beyond explicit knowledge to implicit knowledge. Certainly, with hearing and pronunciation practice, there is value in having consistent, clear, and accurate models.

*Quantity:* Hearing and pronunciation development requires spaced repeated practice. In the initial stages, it is necessary to spend time on a problem sound and its components to get as close as possible to an intelligible pronunciation.

*Quality:* The major quality feature for sounds is informed observation and informed production, where being informed involves knowing the various components of the sound. This is a kind of analysis.

## How can hearing and pronunciation practice be done well?

To teach pronunciation well, a teacher needs some knowledge of articulatory phonetics. This is included in most courses in introductory linguistics. The classic text is Daniel Jones's (1918) *An Outline of English Phonetics*. Pronunciation practice involves getting guidance in the pronunciation of particular sounds, in isolation, in syllables, and in words.

1 The first step in this process is gathering information about the target sound and the sound it is replaced by. This useful information can be found by answering these questions.
   a Does the learner have the wanted sound in the first language? What is the nearest sound?
   b What sound does the learner put in place of the wanted sound?
   c What is the difference between the wanted sound and the unwanted sound?
   d Does the learner make this mistake in initial, middle, and final position?

The table shows how consonants can be analysed, using /ð/ as an example.

| Sound | Voiced/voiceless | Position | Type of sound |
|---|---|---|---|
| ð | Voiced | Top teeth<br>Front of tongue | Long |

A more technical analysis would involve terms such as *labio-dental* and *continuant*, but more common, more transparent words are better for teaching purposes. The sound that the learner puts in place of the wanted sound can be described in a similar table, and that usually makes the difference between the two sounds more obvious. Here is the analysis for /z/, often a substitute for /ð/.

| Sound | Voiced/voiceless | Position | Type of sound |
|---|---|---|---|
| z | Voiced | Tooth ridge<br>Front of tongue | Long |

The difference between the two sounds involves the position of the tongue.

2  The second step in learning to pronounce a sound is hearing practice, using the distinguishing technique and later the identifying technique.
3  The third step is listening to the sound in a nonsense syllable and then repeating it after the teacher. If this works, then there is no need for further steps with that sound.
4  If listening and repeating does not work after about three attempts, then the fourth step is getting the learner to observe the teacher's mouth, as well as the teacher giving a simple explanation of how the sound is made. This simple explanation should not involve much of the terminology of phonetics but should involve explanations, such as "It is a long sound" for continuants, "Put your tongue between your teeth" for the labio-dentals, and "Put your tongue against the tooth-ridge". This step can also involve getting the learner to consciously sense where the tongue is in the mouth. The fifth step is used if the fourth step does not work.
5  The fifth step involves forcing the sound. Forcing the sound involves using some physical way of making sure that the position of the parts of the mouth and the type of sound are correct. This step is sometimes necessary for sounds such as /r/ and /ð/. The essence of forcing is that it stops the tongue being where it should not be. Here are some suggestions for forcing particular sounds.

/r/ Place your finger or a pencil under your tongue and push it back so that it cannot touch the tooth ridge. This stops the learner making /l/. /r/ is a long sound.

/ð/ Put your tongue between your teeth. Bite down gently. Your teeth should touch the front of the tongue not be right at the tip of the tongue. Another way is to place your forefinger upright against the tip of your nose. Your tongue should come far enough out of your mouth to touch your forefinger. This stops the learner making /z/ or /d/. /ð/ is a long sound, so you should be able to make it continue for a long time.

/w/ Point your forefinger at your mouth. Make your lips form around the end of your finger. This stops the bottom lip from touching your top teeth and thus avoids /v/.

/l/ Press the tip of your tongue hard against the back of your top teeth. Make a long sound. This stops the tongue curling back to make /r/.

These descriptions all use simple language and make it difficult for the learner to make the unwanted sound.

## *How can I check that hearing and pronunciation practice is working well?*

The goal of hearing and pronunciation practice is accuracy, so learners should be able to identify and produce wanted sounds in a comprehensible way. Ultimate success occurs when the sounds are produced accurately in largely unmonitored speech. However, careful accurate use is a good step towards this.

## What are the variants of hearing and pronunciation practice?

There are several activities which are variants of the two hearing activities of distinguishing and identifying. They involve the use of real words rather than nonsense syllables, pictures, triplets (three sounds rather than two), and multiple choice. Unfortunately, these other activities bring their own problems with them. Using real words can bring previous mispronunciations of those words to the fore. Along with pictures, they can also encourage a focus on meaning rather than form, when the goal of the activity should be to get the spoken form correct. Even with pairs of words in the distinguishing activity, there is a subconscious preference to say the same rather than different when unsure (Briere, 1967). When more than two sounds are compared, a memory factor is involved and sounds next to each other are easier to distinguish than sounds separated by another sound. The two basic hearing activities of distinguishing and identifying using nonsense syllables, at least initially, are enough to develop the required hearing skills.

Sound dictation is a variant of identifying and is useful as an informal testing technique. The teacher says simple nonsense words or real words and the learners write them.

### Learning through discovery

As well as listening to single sounds, learners can be given practice in listening to types of sounds, for example, distinguishing voiced and voiceless sounds, stops and continuants, etc. By learning in this general way, the learners will find it easier to classify the sounds that they hear and will find it easier to hear and remember them. Learners can be taught to discover these types of sounds themselves with a little help from the teacher. Here is an exercise which does that.

*The learners' material:* The learners need to see this list of words.

m<u>ee</u>t <u>th</u>in bag f<u>ee</u>l girl wi<u>sh</u> bus <u>sh</u>arp with <u>th</u>en ten z<u>oo</u>
d<u>ee</u>p <u>p</u>art had lot h<u>or</u>n si<u>ng</u> <u>th</u>ird n<u>or</u>th yes rob g<u>oo</u>d oz*
win b<u>oo</u>k <u>sh</u>ut gas van av* am r<u>oo</u>m b<u>ir</u>d f<u>ee</u>t if k<u>ee</u>p
__ = two letters which make just one sound; *th* and *oo* each have two pronunciations.
\* = nonsense words

*The teacher's notes:* (The learners do not see these notes.)
/ʒ/, /ə/ (schwa), diphthongs and *ch* /tʃ/, and *dg* /dʒ/, are not included in the list.
a = /æ/, e = /e/, i = /ɪ/, o = /ɒ/, u = /ʌ/, ee = /iː/, oo = /uː/ or /ʊ/, ar = /ɑː/, or = /ɔ/, ir = /ɜː/

*The exercise:* The teacher can present this orally, giving examples and help. The answers to some of the questions are given here in brackets. However, the teacher should let the learners find these for themselves.

1 Make a list of all the other letters and letter groups in the words that do not use the following letters: vowels: *a e i o u*, semi-vowels: *y w r h l*. These are consonants.
2 Practise pronouncing the consonant sounds in your list. You should have 16 different sounds. How many are written with one letter? (12) How many are written with two letters? (4- *th, ng, sh, th*). Be careful, *th* has two pronunciations.
3 Say the sound /ɑː/ as in car. While you say the sound put your hands over your ears and listen to the sound in your head and feel your throat. Then say /s/. Now you cannot hear the same noise in your head. Divide the sounds in your list into two groups. In one group, put the sounds that make a noise in your head when your ears are covered. These are called voiced sounds. In the other group, put the sounds that do not make a noise in your head. These are called voiceless sounds (other examples: /m/ /b/ – /p/ /f/).

4  Say the sounds in both groups while you hold your nose so that air cannot come out of your nose. If you cannot say any of the sounds because you are holding your nose (example /n/), draw a circle around these sounds in your lists. These sounds are called nasal sounds because the sounds come through your nose. There are three of them (/m n ŋ/). There is something else that is the same in all of them. What is it? (Voiced)
5  Some sounds can be said for a long time without changing the sound or moving the mouth (example /s/). Other sounds are short. They are like small explosions (example /p/). Draw a square around all the long sounds in your list. (Long sounds should be looked for first, otherwise continuants are turned into stops.) The short sounds are called stops, because at the beginning of the sound the movement of the air in the mouth is stopped. The long sounds are called continuants, because they continue. That is, they are long. You should have six stop sounds (/p b t d k g/).
6  Now, say all the voiceless sounds in your list. Say the voiceless sounds again. This time hum while you say each sound, or cover your ears and make the voiceless sound become voiced. If you do this, you will find that it is exactly the same as a sound in the voiced list (examples /s/ – /z/, /k/ – /g/). Write the pairs of sounds that are the same except that one is voiceless and the other is voiced. Make pairs of stops first and then continuants. The nasals do not make pairs.
7  Now, look at the words in the first list again. Some consonant sounds can be at the beginning and the end of a word. Some can be only at the beginning of a word and not at the end. (4- /h/ /j/ /r/ /w/) Some can only be at the end of a word and not at the beginning. (1- /ŋ/) Draw a triangle around the sounds that can only be at the beginning of a word and not at the end. Draw a diamond around the sounds that can only be at the end of a word and not at the beginning. Compare this with the sounds in your language.
1a  These letters are used to make vowels in the words in the list, *a e i o u r*. Look at the words in the list and write all the vowel sounds. Five vowel sounds use only one letter (example *u*). Six vowel sounds use groups of two letters (example *ee*). Be careful one group *oo* has two pronunciations.

When the learners have followed all these steps and know some of the sounds of English, they can look at other carefully chosen lists of words to see how one sound can have several spellings and one spelling can have several sounds. They can try to see the connections between sounds and spelling. Appendix 1 of Nation and Macalister (2021) has detailed information on this. See also Bauer (2023).

### Are there digital applications of this technique?

Computer Assisted Pronunciation Training (CAPT) can provide greater quantity of practice, greater variety of models, and innovative ways of getting guidance and feedback (Levis & Rehman, 2023).

By typing "How do you say *priest*?" into Google, you can get the pronunciation of any word accompanied by a picture of someone saying the word. You can also slow down the pronunciation.

By typing "Learning articulatory phonetics" into Google, you can find sites that will help teachers learn about the different kinds of sounds and the phonetic alphabet.

English Accent Coach is an interactive game that provides practice in identifying sounds.

The internet increases the opportunity to hear a range of different speakers and different accents.

### Revisiting and linking to other activities

In this chapter, we have looked only at individual sounds and not at suprasegmentals. Intonation is particularly important in managing turn-taking and interaction, in signalling topic shifts, and in conveying pragmatic meaning. Levis (2016) argues that current research on intonation is still not well represented in teaching materials. We also have not looked at pronunciation and connected speech, although this can be a focus in techniques such as prepared talks and informal conversation. A focus on pronunciation in connected speech can involve the difference between citation forms and their non-stressed use in connected speech, linking (gunna), deletion (can e do it), insertion (two wapples), modification or blending, and reduction.

### What does research say about the effectiveness of hearing and pronunciation practice?

The historical trends in pronunciation teaching have been unusual in that they have tended to be more cumulative than in other parts of the foreign language learning field. That is, the focuses of previous trends have been retained and have been enriched and added to by newer trends (Levis, 2016).

Thomson and Derwing (2015) and Lee, Jang, and Plonsky (2015) provide comprehensive reviews of research. The vast majority of studies, the majority of which focused on discrete pronunciation features, showed substantial improvement as a result of instruction in pronunciation. Improvement was largely measured in terms of accuracy (accent reduction) rather than intelligibility or comprehensibility. However, these criteria are closely related to each other. A lot of the assessment involved reading aloud or picture description, which is different from communicative use, but nonetheless, this careful mode of speaking can be a stepping-stone to more communication-focused use. Learners' gains were large when a single sound or feature was targeted, when there was a longer treatment, and when feedback was provided. These findings are in line with meta-analyses of other aspects of language learning, such as the learning of vocabulary and grammar.

There has been a lot of discussion on how to set priorities in pronunciation practice with the criterion of accuracy being replaced by more communicative criteria such as intelligibility (how recognizable is it?), comprehensibility (how easy is it to understand?), and functional load (how likely is it to be a source of confusion?). It is important to focus on areas where help is needed, and where help is likely to have a big effect on intelligibility. The effect of the learners' first language is critical here.

Listening to a wide variety of voices can help in learning new sounds and the pronunciation of words (Uchihara, Webb & Trofimovich, 2021). The deliberate use of a wide variety of speakers is called High Variability Perceptual Training (HVPT) and lies behind the design of the English Accent Coach app. The internet is particularly useful in providing opportunities for a variety of input (Derwing, 2017).

Newton (2017) looks at how pronunciation can develop as a result of communicative interaction.

There is a journal called the *Journal of Second Language Pronunciation* published by John Benjamins.

## Research questions

### *Motivation principles (Engagement)*

For learning to occur, there needs to be a willingness to focus on what needs to be learned, and to give it quantity and quality of attention.

1 *Motivation: The degree of engagement with the task affects the likelihood of learning occurring.* Are learners strongly motivated to improve their pronunciation? Do learners notice improvement in their and others' pronunciation?
2 *Self-efficacy: Our confidence in our own skills of learning affects our success in learning.* Is contrastive analysis a good predictor of the difficult sounds for learners of the same L1? Is the sequence of distinguishing, identifying, copying, and guidance the most effective sequence for improving the pronunciation of particular sounds?

### *Focus principles (Usefulness)*

Learning requires giving attention to what needs to be learned.

3 *Focus: We learn what we focus on, and in addition, our learning is more useful if it closely resembles the use that we need to make of what we learn*

*(transfer-appropriate)*. How can deliberate training in pronunciation be transferred to normal spoken use? To what degree does training learners in elementary articulatory phonetics improve their pronunciation? How quickly do the distinguishing and identifying techniques result in accurate perception of sounds?
4 *Accuracy: Our learning is more efficient if the information we are focusing on is complete, accurate, and comprehensible.* Is accurate perception essential for accurate pronunciation?

### Quantity principles (Amount)

5 *Repetition: The more repetitions, the stronger the learning.* When trying to improve pronunciation of a sound by copying a model, how many unsuccessful repetitions of the model signal that no improvement is likely to occur without a different intervention?
6 *Time-on-task: The greater and longer the attention, the stronger the learning.* How long does it take to improve the pronunciation of particular sounds?

### Quality principles (Connections)

Elaboration and analysis increase and strengthen connections between the item to be learned and other knowledge making it easier to access the item.

7 *Elaboration: This includes enriching the encoding of an item through variation.* Which is the most effective way of improving pronunciation through listening to a model, listening to the same model, or listening to a range of models?
8 *Analysis: This involves relating the familiar parts to the unfamiliar whole.* Is the deliberate learning of basic articulatory phonetics worth the effort in improving pronunciation?

The most needed research on pronunciation is how deliberate training on pronunciation features transfers to normal language use.

# 12
# 4/3/2

### What is 4/3/2?

In the 4/3/2 technique, the learners work in pairs with one member being the speaker and the other being the listener. The teacher says, "Go!" and each learner who is the speaker delivers their talk. They have four minutes to do this. Each learner who is the listener simply listens and does not interrupt or ask questions. At the end of four minutes, the teacher says, "Change partners!" and the listeners move to a new partner. The teacher says, "Go! You now have three minutes." and each speaker delivers exactly the same talk again, but this time to their new partner. After three minutes, the teacher stops the learners, they change partners, and the speakers give the same talk again to their new partner for two minutes. Note that the listeners always listen, and the speakers do not become listeners during the activity. On a different day, the listeners can take their turn at being speakers and deliver their talk three times to different listeners.

The reason for the speakers delivering the same talk three times, one after the other, with no interruptions and to a new listener is so that they cover exactly the same content each time. This gives them a chance to increase their speed through largely verbatim repetition. Thai and Boers (2016) found that a very large percentage of the words in the second and third parts of the talk occurred in verbatim contexts from the earlier parts.

The 4/3/2 activity was originally devised by Keith Maurice (1983). He used 5/4/3, but delivering a five-minute talk proved to be a bit too demanding for lower-proficiency learners, so it was reduced to 4/3/2. Some teachers have used

3/2/1½. In the original version of the activity, the members of each pair took turns in speaking. We changed this, so that each speaker gave their talk three times without the interruption of listening to someone else's talk in order to encourage verbatim repetition.

The 4/3/2 technique fits into the fluency development strand and aims at developing spoken fluency. It is an experience technique like most fluency development techniques because it involves language that is already well within the learners' knowledge. The learning goal is developing fluency with known language – a skill development goal. Research on 4/3/2 indicates that increases in fluency in 4/3/2 may come at the expense of accuracy, and so 4/3/2 is best paired with a repeated activity, such as 3/3/3 which allows opportunity for accuracy improvement as well as with additions to the technique, such as planning and corrective feedback, which give some attention to accuracy. Ultimately, fluency needs to be fluency with accuracy.

4/3/2 is a group work technique using pairs and involving individual performance. Group work techniques involving individual performance are used so that lots of learners have a chance to perform at the same time. This can make it a somewhat noisy technique in a large class.

## What are the learning goals of 4/3/2

4/3/2 is a technique for developing spoken fluency, that is making the best use of what is already known. Like all techniques in the meaning-focused input, meaning-focused output, and fluency development strands, it involves incidental learning.

The major learning goal of 4/3/2 is increasing the speed of speaking using known language features (see Table 12.1). Fluency development activities also strengthen knowledge of familiar vocabulary and grammatical features and encourage the use of multiword units as the learners move from operating at the word level to operating at the phrasal level.

**TABLE 12.1** The goals of 4/3/2

| Goals | Specific focuses |
|---|---|
| Language | Strengthening and enriching partly known vocabulary and grammar<br>Encouraging the use of multiword units |
| Ideas |  |
| Skills | *Developing spoken fluency* |
| Text |  |

Note: The major goal is in *italics*.

## How does 4/3/2 help learning?

4/3/2 involves language use and language use can result in incidental language learning. There are several possible explanations of why language use helps language learning, but from a teaching perspective, it may be sufficient to accept that it does, and look for ways to provide plenty of opportunities for language use. Applying the principle of the four strands is one way of doing this. In essence, 4/3/2 helps develop fluency in speaking through quantity of accurate easy practice. Quantity of easy practice may also result in the strengthening of vocabulary knowledge and developing knowledge of multiword units.

*Motivation:* Changing partners in 4/3/2 can keep up the motivation to repeat the same talk without making substantial changes, as each delivery is a genuine piece of communication because the content is new to the listener. The topics chosen for 4/3/2 should be very familiar.

*Focus:* The familiar topic and time pressure in 4/3/2 keeps the focus on fluency. Because research shows that there is little if any improvements in accuracy during 4/3/2, it is worth running the activity so that the chances of using accurate language are high. We will look more closely at this later in this chapter.

*Quantity:* 4/3/2 relies on repeated practice of easy material. Repetition helps learning and there is plenty of evidence that repeating tasks either immediately and after some delay results in improvements in fluency (Ellis, 2018). The effects of repetition on accuracy and complexity are helped by time to reflect, and feedback.

*Quality:* The repetition with time pressure encourages the learner to work with a more efficient unit of processing. It is likely that fluency development techniques such as 4/3/2 provide encouragement to make more use of multiword units and formulaic sequences, because working at a level higher than the single word is an efficient way of coping with limited time.

## What are the requirements of 4/3/2?

There are five criteria that define a fluency development technique. The criteria are listed in order of importance, with the most important criterion by far being the easiness of the activity.

1  A fluency technique uses known language features.
2  A fluency technique involve accurate use.
3  A fluency technique involves some pressure to perform at a faster than usual level.
4  A fluency technique is meaning-focused.
5  A fluency technique involves a large quantity of activity.

The 4/3/2 technique meets these five criteria because:

1 the talk involved is on topics that are very familiar to the learners and that involve language they already know.
2 preparation for the talk and reflection between the talks increases accuracy
3 the reducing amount of time from four minutes to three minutes to two minutes pushes the learners to speak faster.
4 the talk is delivered to a different listener each time so there is genuine communication of the message.
5 each activity involves four plus, three plus, two minutes of talking (nine minutes) as well as nine minutes of listening, within a ten-minute activity.

4/3/2 clearly meets most of the fluency criteria.

### *How can you prepare for 4/3/2?*

Before doing 4/3/2, the teacher needs to work out a system for deciding who will be speakers and who will be listeners. The teacher also needs to work out a way of changing partners that will cause the least disruption. If the learners are sitting in rows, then the learners at the ends of the rows should be the ones who move.

3/3/3 is an activity which involves repeating the same talk to a different partner but with no pressure through decreasing time. The lack of time pressure provides an opportunity for a more reflective second and third delivery of the talk so that performance errors can be corrected and more appropriate words or expressions can be chosen. Thai and Boers (2016) also recommend having some kind of intervention between the first delivery and the second delivery that provides an opportunity for improvements in accuracy and complexity. Such an intervention could take a variety of forms, including feedback from the listener, reflection by the speaker and making notes on a cue sheet, and the speaker listening to a recording of the four-minute talk before giving the same talk for three minutes.

There can also be interventions before the 4/3/2 activity is done. 3/3/3 with an intervention could be preparation for 4/3/2. That is, the same topic covered by 3/3/3 can later be redone as 4/3/2. Preparation for 4/3/2 or 3/3/3 could involve preparing a written version of the talk and getting feedback on it. It could involve giving a four-minute presentation on the topic which is recorded and then listening to the recording, perhaps with a partner, to consider improvements to the recording, and perhaps recording again. On another day, the same topic is then redone as 4/3/2.

Preparation could also involve learners working in pairs, with one learner interviewing the other about the topic before it is then done as 4/3/2.

The major requirement for the activity is a list of familiar topics that involve language that is already within the learners' knowledge. One way of ensuring this is choosing topics from those already covered in the language course.

The classroom needs to be arranged so that one member of each pair can quickly move to pair up with another member.

## *What texts should be used for 4/3/2?*

Boers and Thai (2017) have shown that topics chosen for 4/3/2 need to be easy otherwise fluency will be affected, and fluency development may involve making incorrect forms fluent. Thai and Boers (2016) got learners to rate topics for familiarity and this rating was used in the choice of topics. If the language classes are based around themes, then basing the topics for 4/3/2 on themes already well covered will be helpful. Similarly, basing the 4/3/2 topic on a piece of previously covered intensive reading or a piece of project work can ensure that the learners get the greatest benefit from 4/3/2.

## *How much time should be given to prepare 4/3/2 in a general language course?*

4/3/2 fits into the speaking part of the fluency development strand. If it was the only spoken fluency development activity, it would occupy one-quarter of the time in the fluency development strand which is one-sixteenth of the total course time. There are, however, other spoken fluency development activities, such as revisiting the same activity again on a different day, speaking as part of project work, prepared talks, and speaking as part of the linked skills activity. Because 4/3/2 can be done in a little over ten minutes, it is worth scheduling it as a regular weekly or two-weekly activity.

## How can 4/3/2 be done well?

1. The teacher prepares the learners for the activity by working out a topic with them and making sure they are well on top of the ideas and language of the topic.
2. The teacher explains the 4/3/2 activity and indicates who will be the listeners and the speakers and how to change partners when told to do so.
3. The teacher says, "Go!" and each learner who is the speaker delivers their talk. They have four minutes to do this. Each learner who is the listener simply listens and does not interrupt or ask questions.
4. At the end of four minutes, the teacher says, "Stop! Change partners!" and the listeners move to a new partner. The teacher says, "Go! You now have three minutes." and each speaker delivers exactly the same talk again, but this time to their new partner.
5. After three minutes, the teacher stops the learners, they change partners, and the speakers give the same talk again to their new partner for two minutes. Note that the listeners always listen and the speakers do not become listeners during the activity.

6 On a different day, the listeners can take their turn at being speakers and deliver the same talk three times to different listeners.

## How can I check that a 4/3/2 activity is working well?

Because 4/3/2 is a fluency development activity, then speed of speech is the best measure. For monitoring purposes, this need not be measured through counting words per minute but can be judged simply by observing the activity. The second aspect to look for is accuracy, because fluency activities should involve accurate fluent use. This also can be judged by observation.

## What are the variants of 4/3/2?

### Different skills

4/3/2 involves doing the same activity three times in a row with no breaks in between. There are fluency development techniques using different skills which use a different time pressure or no time pressure. Repeated reading is intended for learners who are developing written word recognition skills. The same text around 150 words long is read aloud three times. The time taken to do each reading is noted. If the listener is of a higher-proficiency level than the reader, then long hesitations and errors can also be noted, looking for improvement over the three readings.

Repeated writing is a form of writing practice for time-controlled exams, where each question has a certain mark value and needs to be completed within a fixed time. The time taken to write each answer is noted with the goal of fitting the answer within the time limit.

Speeded listening involves listening to the same recorded spoken text three times increasing the playback speed with each re-listening.

### Repeated speaking techniques

There are repeated speaking activities which involve a circulating audience of individuals or small groups. Usually, no time pressure is involved. In the *Headlines* technique, around one-third of the learners are speakers and two-thirds are listeners. The speakers each think of an exciting or amusing thing that happened to them and then each writes a headline in large letters filling a piece of A4 paper. The headline should be something striking that will attract the interest of the listeners, such as *Burning bed brings pleasure* or *Rain of terror*. Each speaker then sits with their headline displayed in front of them, and the speakers move around individually or in pairs or small groups saying, "Tell me your story". Each speaker will need to tell their story based on the headline several times to different listeners.

*Marketplace* is a similar technique, but this time the speakers are advertising things for sale. These can be overseas holidays, cars, kitchen equipment, movie or concert tickets, and so on. Each speaker has to give their sales pitch several times to different buyers. The buyers can ask questions about the value and quality of what is being sold. The buyers listen to several sellers all selling similar things and decide which one they will buy.

### How can 4/3/2 be used at all levels of proficiency?

Low proficiency learners can work with memorized talks and with shorter times for each delivery (3/2/1½). Higher-proficiency learners can have little or no time for preparation and longer speaking times (5/4/3).

### How can 4/3/2 be used in large classes?

The major problem with 4/3/2 in large classes is the noise created by half of the class all speaking at the same time. This problem can be partly solved by the learners being aware of the need to speak quietly, and the teacher using well-known signals, such as tapping on the desk, to bring down the noise level.

### Are there digital applications of this technique?

If 4/3/2 is done as an individual activity by learners working alone, the learner can talk for four minutes, listen to a recording of the talk briefly noting possible improvements, and then make the three-minute delivery, and so on.

Digital timers on cell phones now make the timing of 4/3/2 much easier.

### Revisiting and linking to other activities

Because 4/3/2 is a fluency development activity, it is a useful way of revisiting material covered in previous lessons. It brings the old material closer to being learned. So, 4/3/2 is a useful way of revisiting reading and listening passages in previous units of the coursebook.

4/3/2 can also be linked to writing. The learners use what they have written as their content for the 4/3/2 talk.

### What does research say about the effectiveness of 4/3/2?

Repetition activities provide opportunity to reduce the cognitive load of a task, thus allowing attention to be directed towards the difficult parts. For example, once the ideas in a talk have been worked out, it is then possible to give attention to how well they are expressed. Drawing on Skehan's trade-off hypothesis, Thai and Boers (2016, p. 369) suggest that "the simultaneous enhancement in the three speech qualities of complexity, accuracy, and fluency is unusual". This fits well with Barcroft's idea that we learn what we focus on. Thai and Boers (2016), and Boers (2014) present evidence that the use of decreasing time in 4/3/2 has negative effects on the development of accuracy and complexity, possibly because time pressure encourages verbatim repetition and discourages changing parts of the talk which could be improved. The pedagogical implications of this are that if we want learners to improve their speaking fluency, then we should use 4/3/2 with its increasing time pressure. If we want to improve accuracy and complexity as well, we should not include time pressure but should just use repeated tasks. Repeated tasks will increase fluency but not to as large a degree as with time pressure. In addition, adding some deliberate attention between the repetitions, particularly between deliveries 1 and 2, in the form of corrective feedback or study of a language feature, is likely to result in more improvements in accuracy and complexity (Tran & Saito, 2021). Macalister (2014) noted that the step from three minutes to two minutes may be too big a step, forcing the learners to cut more than they should. 4/3/2½ may be more effective.

The effects of repetition can be both short term and long term. De Jong and Perfetti (2011) argue that fluency development studies need to look at the long-term delayed effects of repetition because immediate spoken repetition can be explained by priming effects, whereas delayed effects are more likely to occur through proceduralization and automatization. Proceduralization and automatization are explanations of how language use can help learning. Priming means that items are brought to the forefront of memory making them easier to access in the short term. De Jong and Perfetti found evidence of both short-term and long-term effects in their study of 4/3/2.

DeKeyser (2015) uses the DeJong and Perfetti study as a good example of how Skill Acquisition Theory can explain aspects of language learning. Skill Acquisition Theory sees learning proceeding through the stages of declarative knowledge, procedural knowledge, and automaticity. The DeJong and Perfetti study showed that through repeated practice, declarative knowledge could become procedural knowledge. The measures used which showed proceduralization were mean length of run and stable length of run, basically measures involving amount of speech without pauses. Practice did lead to increases in length of run which were maintained on a delayed post-test, and which transferred to different stories. Skill Acquisition Theory is not the only way of explaining these findings, but it is a way that fits nicely with the findings.

Wood (2009) found that sustained teaching of multiword units contributed to increases in fluency, suggesting that a useful intervention may involve memorization of relevant multiword units.

## Research questions

### *Motivation principles (Engagement)*

For learning to occur, there needs to be a willingness to focus on what needs to be learned, and to give it quantity and quality of attention.

1 *Motivation: The degree of engagement with the task affects the likelihood of learning occurring.* Do learners enjoy doing 4/3/2? Do they see it as an activity that should be used regularly during a course?
2 *Self-efficacy: Our confidence in our own skills of learning affects our success in learning.* Does preparation for 4/3/2 increase feelings of self-efficacy?

### *Focus principles (Usefulness)*

Learning requires giving attention to what needs to be learned.

3 *Focus: We learn what we focus on, and in addition, our learning is more useful if it closely resembles the use that we need to make of what we learn (transfer-appropriate).* Does a deliberate focus on avoiding just one kind of error slow down the delivery of the talk?
4 *Accuracy: Our learning is more efficient if the information we are focusing on is complete, accurate, and comprehensible.* What are the most effective interventions with 4/3/2 in terms of the effect on accuracy and complexity without greatly sacrificing fluency? Possibilities include speak and record followed by review of the first delivery, record and transcribe, and correct and then do 4/3/2.

### *Quantity principles (Amount)*

5 *Repetition: The more repetitions, the stronger the learning.* Does coming back to exactly the same 4/3/2 talk again at a later date result in further increases in fluency? Does repetition without time pressure (3/3/3) result in the same amount of fluency increase? 4/3/2 involves three deliveries of the talk. Does having four or five deliveries result in more improvement?
6 *Time-on-task: The greater and longer the attention, the stronger the learning.* How often should the 4/3/2 activity be used in a course?

### *Quality principles (Connections)*

Elaboration and analysis increase and strengthen connections between the item to be learned and other knowledge making it easier to access the item.

7 *Elaboration:* This includes enriching the encoding of an item through variation. How much elaboration occurs during 4/3/2?
8 *Analysis:* This involves relating the familiar parts to the unfamiliar whole. Does feedback between deliveries result in fluency and accuracy improvements? Are there signs of multiword unit learning from 4/3/2?

The most needed research on 4/3/2 would be on how to make sure that 4/3/2 involves accurate use of the language.

# PART 3
Reading

# 13
# EXTENSIVE READING

## What is extensive reading?

Nation and Waring (2020, p. 3) define extensive reading as involving "each learner independently and silently reading a lot of material which is at the right level for them". This definition implies that at the beginning and intermediate levels, the learners need to be reading vocabulary-controlled material such as graded readers, where most of the vocabulary is already known or partly known.

Extensive reading fits into the meaning-focused input and fluency development strands of a course, with around two-thirds of the time in an extensive reading programme involving meaning-focused input and one-third fluency development. The meaning-focused input material should involve text coverage of around 98% of the running words, meaning that around two words or fewer per 100 running words are unfamiliar. The fluency development material should not involve any unknown words. Extensive reading tasks are experience tasks where the material is designed or chosen to be largely within the learners' previous experience, particularly regarding vocabulary and grammar knowledge.

In many ways, the extensive reading programme should be the main part of a language course, with some activities preparing learners for graded reading, lots of reading going on, and a wide range of activities based on the information gained from extensive reading.

## What are the learning goals of extensive reading?

As Table 13.1 shows, the major learning goal of extensive reading is development of the reading skill through large amounts of comprehensible reading.

DOI: 10.4324/9781003496151-17

TABLE 13.1 The goals of extensive reading

| Goals | Specific focuses |
| --- | --- |
| Language | Learning new vocabulary, multiword units, and grammatical features |
|  | Strengthening and enriching partly known vocabulary and grammar |
| Ideas | Gaining information and enjoyment from reading |
| Skills | *Reading with comprehension at a reasonable speed* |
| Text | Developing familiarity with fiction and non-fiction genres |

*Note*: *Italics* indicates the major goal.

An important secondary goal is strengthening and enriching vocabulary knowledge while learning some new vocabulary.

For learners at the beginning and intermediate levels with vocabulary sizes of less than 5,000-word families, specially written or carefully chosen reading material is needed. In most unsimplified material, the number of unfamiliar words is too large, and the density of unfamiliar words is too high for comprehensible reading at a reasonable speed of at least 150 words per minute and preferably around 250 words per minute.

## How does extensive reading help learning?

In essence, extensive reading helps develop the reading skill through highly transferable quantity of attention to the reading skill. Extensive reading also helps vocabulary learning through varied retrieval of vocabulary. Here variation is a quality of learning factor, and the weakness of vocabulary learning through extensive reading is that around half of the different words met will occur only once in any particular book.

The development of the reading skill comes from doing lots of reading. Learners can consult glosses or dictionaries as a part of extensive reading, but this look-up should not occur often. If it occurs often, it is a sign that the reading material is not at the right level for the learner.

The fluency development aspect of reading skill can be dealt with in two ways in an extensive reading programme. One way is through reading texts which are well within the learners' language knowledge or which have been read before, with the aim of reading them quickly. The other complementary way is to include a speed reading course within the extensive reading programme. We look closely at speed reading courses in Chapter 15. Including both of these ways of increasing reading speed is a good idea.

While doing extensive reading, vocabulary learning occurs through guessing from context clues, through dictionary or glossary look-up, and through repeated meetings with words in varied contexts. Dictionary look-up after guessing greatly improves vocabulary learning (Mondria, 2003). For a detailed analysis of guessing from context and extensive reading from a vocabulary learning perspective, see Webb and Nation (2017, pp. 90–96) and Nation and Waring (2020, Chapter 9).

*Motivation:* Extensive reading works well if learners enjoy reading. Most graded readers are interesting and enjoyable texts, and an annual competition run by the Extensive Reading Foundation awards prizes for the best graded readers. The winners can be found on the Extensive Reading Foundation web site. Vocabulary control is a critical factor helping self-efficacy, because vocabulary control largely ensures that learners will not face a large unknown vocabulary burden when reading the texts.

*Focus:* The focus in extensive reading should be on comprehending the text with a good degree of comprehension (accuracy). This is a highly transferable skill.

*Quantity:* Learners should do large amounts of extensive reading, and thus get good at reading. From a vocabulary perspective, research has shown that learning a large vocabulary through extensive reading is possible as long as learners do reasonable amounts of reading. The amount of reading needed to get at least 12 repetitions of the words at a particular 1,000 word level increases from one 1,000 word level to the next. For the 2nd 1,000 word level, learners need to read around 42 minutes a week if reading at the slow reading speed of 100 words per minute (Nation, 2014b). For the 3rd 1,000 level this increases to one hour and 16 minutes per week at the same slow speed. At 200 words per minute, learning words at the 4th 1,000 level would require around one hour and five minutes a week. These figures are calculated on 40 weeks of the year and five days a week. Extensive reading should be an activity that occurs at least every week and preferably almost every day.

*Quality:* The kind of learning involved in extensive reading is largely incidental learning, where the learner is focused on reading and enjoying the text. The varied contexts of the vocabulary involved in extensive reading helps learning through elaboration.

## What are the requirements of extensive reading?

### How can you prepare for extensive reading?

There are several booklets available providing guidance about setting up an extensive reading programme. The most readily available is on the Extensive Reading Foundation web site (https://erfoundation.org). Look under *What is ER?* for *ER Guides*. Some of the major ELT publishers, such as Oxford University Press and Cambridge University Press, have their own free guides to graded reading.

By far, the easiest way to set up a graded reading programme is for a school or class to subscribe to *Xreading.com*. A subscription needs to be paid to do this, but the subscription rates are very reasonable and there is no need to buy graded readers. Through this programme, learners have access to hundreds of electronic graded readers at a wide range of levels. The programme monitors the learners' reading and keeps records, provides tests for each book, has reviews for most books, and provides spoken versions of the books for listening at different speeds. The programme records which books and the number of books each learner reads, the number of words they have read, the time taken to read each book and their reading speed. With a subscription, learners can read as many books as they want, and they can all read the same book at the same time if they wish. Xreading also includes speed reading courses that track the learners' reading speeds.

### What texts should be used for extensive reading?

Most graded readers are narrative texts, but many publishers include non-fiction texts among their offerings. These publishers include National Geographic Learning, Oxford University Press, Collins ELT, Compass Publishing, and Macmillan ELT. The Extensive Reading Foundation web site has a wealth of information on graded readers.

### How much of the course time should be given to extensive reading in a general language course?

A well-balanced language course spends an equal amount of time on each of the four strands of meaning-focused input, meaning-focused output, language-focused learning, and fluency development (Nation, 2007). Meaning-focused input involves learning from listening and reading where the learners' main attention is focused on the message. That is, their focus is on comprehending what they listen to or read.

Meaning-focused input should make up one-quarter of the time on a course. Around half of this time should be spent on reading (the other half is spent on listening) and most of this reading should be extensive reading. The fluency development strand should make up one-quarter of the time on a course and this time should be shared between listening fluency development, speaking fluency development, reading fluency development, and writing fluency development. Most, but not all, of the reading fluency development time should be spent doing extensive reading of very easy books where there are no unknown language items and where the topic is to some degree familiar to the learners. There should also be a small language-focused learning aspect to extensive reading where learners learn about the goals of extensive reading, about the importance of reading a lot, about the importance of reading at the right level, and about the importance of noting down any new words which are met on word cards so that they can be deliberately studied later. In total, adding these three strands together means that just under one-quarter of the total course time (which includes time for doing homework) should be spent on extensive reading for meaning-focused input and for fluency development.

### How can extensive reading be done well?

To work properly and to get the most benefit from extensive reading, learners should do large amounts of extensive reading, and they should do it every week. The teacher should monitor this reading in a minimally intrusive way to make sure it is done. In an ideal extensive reading programme, learners will enjoy the reading, do it regularly, and progress through the various word levels of the graded readers.

Much of the following information about setting up an extensive reading programme comes from *Extensive Reading and Graded Readers* by Paul Nation and Rob Waring (Compass Publishing, 2013).

The three most important things to give attention to when setting up an extensive reading programme are that (1) there are plenty of texts at the right level for the learners, (2) the learners are given the time and encouragement to do plenty of reading, and (3) there are two strands to the extensive reading programme – the meaning-focused input strand where learners read texts which are at the right level for them with a few words just beyond their present knowledge, and the fluency development strand where the learners read texts which are very easy but they read them as quickly as possible.

Very simply, the steps involved in extensive reading are these.

1. Get plenty of books at the right levels for the learners.
2. Set aside a regular time for silent reading, about 20 minutes at first, but later extensive reading should make up about a quarter of the total in-class and out-of-class learning time and should mostly be done out of class.
3. Get each learners to choose the book they want to read.
4. Let them get on with the reading without interruption.
5. Each time a learner finishes reading a book, get them to fill in a brief report form or sit a very short test on the book, and then let them choose a new book to read.
6. Encourage them to do plenty of reading.

You need to have plenty of books at the right level for your learners. That is, you need some books which contain a small amount of unknown vocabulary for them, and you need some books that are very easy for them to read and which contain little or no unknown vocabulary. At its most modest level, an extensive reading programme involves having a few more books than there are learners in the class. So, if you have a class of 40 learners then you may need around

50 extensive reading books. This allows each learner to have a book to read, and allows the fastest readers to return their book and exchange it for another without having to wait for someone else to finish reading. Ideally, however, there should be plenty of extensive reading books available at the right levels. The Xreading programme, which involves electronic reading, makes thousands of books available at all levels.

### How do I introduce the learners to extensive reading?

When learners are new to extensive reading, it is very useful to set aside a regular time for such reading. It is important to prepare learners for this reading by explaining that

- it is a time for silent reading,
- the main aim of the reading is to understand and enjoy the book they are reading,
- they should choose a book which is at the right level for them. If a book is too difficult, it should be changed for one which is less difficult,
- there are two types of extensive reading – reading where there are a few unknown words, and reading for fluency – and learners should do both kinds of reading at various times during the extensive reading program,
- the reading is not assessed but the learners must keep a record of what they have read,
- it is important to do large quantities of reading and the best learner is the learner who reads the most,
- learners can look up words in dictionaries while they read, but if they can guess the meaning of the word, then they should just carry on without looking up the word.

At various times it is useful to hold class discussions about the goals and issues in extensive reading, so that learners can see the value in it and commit themselves to doing it properly.

The next step is to get the learners doing extensive reading. First, they choose a book which seems to be at the right level for them and which looks interesting. Then they sit down and quietly read the book. They can look up unknown words in their dictionaries if they wish (bilingual dictionaries and electronic dictionaries are very satisfactory resources for learners), but if they find that they are looking up more than two or three words on the page, they have probably chosen a book which is too difficult for them and should exchange it for another more suitable one. At the end of the reading time, they place a bookmark in the book to mark where they are up to, and continue to read the book for homework if they are allowed to take it home, or read it in the next extensive reading session in class. When they complete a book, they quickly fill in their report form for it, and choose another book to read.

An extensive reading session is as simple as that – the learners get on with the job of reading.

## What texts can be used for extensive reading?

Graded readers are texts written within a controlled vocabulary. Some graded reader series start at the 75 word level, which means that if a learner knows just under 100 words of English, there are books that they can read. Most graded reader series go up to the 3,000-word family level. The mid-frequency readers are at the 4,000, 6,000, and 8,000 levels, and they bridge the gap between the publishers' graded reader series and unsimplified text. Teachers need to know about graded readers and the Extensive Reading Foundation web site is a good place to begin. Nation and Waring's (2020) book on extensive reading includes a chapter on graded readers. Most English Language Teaching publishers have one or more series of graded readers, and it is worth becoming familiar with them. Graded readers are one of the greatest resources available for learners of English as a foreign language.

## Criticisms of the use of graded readers for extensive reading

Graded readers are sometimes criticized for not being authentic texts because they are written using vocabulary and grammar control. Moreover, many graded readers are simplified versions of well-known works of literature. There are two meanings of *authentic* which are important in language teaching and learning. One meaning of authentic is used to refer to material which is written for native speakers or which is produced by native speakers. So, for example, we talk about authentic texts and authentic speech. The other meaning of authentic refers to something that a learner experiences. For example, when the learner has an authentic reading experience, this means that they read a text and experience it in the same way that it was intended to be read (for example, the way a native speaker or highly proficient reader would experience it). That is, they enjoy it or think it is a load of rubbish or boring, they can see how it relates to what they already know, and they can look at it critically. If a learner of English as a foreign language reads an authentic text, they are very unlikely to have an authentic reading experience, because so many words and grammatical constructions in the text will be unfamiliar to them. Somewhere around 40–50% of the different words in a text, no matter how long it is, occur only once, and are unlikely to occur again soon in a following text. Many of these words will be well outside the learners' knowledge and any time spent dealing with them will be time wasted. In an average novel, around 100,000 words long, there will be around

5,000 different word families (Nation, 2018), and around 2,000 of these will be beyond the 3,000 word level. This works out to be around one unknown word in every line of the text. The vocabulary burden of authentic text is far too heavy for meaning-focused input for learners who do not know at least 5,000 or 6,000 words of English (Nation, 2006, 2018). Because of this heavy vocabulary burden of authentic texts, texts within a controlled vocabulary are essential for the learning of English, if learners are to have meaning-focused input at every level of their language-proficiency development.

Some have argued that the discourse of graded readers is distorted as a result of the simplification process (Honeyfield, 1977) or provides impoverished input (Long, 2020). There is no evidence for this, and there is in fact evidence to show that they are like normal English writing (Claridge, 2005).

### How can learners know which books are at the right level for them?

The easiest way to see if a book is at the right level is for a learner to choose a book and if it seems easy to read and there are only a small number of unknown words (no more than three or four words per page) and they understand almost everything, then that is a suitable book.

Ideally, the teacher should know the vocabulary size of their learners, and learners should also know their current vocabulary size. This can be found by taking one of the new Vocabulary Levels Tests which are freely available on Paul Nation's resources pages. The learners' vocabulary size can then be matched to the graded reader levels.

For fluency development, the learners should choose very easy books containing no or few unknown words. Re-reading books that they have read before is also good for fluency development.

### What should the teacher do during an extensive reading session?

Some teachers recommend that they should also read quietly during an extensive reading session to act as a model for the learners. One advantage of doing this is that learners can see that if they talk or misbehave during the extensive reading session, they are interrupting the teacher's reading in the same way that they are interrupting their classmate's reading. This may encourage them to get on with their own reading.

Every so often, the teacher should look at learners' report sheets, or talk quietly with the learners individually to see that they are reading enough and that they are reading at the right level. The teacher should also check to see that each learner is doing some reading for fluency development (by reading very easy books quickly), and some reading for normal language development (by reading books which contain a few unknown words). This checking can be done during the extensive reading session, although the disadvantage of this is that it does interrupt some learners' reading.

The teacher can also use this time to quietly observe the learners and see who is reading well and who is not. It is highly likely that giving some individual counselling and attention to those who are not reading will result in a stronger commitment to the extensive reading programme.

### *How can we make sure that the learners are doing the extensive reading?*

You need some way of the learners keeping a record of what they have read and their brief reaction to it, so that the learners can see how much they have read and the teacher can monitor the amount of reading that they did. One way to do this is to have a table like the following on an A4 sheet of paper.

| *Title of the book* | *Series & Level* | *Purpose* | *Date begun* | *Date finished* | *Comment on the book* | *Interest* |
|---|---|---|---|---|---|---|
| | | | | | | |

In the column headed "Purpose", the learner can indicate whether the book was read for fluency development or for normal reading. In the column headed "Interest", the learner can give the book a ranking from one to five in terms of how interesting the book was for them. This gives the teacher some idea about which are the popular books and other learners can look at their friends' rankings to see what books they might want to read next.

The learners can also log on to a web site that provides tests for each graded reader and keeps a record for the class that the teacher can access (MReader quizzes on the Extensive Reading Foundation web site). The Xreading programme has a very extensive monitoring system that uses the time spent reading the book as a check on whether the learner was really doing the reading.

### *How should I organize an extensive reading library?*

It is important that an extensive reading programme includes texts at a variety of vocabulary levels. Although publishers use different grading schemes and different lists, it is best if an extensive reading programme does not limit itself to one series of readers but chooses the best from a variety of series. The matching of learners' vocabulary levels to graded readers is a very inexact process and always will be so. Any one graded reader only uses some of the words available at a particular level in the scheme, and so having graded readers from different schemes is not a big issue when it comes to finding suitable texts for learners.

The books in an extensive reading library should be clearly labelled so that learners are aware of the level of each book. Although publishers put this information somewhere in the book, it is not always easy to find. Moreover, as not all publishers follow the same scheme, it is best if institutions use their own levelling system. One solution is to label the books with coloured stickers with each colour representing a different level, or with a number on the sticker to indicate a standard set of levels. The Extensive Reading Foundation provides an overall set of graded reader levels on its web site at www.erfoundation.org and these levels can be used as a basis for coloured or numbered stickers.

Each class may have its own extensive reading library, but this is probably a wasteful use of resources, and it is better to have a library on a trolley which can be wheeled from class to class, or an easily accessible central library where the learners can go to borrow books. The advantage of using a central library which has a formal book borrowing system is that the teacher then does not have to keep track of the books.

Whatever kind of library is used, it is important that the books are easily accessible and attractively displayed. Learners may need a lot of encouragement to begin doing extensive reading seriously, and the accessibility and display of books is one part of providing this encouragement.

### *How do I set up an extensive reading scheme if my school has no budget to buy the books?*

The first thing to do is to see what graded readers are already available within the school. By looking carefully within the school library, it may be possible to find some graded readers that the school already owns. If the school has no graded readers and no money to buy them, then one alternative is to ask each learner to buy a graded reader and to make sure that each learner buys a different title. In this way, learners can read the book that they have bought and then lend it to their classmates.

Some publishers make the first chapter of a graded reader freely available on the web.

It is also possible to do fund raising activities in order to raise money for graded readers. Teachers should ask the school principal, the city education board, or the state board which often have grants for these types of projects. Sometimes generous companies will donate money or resources. This is likely to be more successful if teachers co-operate in the fund raising and in the subsequent use of the graded readers. The money spent on subscribing to the electronic reading scheme, Xreading, is typically much less than buying hard copy books.

## How much time should learners spend on extensive reading in a general language course?

Ideally, about one-quarter of the total course time (including class time and homework time) should be spent on extensive reading and listening. This includes extensive reading for fluency development and speed reading courses for fluency development.

Half of the time for meaning-focused input should be spent on extensive reading, and one-quarter of the fluency development strand should be spent on speed reading and reading very easy graded readers (extensive reading for fluency development). The means that around one-eighth (meaning-focused input) plus one-sixteenth (fluency development) of the total course time, three-sixteenths of the total course time should be spent on extensive reading. In a course involving around four hours a week (including homework), extensive reading would take up three quarters of an hour.

While the time spent on extensive reading may initially be class time, over a period of time, extensive reading can become more of an out-of-class activity.

## Should an extensive reading programme include a speed reading course?

It is very useful if an extensive reading programme is accompanied by a speed reading course (see Chapter 15 of this book). The purpose of this is to increase the learners' reading speed so that they can read more fluently and thus read more within the same time. A speed reading course involves passages followed by comprehension questions, and free speed reading courses at various levels can be found on Paul Nation's resources pages. They can also be found in the free app *ESL Speed Reading* and in Xreading. The books in the *Reading for Speed and Fluency* series (Nation & Malarcher, 2007) are published speed reading courses at the 500, 1,000, 1,500, and 2,000 word levels. Speed reading courses should only involve vocabulary that the learners already know because their aim is fluency development.

In a speed reading course, the learners read an easy text, note the time it took to read it, answer some comprehension questions, mark them, and then record their reading speed and comprehension score on a reading speed graph and a comprehension graph. They read around 20 passages in this way over several weeks. The speed goal of a speed reading course is around 250 words per minute. Most learners will achieve speeds greater than this, but the upper limit of normal reading, where the majority of words are attended to, is around 300 words per minute (Nation, 2005).

## How many books should learners read?

Research by Nation and Wang (1999) on the Oxford Bookworms Series suggested that learners should be reading one graded reader a week in order to get enough repetitions of the new words at a level in order to be sure that vocabulary learning occurs. So, when we say that learners should do large quantities of extensive reading, we mean that they should be reading at least one book a week. Books differ in their length and in the Nation and Wang study, the books at the easiest level were around 5,000 words long. If the learners are reading really short books, then at the beginning level they should be reading around 5,000 words a week. A list of the length of thousands of graded readers is available on the Extensive Reading Foundation web site.

This sounds like a lot of reading and it is, but it must be remembered that such reading only involves a small number of unknown words (around two to three unknown words per 100 running words of text) and thus can be read quite quickly. If learners read at the very slow speed of 100 words per minute, it would take 50 minutes to read 5,000 words. At a more normal reading speed, it would take less than half this time.

Extensive reading requires large amounts of interesting input at the right level for the reader. What is the right level will change depending on whether the reading is at the level of meaning-focused input, where around 2% of the running words are unfamiliar, or at the level of fluency development, where there should be no unfamiliar words.

## *How can I check that extensive reading is working well?*

There are two aspects of extensive reading to look at. Firstly, the learners should be doing large quantities of reading, at least one graded reader a week. A good extensive reading programme includes a monitoring system that keeps a record of how much each learner reads. Secondly, most pieces of extensive reading should be done without a lot of dictionary look-up, at a reasonable speed, and with enjoyment. Quietly observing learners while they read can reveal a lot. Through observing a learner and timing how often they turn the page, it is possible to roughly calculate their reading speed. In a well-run extensive reading programme, the teacher should talk to each learner about how much they are enjoying the reading and the obstacles they face. Learners may find it difficult to do extensive reading at home because of the demands of other activities and various distractions. It is worth asking learners about this, and if necessary, providing time for extensive reading at school.

## *What are the variants of extensive reading?*

Reading can occur in various forms and the growth of the internet has transformed what people read, and how much they read. The Xreading programme has made the reading of electronic graded readers a very attractive reality. This is important because even though learners may read web pages, electronic messages, and social network pages, there is no substitute for the sustained reading of graded readers, because the vocabulary control of the books ensures that they will be at the right level for the learners, and the number of books at each level and the length of the books ensure that learners can get the large amounts of input needed for incidental learning to have an effect. Learners need to read several thousand running words per week and the other kinds of reading are unlikely to reach this amount of input. Nonetheless, other kinds of reading are useful, as long as they are adding to the extensive reading programme and not taking time away from it.

### How can extensive reading be done at all levels of proficiency?

Extensive reading can be done from the first few weeks of learning up to the highest proficiency levels. Graded readers begin at the 75 word level and go up to the 8,000 word level. This means that a learner who knows only 75 words of English can read the easiest graded readers without encountering large vocabulary difficulties. Because extensive reading is an independent individual activity, different learners in the same class can be reading at different levels.

### How can extensive reading be done in large classes?

Extensive reading is ideally suited to large classes because it is a quiet independent activity where each learner reads at their own most suitable level and speed. If the reading is done electronically using a programme such as Xreading, there is little work for the teacher to do.

### Are there digital applications of extensive reading?

Teachers should visit the Xreading web site and look at how extensive reading can be carried out and monitored digitally. This is clearly the way that extensive reading should go because it solves most of the problems that teachers face in setting up extensive reading programmes. Digital reading also allows easy word look-up.

### Revisiting and linking to other activities

Revisiting previously read material is an important part of an extensive reading programme. While this can improve reading comprehension and help in the learning of vocabulary, its main effect is to increase reading fluency. Fluency development requires that use of very easy material, some pressure to go faster, a focus on the message, and quantity of practice. Learners need to be aware of the need to increase reading fluency and this awareness is easily fostered with a targeted speed reading course, because in such a course the learners note their reading speed and comprehension levels on a graph and are encouraged to make their speed graph go up by trying to read faster. Learners should be aware that in addition to a speed reading course, doing very easy extensive reading is an important way of supporting fluency development and their goal when doing easy extensive reading is to do it quickly. Part of the easy extensive reading for fluency development should be new books that are way below their current level, and part should involve re-reading books that they have already read and enjoyed.

Extensive reading can be linked to related activities to provide opportunities for repetition of language features. These related activities can include writing book reviews, oral book reviews, group discussion of a book that all have read, and the deliberate learning of unfamiliar vocabulary and multiword units found during extensive reading. Many graded readers have recorded versions, and listening-while-reading or listening before or after reading can provide support for reading or listening, as well as valuable repetition.

### What does research say about the effectiveness of extensive reading?

There is a very large amount of research on extensive reading, and there have been meta-analyses (Krashen, 2007; Nakanishi, 2015; Swanborn & de Glopper, 1999) and a book (Nation & Waring, 2020) which attempt to provide summaries and analysis of this research. The research varies in quality and one way that Nation and Waring (2020) dealt with this was to include a chapter on eight of the exemplary pieces of research that anyone advocating extensive reading should go to first. The research shows that extensive reading can increase motivation to do more reading, improve reading comprehension, increase reading fluency, increase vocabulary size, strengthen and enrich knowledge of words and multiword units, increase overall language proficiency, and have small but positive effects on writing.

There have not been enough detailed studies of the effect of extensive reading on grammar knowledge, although some studies included a grammar measure as part of a range of proficiency measures.

The classic study of learning from extensive reading is the book flood study by Elley and Mangubhai (1981). In this study, young learners of English as a foreign language spent three-quarters of their class time reading interesting books. The learners only studied English for a total of less than four hours a week, and for the experimental group around three of these four hours were spent on reading. Elley and Mangubhai measured the results of the programme using a wide range of tests which looked at reading comprehension, writing skill, grammatical knowledge, oral sentence recognition, and listening comprehension. Compared to a group of learners who followed the traditional class English programme of largely teacher-fronted oral work, the learners in the book flood programme made the equivalent of 15 months progress in nine months, and a year later still maintained these gains. The Elley and Mangubhai study focused on measuring language and skill gains. It did not include a measure of vocabulary growth. However, it was very clear from the study that if learners had reasonably large quantities of interesting language input, a very wide range of learning occurred. Since then, there have been other book flood studies with similar results (Elley, 1991), and there have been studies focusing on vocabulary growth from graded readers and extensive reading (Horst, 2005; Pigada & Schmitt, 2006; Waring & Takaki, 2003). These studies have shown that vocabulary learning of different strengths occurs incidentally during the reading of texts which are at the right level for the learners. These studies also suggest that large quantities reading are needed in order for this vocabulary knowledge to strengthen and expand.

A study by Beglar, Hunt, and Kite (2012) of an extensive reading programme carried out over a period of a year looked at the development of reading fluency. The learners who made the biggest gains in reading fluency were not the learners who read the most, but were the learners who read the most text written within a controlled vocabulary. The learners who read a lot of difficult unsimplified text did not make the same fluency gains.

It is clear from the research that teachers can expect more than just improvement in reading from an extensive reading programme. They can expect that learners will grow in their knowledge of the language, will develop good reading skills, will come to enjoy reading, and will also show an improvement in other skills besides reading.

The studies of the effectiveness of extensive reading are necessarily looking at the effects of incidental learning and as a result the findings of short-term studies show small amounts of learning. Learning requires a focus on what is to be learned, quantity of attention and quality of attention. Extensive reading requires large amounts of reading to be most effective because the focus on what is to be learned is incidental rather than deliberate, and quantity of input increases the repetition of vocabulary and multiword units. One of the strengths of learning through extensive reading is that the quality of the meetings with language features is quite high because of the varied contexts in which these features occur. Although the gains from the short-term studies are small, they are consistent, and when measured through tests of varying strengths show a range of strengths of learning for many items (Waring & Takaki, 2003).

There is plenty of evidence to suggest that the single most effective improvement that a teacher could make to a language course would be to include a substantial extensive reading programme. The availability of the web-based extensive reading programme called Xreading has made the introduction of such a programme much easier.

## Research questions

### Motivation principles (Engagement)

For learning to occur there needs to be a willingness to focus on what needs to be learned, and to give it quantity and quality of attention.

1 *Motivation: The degree of engagement with the task affects the likelihood of learning occurring.* How can we increase learners' motivation to do extensive reading? Interventions could include peer discussion of book reports, making word cards while reading, and reflection on reading. How can teachers be encouraged to set up extensive reading programmes?
2 *Self-efficacy: Our confidence in our own skills of learning affects our success in learning.* Is the quantity of successful reading directly related to the willingness to keep reading?

### Focus principles (Usefulness)

Learning requires giving attention to what needs to be learned.

3 *Focus: We learn what we focus on, and in addition, our learning is more useful if it closely resembles the use that we need to make of what we learn (transfer-appropriate).* Can extensive reading begin directly from vocabulary learning? How quickly is deliberately learned vocabulary integrated into normal reading? This question could be answered using multiple-measures of vocabulary knowledge and eye-tracking.
4 *Accuracy: Our learning is more efficient if the information we are focusing on is complete, accurate, and comprehensible.* At what level can learners move comfortably from graded readers to unsimplified texts?

### Quantity principles (Amount)

5 *Repetition: The more repetitions, the stronger the learning.* Does the repetition of grammatical features affect the learning of grammar through extensive reading?
6 *Time-on-task: The greater and longer the attention, the stronger the learning.* Does the time spent on a word (eye-tracking) reflect the strength of knowledge of the word? What kinds of deliberate learning and how much deliberate learning occurs during extensive reading? Use eye-tracking, and dictionary look-up tracking. What factors affect look-up?

### Quality principles (Connections)

Elaboration and analysis increase and strengthen connections between the item to be learned and other knowledge making it easier to access the item.

7 *Elaboration: This includes enriching the encoding of an item through variation.* Does the variety of types of text read affect improvement in the reading skill?
8 *Analysis: This involves relating the familiar parts to the unfamiliar whole.* Does pre-teaching word parts affect skill at dealing with derived forms in extensive reading?

There is a very large amount of research on extensive reading showing its value for language learning. The most needed research on extensive reading is on how to convince teachers and learners to do it.

# 14
# INTENSIVE READING

### What is intensive reading?

Intensive reading involves reading a short text very carefully giving deliberate attention to a variety of language features and reading strategies. It is usually done as a teacher-led activity but can be done as individual work with the help of a dictionary, usually a bilingual dictionary. It is a very old technique and versions of grammar translation involve intensive reading using the first language as the means of dealing with the language features in the text.

Intensive reading fits into the language-focused learning strand of a course because although one of the goals may be comprehension of the text, this is done with considerable deliberate attention to language features. It is a guided activity because assistance is provided in understanding the text, its vocabulary, its grammatical features, and organization.

The two main issues with intensive reading are that it can occupy too much time in a language course, and that it tends to give too great a focus on comprehending the text rather than remembering useful language features (Nation, 1979). We will look at each of these two issues again in this chapter.

In this chapter, we look at intensive reading as a teaching technique, where the teacher largely decides what aspects of the text will be focused on and interacts with the learners on these aspects. An alternative kind of intensive reading is that provided in many course books where a text is accompanied by several related exercises, but that is not the focus of this chapter.

DOI: 10.4324/9781003496151-18

## What are the learning goals of intensive reading?

There are two major ways of going about intensive reading. One way sees the goal of intensive reading as involving comprehension of the text, and comprehension is usually achieved by translating the text and dwelling on its difficult features that are barriers to comprehension. The other way sees intensive reading as an opportunity for focusing on language features that are likely to occur in other texts. That is, the goal of intensive reading is not so much to understand today's text but to make the reading of tomorrow's text easier (Nation, 1979). In this book, the main focus is this second goal – focusing on the most useful generalizable features of the language so that the learners find it easier when they do tomorrow's reading task. Intensive reading is ideally suited to strategy development because strategy development requires coming back to the same strategy many times, and practising it on new material. A benefit of a focus on strategies is that such a focus has two useful outcomes – the learning of a useful strategy and the learning of the particular items that are focused on using the strategy. So, if the guessing from context strategy is practised during a session of intensive reading focusing on the word *manipulate*, then the learners get practise in the guessing from context strategy, and they also get a chance to begin learning the word *manipulate*.

As Table 14.1 shows, the major learning goals of intensive reading are the development of language knowledge and the development of reading strategies.

The skills goal of reading difficult text is a kind of strategy goal. The way that the teacher models coping with the difficulties in the text can be an example of how learners could approach the difficult texts they may need to deal with.

The text or discourse goal involves giving deliberate attention to the kind of information in the text, the way the information in the text is organized, the language features associated with a particular kind of text, and not so obvious messages in the text, such as the stance, assumptions, and attitudes of the writer, the degree of formality, and the writer's goals.

**TABLE 14.1** The goals of intensive reading

| Goals | Specific focuses |
|---|---|
| Language | *Learning new vocabulary, multiword units, and grammatical features* |
|  | *Learning and practising reading strategies* |
| Ideas | Gaining information from reading |
| Skills | Reading difficult text |
| Text | Gaining familiarity with text types and text organization |

*Note*: *Italics* indicates the major goal.

## How does intensive reading help learning?

Intensive reading focuses on deliberate learning. In essence, intensive reading helps language learning through quality of deliberate attention on language features. In addition, focusing on strategies provides an opportunity for learners to take control of their own learning and thus extend this deliberate learning beyond teacher-guided intensive reading.

*Motivation:* From the learners' perspective, the apparent goal of intensive reading is to make the reading text comprehensible, and this can act as a motivation. The teacher's goal, however, is to make tomorrow's text easier, that is, to teach useful language features and strategies that will increase learner proficiency. It is useful if the learners are also aware of this wider goal, as this can also increase motivation. Because the teacher supports the learners in intensive reading, learners should experience success in the activity.

*Focus:* The focus of attention in intensive reading is on language items and strategies. The information given is likely to be accurate and comprehensible. When the intensive reading instruction is done in the first language, this will increase comprehensibility. The focus is on deliberate knowledge and for some language features, especially some grammatical features, deliberate knowledge may not readily transfer to language use. It may, however, be useful for self-monitoring.

*Quantity:* The teacher should focus on a rather small number of features and strategies so that plenty of attention can be directed to these. Deliberately focusing on language features can result in quantity of attention being given to a language feature and this helps learning. Often however, this quantity of attention does not involve spaced repetition, which may mean that what is learned may be eventually forgotten. However, by coming back to the same strategies, repetition can be used to help learning. For example, with regard to vocabulary, doing word part analysis on unfamiliar words helps the learning of a relatively small number of useful word parts and provides practice in word analysis (cutting words into parts) and relating the parts to the whole. Similarly, seeing a word as part of a word family, and looking at several examples of its use in a sentence help learning. Intensive reading provides a very useful opportunity for focused deliberate learning, and this makes it a valuable part of a language course. It can also be an opportunity for learners to get answers to questions about aspects of the language that puzzle them.

*Quality:* Intensive reading involves giving deliberate attention to language features and strategies. This deliberate attention can involve gaining knowledge about some of the phonological, orthographic, morphological, lexical, and grammatical systems that lie behind language use. This elaboration of knowledge about a language feature adds to the quality of attention making it more memorable. The two criteria that can be used to help decide what features to focus on are regularity of the rule or pattern-getting attention, and frequency, either of the pattern or rule, or the frequency of a particular item, such as a high-frequency word or multiword expression.

## What are the requirements of intensive reading?

Intensive reading is often contrasted with extensive reading. Extensive reading involves reading long texts which are at the right level for the reader so that the reader can read independently and still pick up some unfamiliar language features incidentally. Extensive reading texts should contain 2% or fewer unknown words. Intensive reading involves texts a few hundred words long where there are many unknown words and unfamiliar grammatical features, and so the reader will need some form of assistance in reading the text and will need to puzzle over parts of the text. While texts for extensive reading are usually vocabulary-controlled texts, intensive reading texts are often texts written for native speakers, although in course books these texts may be adapted in several ways. In course books, intensive reading texts are accompanied by a variety of exercises including comprehension questions.

### How can you prepare for intensive reading?

A teacher needs to have a short list of useful language learning strategies that are focused on in intensive reading and needs to keep coming back to the same strategies. A useful list would include vocabulary learning strategies, such as guessing from context, word part analysis, and looking for core meanings. Grammar-based strategies would include recognizing finite verbs and knowing the rules that apply to them such as the number of conjunctions needed (one less than the number of finite verbs), and the need for finite verbs to agree with their subjects and with each other. Other grammar-based strategies involve recognizing reference words and knowing that they must agree, and knowing the rules relating to countable and uncountable nouns.

Before using an intensive reading text, the teacher should quickly mark it up to highlight the points that will be focused on. It is worth doing this for a few minutes before the class so that any points of difficulty can be checked and some avoided if discussion of them will upset previous learning.

### What texts can be used for intensive reading?

A variety of short texts can be used for intensive reading. If a learner is working alone, then reading texts of the same genre or on the same topic can reduce the difficulty of the texts. For example, reading several recipes gives plenty of opportunity to meet the same words and constructions again. Reading some children's books can also reduce the learning load, and reading the same short book several times gradually turns intensive reading into fluency development.

When the teacher works with a class, intensive reading texts can come from current events, such as newspaper reports, transcriptions of TV reports, or from the kinds of texts that learners will later have to deal with.

Course books tend to use a variety of interesting topics to work with, including dialogues. Because the goal of intensive reading is language-focused learning, the topics of the texts used for intensive reading are not of great concern, the main requirement being a text with useful language features to focus on. Nonetheless, if the topic of an intensive reading text is one that engages learners, then this helps with motivation.

### How much time should be given to intensive reading in a general language course?

Intensive reading is part of the language-focused learning strand. This strand should take up around a quarter of the course time. Intensive reading shares the time in the language-focused learning strand with activities such as getting feedback on writing, using word cards for vocabulary learning, pronunciation practice, spelling, memorizing dialogues, studying grammar, and developing language learning and use strategies. At the most, intensive reading should take up about one-quarter of the time in this strand, meaning that it should not occupy more than about one-sixteenth of the total time in a language course. As we saw in Chapter 13 on extensive reading, much more time should be given to extensive reading.

### What are the focuses of intensive reading?

Intensive reading can have a wide range of language focuses and a teacher needs to decide which ones need to get the most attention for any particular group of learners. For learners going on to university study, for example, a focus on strategies (see column 3 of Table 14.2) may be a wise choice, particularly on notetaking, the word part strategy, and topic types. Younger learners may respond well to a focus on comprehension with attention to sound-spelling correspondences and high-frequency vocabulary. Advanced learners may see value in looking at the genre and organization of text with a view to improving their writing skill. Chapter 3 of Nation and Macalister (2021) looks in detail at intensive reading.

Because of the usefulness of intensive reading for strategy training, the right-hand column in Table 14.2 suggests strategies that could be focused on. The following discussion focuses on points in Table 14.2.

Predicting involves looking at the title of the text and the first sentence and then predicting what the text is likely to cover. Nation (1993) looks at the range of clues which may be available as a basis for prediction. These include the indefinite noun groups in the topic and first sentence, the conjunction relationship

TABLE 14.2 Useful focuses in intensive reading

| Focus | Items | Strategies |
|---|---|---|
| Comprehension | Question types | Predicting |
|  | Question forms | Standardized reading procedures |
|  |  | Notetaking |
| Sound-spelling | Regular sound-spelling correspondences | Spelling rules |
|  |  | Free and checked vowels |
| Vocabulary | High-frequency vocabulary | Guessing from context |
|  | Underlying meaning of words | Using word cards |
|  | Word parts | Word part strategy |
|  | Multiword units | Dictionary use |
| Grammar and cohesion | High-frequency grammatical features | Dealing with sources of difficulty (clause insertion, what does what?, coordination, cohesion) |
| Information content | Topic-type constituents | Topic type |
| Genre | Features that typify this type of text | Generalise to writing – reading like a writer |

between the first sentence and the following sentence, and topic type and genre which may be indicated by the topic.

There are several standardized reading procedures that can be practised as a way of giving first-language learners a framework to follow when they read a non-fiction text. The procedures are often best practised in a teacher-led group or in pairs, so that there is opportunity for discussion of the steps and their application. These procedures include reciprocal teaching (Palincsar & Brown, 1986), and concept-oriented reading instruction (CORI) (Guthrie, 2003). They involve going through a series of steps, each of which focuses on a different aspect of comprehending a text. These can include stimulating prior knowledge, predicting, dealing with unknown vocabulary, mapping the main points in the text, clarifying parts of the text, and summarizing. The value of such a procedure is that all the useful sources of information are covered.

Notetaking from a text is usefully related to notetaking from lectures. The essence of notetaking is to process the text in a thoughtful way. That is, notetaking involves more than simply noting the main points of a text, but involves placing some kind of organization or structure on the notes that reflects the nature of the text the value of the ideas to the notetaker. This structure could involve headings of various levels, an information transfer table (see Chapter 17 on information transfer), or a concept diagram as used in semantic mapping. Researchers on notetaking point out that it is the making of the notes (encoding) that is the important effect of notetaking rather than the resulting storage of information. If the notes were thrown away immediately after notetaking, it would not matter too much because the important aspect of thoughtful encoding had already been done.

The strategy aspect of the sound-spelling focus in intensive reading involves learning the regular spelling patterns and a few spelling rules. The checked-free vowel rule in English is a very useful rule that helps with the doubling of consonants, final silent *e*, and the spelling of some difficult words like *occurrence*.

The various vocabulary strategies of guessing from context, learning from word cards (see Chapter 23), word parts, and dictionary use are dealt with in detail in Nation (2021). Each strategy deserves small amounts of repeated practice over several months to ensure that the strategies are well understood, well practised, and used effectively.

Grammar strategies related to reading largely involve being able to break complicated sentences into parts so that the main sentence pattern stands out more clearly. Difficulties can occur with relative clauses coming after the subject, coordinated clauses, and multi-clause sentences.

Topic types are looked at in Chapter 17 on information transfer. Nation and Macalister (2021, Chapter 10) also look at topic types in detail. Knowing a small number of relevant topic types helps in predicting what will occur in a text, in taking notes, and in preparing for writing.

Some types of writing follow a pattern. Reports of experiments follow a very well-defined pattern of Summary, Background, Review of research, Research questions, Procedure, Results, Discussion, References. Newspaper reports tend to put the most important information first, often in a non-chronological order. They also tend to alternate reporting with quotation. Stories and narratives tend to follow chronological order.

So far, we have looked at the strategies column in Table 14.2. Let us now look at the items column, which is column two.

Comprehension questions are often used in intensive reading, but as we have noted above, comprehending today's text does not necessarily make it easier to comprehend tomorrow's text, particularly if it is on a different topic. The focus should be on generalizable features of the text. The comprehension questions themselves can be a useful focus in intensive reading, namely the grammatical form of the questions, and the type of information that each question seeks (information directly stated in the text, inferences from the information in the text, and moving beyond the text into application or evaluation).

Some words are difficult to pronounce, perhaps because they do not follow spelling rules, or because the learners' first language affects their pronunciation. These words can be noted on the whiteboard during intensive reading, and near the end of the lesson the learners can be given a chance to pronounce them again individually and get feedback from the teacher on their pronunciation.

Vocabulary can be a focus in intensive reading. Unfortunately, the most salient words tend to be low-frequency topic-related words that are unlikely to occur in other texts. They, thus, do not deserve much teaching time. The time is better spent on high-frequency words that are highly likely to occur in other texts. Nation (2004) outlines principles and procedures for dealing with vocabulary in intensive reading. It is helpful to break complex words into known parts as a mnemonic device for helping such words stick in memory. It is also helpful to look at the core or underlying meaning of high-frequency words to show learners the width of their application in use. For example, the word *manipulate* can refer to physical movement as in using a tool or piece of equipment. It can also refer to medical treatment as in physiotherapy, and it can also refer to psychological manipulation and control. These different uses all share a common underlying meaning of controlling the movement of someone or something. Being aware of the idea that words with the same form are highly likely to have a common underlying meaning is an important part of vocabulary learning.

A multiword unit is a sequence of two or more words that tend to occur together. There are many terms for multiword units, including collocations, formulaic sequences, and lexical bundles. Most multiword units are compositional, that is, the meanings of the parts contribute greatly to the meaning of the whole multiword unit. There are less than 100 true idioms in English where the meanings of the parts seem unrelated to the meaning of the whole, for example, *cats and dogs* as in *raining cats and dogs* (Grant & Nation, 2006). There are several multiword units where the parts of the unit contribute to the meaning of the whole, but the whole unit has some additional meaning that is not obvious from the parts. Martinez and Schmitt (2012) provide a well-researched list of the most useful of these. They include *last night, in addition, you see, for instance*. During intensive reading, it is worth looking at the compositionality of multiword units and their meaning. Some multiword units are well worth memorizing.

Sometimes the term *idiom* is used to refer to figurative uses of expressions, such as *give them the green light, toe the line, the ball is in your court*. Strictly speaking these are not idioms, because the meaning of the whole is related to the meaning of the parts. They seem like idioms because they have a literal meaning and a closely related figurative meaning. These figurative uses are best dealt with in intensive reading by looking at the literal meaning and its origin, and then seeing how the figurative meaning relates to this. For example, *the ball is in your court* comes from the game of tennis and refers to the idea that you must now hit the ball or serve the ball because the ball is in your part of the tennis court. The figurative meaning is of course closely related to this idea and means that you must now do what must be done. A reasonable proportion of figuratives use devices such as alliteration and rhyme to make them memorable (*bouncing bundle of joy, bite the bullet, blue moon*). This should be pointed out to learners.

There are many possible focuses in intensive reading and each text will bring its own interesting and notable features. The teacher needs to be aware of the range of possibilities and needs to keep in mind the principle of looking for features that will recur in other texts.

**How can intensive reading be done well?**

The maximum benefits can be gained from intensive reading if:

1 the intensive reading text contains useful unfamiliar language features to focus on,
2 there is a focus on useful generalizable language features and on language learning strategies, rather than on comprehension of the text,
3 the same intensive reading text is returned to several times to get verbatim and varied repetition of the language features it contains,
4 the same language strategies and language features are revisited in several intensive reading texts, and
5 the features focused on in intensive reading are also met for incidental learning in the meaning-focused parts of the course.

There are many ways of doing intensive reading, and the teacher needs to develop a procedure that covers what needs to be covered and becomes a familiar procedure to the learners so that they know what to do.

1 Choose a useful text for intensive reading that is long enough to have a sufficient number of useful language features to focus on, as well as opportunities to practise a reading or language learning strategy.
2 Before the class, mark up your copy of the text, indicating the points you want to focus on, and how you will focus on them. The points noted may include five or six useful words (some of which can be broken into parts), one or two multiword units, a word to guess from context applying the steps of the guessing from context strategy, four or five reference words such as *it*, *they*, *he*, *this* for learners to find what they refer to in the text, and a long sentence to break into parts to make its meaning clear. If the text has a clear topic-type structure, this may also be a focus.
3 Provide learners with a copy of the text and let them look quickly through the text.
4 Go through the text with the learners setting them a task to do from your list of points and discuss and deal with that point before setting them the next point to focus on. As words and phrases come up note them on the whiteboard to return to later.
5 At the end of the session, go around the class getting learners to pronounce any word or phrase they wish from the list on the whiteboard. Provide praise and feedback. Get learners to break the words on the whiteboard into parts.

Give the learners a minute to look at the words, then rub them off the whiteboard and get the learners to note them from memory on a piece of paper, trying to put them in the same arrangement as they were on the whiteboard.

*How can I check that an intensive reading activity is working well?*

Intensive reading involves deliberate learning, and its goal is to make reading tomorrow's passage easier. The teacher thus needs to look at how learners are progressing in their understanding and use of strategies, and how well they deal with the difficulties they meet in the text. Eventually, learners need to be able to do intensive reading well without the teacher's guidance, so the teacher should be looking for signs of this emerging independence. If the learners do activities like guessing from context, what does what?, sentence analysis, and dictionary look-up successfully, then the teacher can feel happy about their progress.

**What are the variants of intensive reading?**

Intensive reading can be done as an individual activity with the help of a dictionary and occasional access to a teacher or tutor, as a pair activity with learners puzzling out difficulties together, or as a teacher-led class activity. Learners working independently sometimes work their way through a whole book. Nation (2018) looks at the values and difficulties in doing this, concluding that if learners choose the book wisely with a view to their future use of the language and with an awareness that around half of the different words in the book will occur only once, then this can be a useful activity. Otherwise, it is a formidable reading task because there could be around 1,000 unknown words, most of which are likely to occur only once in the book.

Some language courses that focus on gaining a reading knowledge of the language involve the intensive reading of a whole book, usually not too long, with the commentary on the language features and content being carried out in the first language. These courses were common in university study. This practice has had the effect of being a motivator for more communicative approaches to language teaching, because such language courses involved little if any communicative use of the language.

Many of the activities related to a reading text in a course book are intensive reading activities. These include comprehension questions, grammar-based activities such as fill the blanks, complete the sentence, or join the parts of the sentence, or vocabulary-focused activities such as matching words and meanings, or finding words in the text with a particular meaning. Paribakht and Wesche (1996) developed a taxonomy of such exercises. These ready-made activities are probably not very effective for language learning (Webb, Yanigasawa & Uchihara, 2020), and vary greatly in their effectiveness.

Intensive reading can be done with the teacher using the first language to comment on features in the foreign language text. Using the first language will help the explanation be understood and is likely to be much more efficient than having the teacher and learners both using the foreign language to understand the foreign language. Certainly, using the first language to explain word meanings is more effective than using the foreign language. Similarly, using the first language to understand a strategy is also likely to be efficient and effective. The objection to using the first language in intensive reading is that it takes away an opportunity for foreign language use. If there is plenty of foreign language use in other parts of the course, then it makes sense to use the first language in intensive reading.

### *How can intensive reading be used at all levels of proficiency?*

When we look at the wide range of possible focuses (Table 14.2), we can see that intensive reading can be used at all levels of proficiency. For learners beginning to read the foreign language, intensive reading can focus on word recognition and basic phonics. It can also involve a small amount of vocabulary development. At the other end of the scale, for advanced learners studying in a specialist subject area, intensive reading can involve analysing grammatical difficulties in complicated text, focusing on specialist vocabulary and how to learn it, dealing with condensed text, and critiquing the organization and signalling in the text. The use of the first language makes intensive reading possible at even the most elementary levels.

### Are there digital applications of this technique?

Tom Cobb's web site *The Compleat Lexical Tutor* (Hypertext) provides several tools that support learning from short texts. These include analysis of the vocabulary in the text into word frequency levels, the use of a concordancer, text-to-voice, a dictionary, and vocabulary consolidation activities. It is worth doing further work on an intensive reading app, where a text provided by the learner or teacher can be uploaded, and then a variety of focuses can be worked through to assist learning from the text.

### Revisiting and linking to other activities

Texts which are used for intensive reading can be revisited several times over several months with them eventually becoming texts for fluency development. Revisiting the text can involve simply reading the text again (a kind of verbatim repetition) or using the intensive reading text as the beginning of a series of related tasks (varied repetition). For example, after the learners have worked on the intensive reading text, in the following week, part of it can be used for dictation. A later revisiting could involve listening to the text and answering a couple of comprehension questions. A later revisiting could involve using the text as a starting point for piece of related writing. Chapter 21 on linked skills activities includes several activities that use a short written text as a starting point.

## What does research say about the effectiveness of intensive reading?

Several studies focusing on extensive reading have compared extensive reading and intensive reading (Al-Homoud & Schmitt, 2009; Bell, 2001; Huffman, 2014; McLean & Rouault, 2017; Robb & Susser, 1989; Suk, 2017). Generally, comprehension scores for both treatments on an independent text are similar (Al-Homoud & Schmitt, 2009; Lai, 1993), but sometimes this was because of a ceiling effect where learners in both treatments got very high scores (Huffman, 2014; Suk, 2017). Bell (2001) using cloze, true/false, and multiple-choice measures found that his extensive reading group made greater gains in comprehension than his intensive reading group on all measures. The gains were substantial and were not limited by ceiling effects. De Morgado (2009) found a small but significant comprehension improvement for the extensive reading group but none for the intensive reading group.

Usually, in studies comparing extensive reading with intensive reading, intensive reading results in vocabulary gains (Al-Homoud & Schmitt, 2009); however, the gains tend to be greater for the extensive reading group because of the large amount of input they receive (Suk, 2017).

In research comparing deliberate learning with incidental learning, deliberate learning typically results in more learning, simply because it involves a greater quantity of attention to particular features (Paribakht & Wesche, 1996; Wesche & Paribakht, 2000). If intensive reading is done well, it can be a very effective part of the course because it allows a deliberate focus on language features which occur in context, and provides opportunity for a repeated focus on the same strategies and language features, with the learners able to get help tailored to their needs.

The intensive reading technique should be seen as an alternative to commercially prepared text-based exercises. Such exercises in course books help learning, but their success rate is not as high as it should be (Webb, Yanigasawa & Uchihara, 2020). It is likely that teacher-led and pair-work intensive reading will engage learners much more, will allow much more opportunity for repetition, and will more directly address the problems that learners face in their reading. This is a very useful focus for future research.

### Research questions

*Motivation principles (Engagement)*

For learning to occur, there needs to be a willingness to focus on what needs to be learned, and to give it quantity and quality of attention.

1 *Motivation: The degree of engagement with the task affects the likelihood of learning occurring.* Do learners see value in intensive reading?
2 *Self-efficacy: Our confidence in our own skills of learning affects our success in learning.* How willing are learners to indicate the points of difficulty they find in an intensive reading text?

*Focus principles (Usefulness)*

Learning requires giving attention to what needs to be learned.

3 *Focus: We learn what we focus on, and in addition, our learning is more useful if it closely resembles the use that we need to make of what we learn (transfer-appropriate).* Is intensive reading cost effective? That is, how much learning occurs from intensive reading and how much time is involved? Which intensive reading activities offer the best return for effort and time? Should intensive reading involve focusing on points decided on by the teacher or should it be learner-led?
4 *Accuracy: Our learning is more efficient if the information we are focusing on is complete, accurate, and comprehensible.* Is intensive reading best done using explanation in the first language?

*Quantity principles (Amount)*

5 *Repetition: The more repetitions, the stronger the learning.* Is returning to a small number of focuses the best way of increasing learning from intensive reading?
6 *Time-on-task: The greater and longer the attention, the stronger the learning.* Is the time spent on particular words in intensive reading related to the amount of knowledge gained about those words?

*Quality principles (Connections)*

Elaboration and analysis increase and strengthen connections between the item to be learned and other knowledge making it easier to access the item.

7 *Elaboration: This includes enriching the encoding of an item through variation.* Do concordances have strong positive effects on learning from intensive

reading? That is, does seeing more contexts greatly assist vocabulary and grammar learning?
8 *Analysis: This involves relating the familiar parts to the unfamiliar whole.* How much word part analysis practice is needed to develop skill in word part analysis while reading?

The most needed research on intensive reading would be on showing the effect of intensive reading on developing language learning strategies.

# 15
# SPEED READING

Speed reading is part of the fluency component of a reading course. It fits into the fluency development strand and easily meets the five fluency criteria of very easy material, a good level of accuracy, pressure to go faster, a focus on meaning, and quantity of practice (see Table 15.1). Speed reading is an individual, largely independent activity. It involves experience tasks because the materials used are vocabulary and grammar controlled to be well within the learners' knowledge. The fluency strand should make up around a quarter of the time in a language course and reading fluency should make up about one-quarter of the fluency strand, the other three-quarters of the fluency strand covering listening, speaking, and writing fluency.

## What is speed reading?

In a speed reading course, learners read passages about a page long, which are on largely familiar topics, and which are written within a vocabulary that they already know. Each reading is timed. As each reader completes the reading, they note the time it took them and then turn over the passage and answer the comprehension questions on the other side. The learners should not look back at the text when they answer the questions. The questions are not too difficult and are also written within a controlled vocabulary. The learners look at the answer sheet to mark their answers to the comprehension questions and look at the time conversion chart to convert their reading time into words per minute. They enter the number of the passage they read, their reading speed, and their comprehension score on a graph.

**TABLE 15.1** How speed reading meets the fluency criteria

| Criteria | Features of speed reading |
|---|---|
| Easy material | The reading texts are written within a strictly controlled vocabulary |
| Good comprehension | The texts are easy and the comprehension questions are not tricky, so learners find it easy to score 7 or more out of 10 |
| Pressure to go faster | Speed in words per minute is recorded on a graph |
| Meaning-focused | Each passage is followed by comprehension questions |
| Quantity of practice | Each speed reading course has 20 passages |

The teacher moves around the class looking at graphs and giving comments and encouragement to the learners. The whole activity takes about seven to ten minutes. The same activity will happen two or three times in the same week and will continue for a total of around seven to ten weeks until all of the 20 texts have been read.

### What are the learning goals of speed reading?

Speed reading is a fluency development activity.

As Table 15.2 shows, the major learning goal of speed reading is to increase reading fluency so that learners are reading at a speed of around 250 wpm. A secondary goal of speed reading is to strengthen knowledge of words and grammatical constructions that are already known or partly known. A speed reading course is likely to affect the size of the unit of language that learners work with as they read, moving from them needing to look at each letter, to being able to work at the level of the word, to being able to work at the level of the phrase.

### How does speed reading help learning?

In essence, speed reading helps develop fluency in reading through quantity of practice with easy materials. It is also likely to have the effect of helping the learning of multiword units.

*Motivation:* Speed reading courses are really good for motivating learners to read, because almost every learner will make substantial progress in a speed reading course. The graph is a really good motivator. Because the material used in speed reading courses is well within the learners' knowledge and the questions are deliberately easy, learners can see progress and feel good about it.

*Focus:* The focus in a speed reading course is on comprehending the text with a good but not necessarily perfect level of comprehension (around seven out of ten) at a reasonable reading speed (around 250 wpm).

**TABLE 15.2** The goals of speed reading

| Goals | Specific focuses |
|---|---|
| Language | Strengthening and enriching partly known vocabulary and grammar |
|  | Pushing learners to work with a larger unit of processing than single words |
| Ideas |  |
| Skills | *Reading with fluency* |
| Text |  |

*Note:* The major goal is in *italics*.

*Quantity:* Each speed reading course involves 20 passages, so the learners get plenty of reading practice. Quantity of practice is the main factor affecting learning from doing a speed reading course. During their years of study of English, learners may do several speed reading courses, each one at a more advanced level, but all involving basically the same procedure.

*Quality:* During a speed reading course, learners read 20 different texts on different topics, meeting familiar vocabulary and grammatical constructions in a wide variety of contexts and enriching knowledge of them.

## What are the requirements of speed reading?

There is a video showing a speed reading course in action on Paul Nation's resources pages. Look under Language Teaching Videos.

### *How do you prepare for speed reading?*

The main preparation for speed reading involves the teacher reading about the nature of speed reading and speed reading courses, and looking at the free speed reading courses developed by Sonia Millett on Paul Nation's resources pages. Each of the speed reading courses on the resources pages has an introduction with guidance for the teachers and learners. This is the first thing to read, because it shows what you have to do to run a speed reading course. Then, it is worth reading a bit of the research on speed reading. The articles by Bismoko and Nation (1974), Chung and Nation (2006), Nation (2005, 2009), and Tran and Nation (2014) are all freely available under Publications on Paul Nation's resources pages. There is no need to read all of these, but they are useful in showing the effects of speed reading. Reading about the nature of speed reading will help guide you in giving advice to your learners during the course.

The same passages are also available in a free app called ESL Speed Readings. It is worth downloading the app and doing at least part of a speed reading course to get an idea of what speed reading training is like.

The next important step is finding out how much vocabulary your learners know, so that you can choose a suitable course for each learner. Use one of the Vocabulary Levels Tests on Paul Nation's resources pages. You need use only two or three of the levels – the 1,000 and 2,000 levels or the 2,000 and 3,000 levels. If you are lucky and all your learners are at a roughly similar level, then you need only choose one speed reading course. It does not matter too much if some of the really proficient learners in your class are doing a really easy speed reading course.

*What texts can be used for speed reading?*

A speed reading course must have easy texts that are well within the learners' vocabulary level. Usually, all the passages in a speed reading course are exactly the same length, and they are written within a controlled vocabulary. On Paul Nation's web resources pages, there are free complete speed reading courses written and prepared by Sonia Millett at the 500 word level, the 1,000 word level, the 2,000 word level, the 2,000 plus Academic Word List level, the 3,000 word level, and the 4,000 word level. These passages are also available through a speed reading app developed by T. J. Boutorwick called *ESL Speed Readings*, and as a part of the online extensive reading programme, *Xreading*. *Reading for Speed and Fluency* by Paul Nation and Casey Malarcher (2007, Compass Publishing) has texts at the 500, 1,000, 1,500, and 2,000 word levels, with passages grouped by themes to lighten the topic content load.

Teachers need to know their learners' vocabulary sizes in order to choose a speed reading course at the right level. The learners' vocabulary sizes should be well beyond the level of the speed reading course. So, a learner who knows 1,000 words should be doing speed reading using a 500 word level course. A learner who knows 2,000 words should be doing a 1,000 word level course.

*How much time should be given to speed reading in a general language course?*

A speed reading course is a very useful component of an extensive reading programme. It provides a strong focus on fluency development. Easy extensive reading should also be part of an extensive reading programme, and should make up about a third of the time in an extensive reading programme. The logic behind the one-third of the recommendation is this: (1) Half of the meaning-focused input strand should be extensive reading. That is, one-eighth of the total course time (one-half of one-quarter). (2) One-quarter of the fluency development strand should focus on reading fluency. That is, one-sixteenth of the total course time (one-quarter of one-quarter).

(3) One-eighth for extensive reading at the meaning-focused input level, and one-sixteenth for reading fluency development is a ratio of 2 to 1. So, in an extensive reading programme, two-thirds of the time should be for extensive reading for meaning-focused input where a small proportion of the words (2%) are unfamiliar, and one-third should be easy extensive reading and a speed reading course for fluency development where none of the words are unfamiliar.

### How can a teacher run a good speed reading course?

A speed reading course takes around ten minutes per session. It should run for around 20 sessions which could be somewhere between seven and ten weeks. It requires no real work from the teacher, and it brings about substantial increases for most learners.

1 The teacher needs to work out what vocabulary level each learner needs to be working at for speed reading. One way to do this is to get the learners to sit two or three levels of one of the Vocabulary Levels Tests. These tests can be found on Paul Nation's resources pages in the section headed Vocabulary tests. The level of the speed reading course should be well within each learner's vocabulary knowledge.
2 All the passages in a speed reading course at a particular level are assumed to be roughly the same level of difficulty and thus the passages can be read in any order. If a teacher has a class of 30 learners, for example, the teacher can print two copies of a 20 passage speed reading course and put each passage and the comprehension questions in a plastic bag, making a total of 40 passages each in their own plastic bag. Each time they do speed reading, each learner chooses a passage that they have not read before. In this way, just two copies of the course can be enough for a whole class.
3 The teacher should explain the fluency goal of a speed reading course and explain how to choose passages, keep a record of what passages have been read, and how to enter their speed and comprehension scores on a graph. If the learners do their speed reading electronically using the ESL Speed Readings app, then the following steps are all done by the programme.
4 When all the learners have a passage to read, the teacher says "Go!" and the learners start reading quietly. When they reach the end of the reading, they note the time taken to read that passage. The easiest way for learners to measure their reading time is to have a large digital timer that they all can see. In the absence of such technology, the teacher can write the following numbers on the whiteboard and erase the minutes as each minute passes and point to the seconds at ten second intervals.

| Minutes | Seconds |
|---------|---------|
| 0 | 00 |
| 1 | 10 |
| 2 | 20 |
| 3 | 30 |
| 4 | 40 |
| 5 | 50 |

5  As each learner finishes reading the short text, they look up at the board, note down the time it took them to read, and then turn over the text and start answering the ten comprehension questions on the back of the sheet without looking back at the text.

6  Speed reading courses come with answer sheets, time conversion tables, and graphs. The teacher needs to make a copy of the graph for each learner, and enough conversion charts and answer sheets (usually about seven or eight for a class of 30 learners).

7  As learners finish their reading and answer the questions, the teacher moves around the class looking at their speed and comprehension scores and giving advice.

### Advice and attention from the teacher

The best comprehension score for speed reading is 7 out of 10, or 70% comprehension. If a learner gets 9 or 10 out of 10, they are reading too slowly and should go faster on the next passage. If they score 6 or 5 or less out of 10, then their comprehension is not good enough. They should not slow down, but they should maintain their speed on the next passages until their comprehension score rises. They could also read the same text again. Teachers should walk around the class as learners are entering their scores on their graphs, looking at the speed and comprehension scores and giving advice and praise.

In most speed courses, there are a few learners who do not make an increase. Their comprehension is usually good, but their speed sits stubbornly at the same level. In one speed reading course, these learners were identified after they had read the first three passages, and the teacher spoke to each of them individually a couple of times, explaining the purpose of the speed reading course and encouraging them to take the risk of reading faster. In that course, all learners made an increase by the end of the course. The individual attention seemed to make a difference.

Learning typically is better if learners understand why they are doing something and know how to take control of their own learning. It is thus worthwhile for the teacher to talk a bit about reading speed, the science behind it, and its value to the learners. This can include talking about eye movements, typical native speaker reading speeds, and the relationship between speed and comprehension. Learners should also understand the fluency goals of a course, the nature of fluency, and how fluency involves making the best use of what is already known. All of these ideas are explained in this chapter.

### How can I check that a speed reading activity is working well?

Speed reading is a fluency development activity, so the best signs of progress can be seen on the learners' speed and comprehension graphs. When looking at the comprehension graphs, it is worth remembering that 7 out of 10 is a good score. A lower score indicates lack of comprehension. A score of 10 out of 10 indicates the learner can probably read faster.

Speed scores of over 300 wpm mean that the reader is skipping some of the text, probably because they bring a lot of background knowledge to the text. The target of speed reading courses is between 250 and 300 wpm.

Looking at the pattern of increase in the speed graph is often interesting, because progress in speed is usually not a steady progression but involves ups and downs.

### What are the variants of speed reading?

Repeated reading is sometimes used as a way of increasing oral reading speed (reading aloud). It is useful for learners beginning to learn to read in English. Repeated reading involves reading the same short text aloud three times, each time trying to go a bit faster and with fewer errors. It is usually done in pairs, ideally with a good reader paired with a poorer reader. If the reader pauses over a word for too long or makes a mistake, their partner can help them. It is not necessary to time each reading, but that can be done occasionally to show progress.

### How can speed reading be done at all levels of proficiency?

There are speed reading courses from the 500 word level up to the 4,000 word level.

### How can speed reading be done in a large class?

Speed reading is easily done in large classes because it can be done electronically using the ESL Speed Readings app or Xreading, or it can be done by using photocopied texts of the speed reading courses from Paul Nation's resources pages. If each speed reading passage is put in a clear plastic bag with the questions on the back, then there is no need for each learner to have a complete set. They can simply choose a passage they haven't read from the level they are working at. At any one time, each learner in the class can be reading a different passage.

### Are there digital applications of this technique?

The app ESL Speed Readings allows learners to choose an appropriate level of course. The learners read and the app records their speed in words per minute and their percentage comprehension score. These are mapped on a graph. The app also allows learners to sit various levels of the Vocabulary Levels Test to help them work out what level of the speed reading texts they should be reading. The speed reading texts were largely developed by Sonia Millett and are also available electronically as a part of Xreading. The texts are also available as pdf files from Paul Nation's web page. They are all carefully vocabulary controlled to fit various word frequency levels, the first 500 word families of English, the first 1,000 word families, the first 2,000, the first 2,000 plus Academic Word List, the first 3,000, and the first 4,000 word families.

Speed reading is well suited to electronic use as the texts appear well even on the small screen of a cellphone, and the recording of reading speed and the marking of comprehension questions is much speedier and more reliable electronically than when learners measure their own reading time and mark their own questions.

### Revisiting and linking to other activities

A speed reading course does not require the learners to re-read speed reading passages except if they did especially badly on a particular passage. Speed reading has the greatest effect if it is also accompanied by plenty of easy extensive reading where learners read very easy graded readers and re-read graded readers that they have already read before.

### What does research say about the effectiveness of speed reading?

One of the most detailed and well supported accounts of the mechanics of reading faster can be found in Rayner et al. (2016). When people read, four types of action are involved – fixations on particular words, jumps (saccades) to the next item to focus on, return sweeps to the next line, and regressions (movements back to an item already looked at). According to Brysbaert (2019), for an adult native speaker of English, the normal silent reading rate in English is 238 wpm for non-fiction and 260 wpm for fiction. A skilled reader

> makes around 85–90 fixations per 100 words. Most words are fixated on, but function words much less often than content words. The longer the word, the

more likely it is to receive a fixation. If the word is very long, it may receive 2 or even 3 fixations.

spends around 200–250 milliseconds on each fixation (about 4 or 5 per second). These vary a lot depending on how difficult a word or sentence is to read.

makes saccadic jumps of around 1.2 words in English (about seven or eight letters. In Finnish, where words are longer, the average jump is 10 letters). This is around the maximum number of letters that can be seen clearly in one fixation. During the jump no items can be focused on. A jump takes about 20 to 35 milliseconds. The basic unit in the jump is the word and languages with quite different writing systems (for example English and Chinese) all tend to have an average of one jump for every 1.2 words.

makes return sweeps from the end of one line to the beginning of the next.

makes around 10 to 15 regressions in every 100 fixations. Regressions occur because the reader made too big a jump (many regressions are only a few letters long), and because there were problems in understanding the text.

skips some short words. The word *the*, for example, may be fixated on around only 50% of the time. This does not mean it is not processed.

There is thus a physiological limit on reading speed where reading involves fixating on most of the words in the text. This is around 320 wpm.

There are many commercial speed reading apps and devices intended for native speakers which propose increasing speed well beyond 250–300 wpm. Some of these involve presenting one word at a time or looking down the centre of a page and so on. Research on eye movements and fixation times does not support these devices. Beyond the speed of 300 wpm, increases in speed will be at the expense of comprehension, simply because it is not possible to see and process all the words in a text. This lack of processing may be made up for by background knowledge, but that is a risky procedure. As Rayner et al. (2016, p. 13) note, "language processing, rather than the ability to control the movements of one's eyes, is the primary driver of reading performance".

"The way to maintain high comprehension and get through text faster is to practice reading and to become a more skilled language user (e.g., through increased vocabulary). This is because language skill is at the heart of reading speed." (Rayner et al., 2016, p. 4).

### *What are good reading speeds?*

In a very thorough and comprehensive review of well over a century of native speaker speed reading studies, Brysbaert (2019) concluded that

the average silent reading rate for adults in English is 238 words per minute (wpm) for non-fiction and 260 wpm for fiction. The difference can be predicted by taking into account the length of the words, with longer words in non-fiction than in fiction.

Brysbaert noted that these reading rates are similar to maximum listening speeds, and so there is no need to propose a special kind of compressed internal speech to account for the internal oral component of silent reading.

The average reading speed for reading aloud is 183 wpm.

These are reasonable goals for foreign and second language learners who are reading material that contains no unknown vocabulary and grammar.

## *What are the advantages and disadvantages of reading faster?*

There are disadvantages of reading faster. The pressure to go faster can be a source of stress. Such pressure can reduce the enjoyment that learners get from reading. It is best to see the skill of reading faster as providing a wider range of choices for a reader. Sometimes it is good to read fast. At other times it is not. Being able to make the choice is an advantage. However, the goal of speed reading courses for non-native speakers is to get them comfortable with reading at a rate comparable to that of native speakers. It does not aim to turn them into super-fast readers.

Research on reading faster has shown that increasing reading speed in one language can result in increases in another known language. This has been tested from the first language to English (Bismoko & Nation, 1974) and from English to the first language (Cramer, 1975; West, 1955). It is likely that the transfer of training here is the transfer of confidence, that is, the confidence that you can read faster and still comprehend.

Reading too slowly at speeds of much less than 100 wpm can have negative effects on comprehension. Anyone who has learned to read another script knows the phenomenon of slowly sounding out the script and then having to go back and read the sentence again more fluently to see what it means.

Here is an example of the results of a classroom study. You can find a similar study in Tran (2012) and Chang and Millett (2013). In a study of a speed reading course (Chung & Nation, 2006), (1) almost all learners increased their reading speed (an average increase of 73 wpm or 52% using a conservative measure), some very substantially, and there was no drop in comprehension as speed increased, (2) most of the increase occurred in the first ten texts but there were still gains to be made by reading at least 20 texts, and (3) most learners made a gradual increase in speed (see Figure 15.1) rather than making sudden jumps or staying on a plateau for a while before making an increase. Thirty-eight (95%) out of 40 students increased their speed; five out of the 38 students more than doubled their speed. Many started with very low speeds.

Tran (2012) and Tran and Nation (2014) found that the reading fluency improvements made during a speed reading course transferred to texts not included

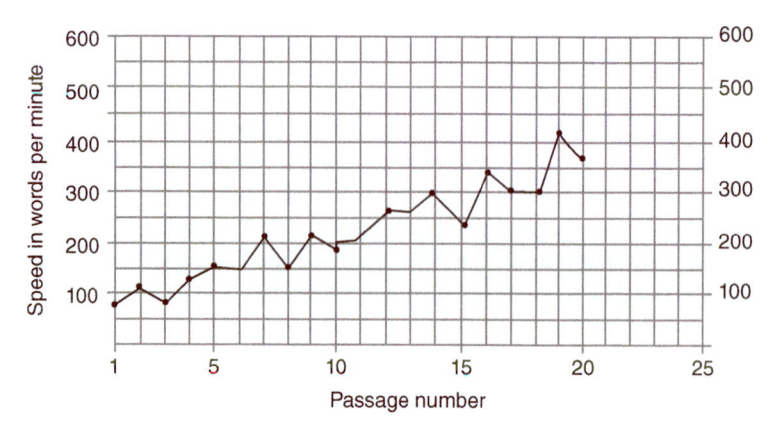

FIGURE 15.1  A learner's graph showing a gradual increase in reading speed.

in the course, and that comprehension still remained at a good level even though speed increased. Tran confirmed Chung and Nation's (2006) finding that different scoring methods all showed an increase in speed. These different scoring methods involved comparing the first text with the last text, comparing the slowest text with the fastest text, and comparing the average of the first three texts with the last three texts. Learners kept increasing their speed in the last ten texts, so it is worth doing all 20 texts in a course.

An increase in reading speed makes it possible for learners to read more in the same time and thus increases the opportunities for learning through meaning-focused input. This is why a well-designed extensive reading programme includes a speed reading component in the form of a speed reading course and about one-third of the time being spent on very easy extensive reading.

## Research questions

### *Motivation principles (Engagement)*

For learning to occur, there needs to be a willingness to focus on what needs to be learned, and to give it quantity and quality of attention.

1 *Motivation: The degree of engagement with the task affects the likelihood of learning occurring.* Are learners motivated enough to complete a self-study speed reading course? How many passages do learners need to read in a speed reading course before they are highly motivated to keep doing the course?
2 *Self-efficacy: Our confidence in our own skills of learning affects our success in learning.* How much of the improvement in a speed reading course is simply based on confidence in being able to read quickly and still have adequate comprehension?

*Focus principles (Usefulness)*

Learning requires giving attention to what needs to be learned.

3. *Focus: We learn what we focus on, and in addition, our learning is more useful if it closely resembles the use that we need to make of what we learn (transfer-appropriate).* What changes as reading speed increases? Is the speed increase explained largely by the reduced time spent on high-frequency words or do the increases occur for all words, even those that are not repeated in the speed reading texts? Why is a speed reading course more effective in increasing fluency of reading than a course reading challenging texts?
4. *Accuracy: Our learning is more efficient if the information we are focusing on is complete, accurate, and comprehensible.* Is there more speed reading improvement in reading very very easy texts than in reading easy texts?

*Quantity principles (Amount)*

5. *Repetition: The more repetitions, the stronger the learning.* Is repeated reading more effective than a speed reading course? Are repeated multiword units treated as single units as reading speed increases?
6. *Time-on-task: The greater and longer the attention, the stronger the learning.* Is there value in doing several speed reading courses at different levels of difficulty during a long language course, or is one course enough?

*Quality principles (Connections)*

Elaboration and analysis increase and strengthen connections between the item to be learned and other knowledge making it easier to access the item.

7. *Elaboration: This includes enriching the encoding of an item through variation.* Is there more fluency improvement in a speed reading course that focuses on a narrow range of topics than in a speed reading course that contains a variety of topics?
8. *Analysis: This involves relating the familiar parts to the unfamiliar whole.* Do individual consultation interventions that deliberately focus on barriers to reading faster help learners read faster?

   The most useful research on speed reading would involve eye-tracking to see what happens to eye movements as proficiency in speed reading increases.

# PART 4
# Writing

# 16
# EXTENSIVE WRITING WITH FEEDBACK

### What is extensive writing?

Extensive writing involves learners doing large quantities of writing to convey information through a variety of fiction and non-fiction genres. It can include writing academic assignments, writing a diary, writing in social media, writing stories, writing formal and friendly letters, note-taking from written and spoken input, filling forms, writing instructions, digital story-telling, blogging, answering examination questions, and collaborative writing. These can involve writing to inform, writing to persuade, writing to maintain social contact, writing to record, and writing to discover.

Writing differs from speaking in that typically when writing, there is time to consider and reconsider how ideas will be expressed. This increases the chances of extensive writing involving deliberate rather than incidental learning.

Extensive writing involves becoming familiar with a relevant range of genres (Hyland, 2004). A genre-based approach to writing has the advantages of providing an opportunity for needs analysis to see what genres are the most useful for the learners in the class, and of providing deliberate analysis and instruction in the structure of texts and the communicative purposes and contexts of this structure. A genre-based approach to writing is based in real-life contexts.

Extensive writing with feedback fits into the meaning-focused output and language-focused learning strands of a course. The feedback is part of the language-focused learning strand, and can provide feedback on spelling, vocabulary, multiword units, grammar, organization, writing conventions, writing strategies, and content. The writing itself is largely meaning-focused output but can also involve language-focused learning when the form of the writing is considered during the writing process.

For each of the four skills of listening, speaking, reading, and writing, there should be an opportunity to gain feedback on the accuracy of the use of the skill. For the receptive skills, this can involve a focus on comprehension difficulties, and for the productive skills, it can involve accurate use of the language.

Feedback on writing provides a very useful opportunity for teachers to provide correction of vocabulary and grammatical errors that is not available when learners speak. Teachers should take this opportunity and use it to improve learners' grammatical accuracy, their control of grammar-based self-checking procedures, and their understanding of the principles of learning. Feedback on writing should also include attention to the organization and content of writing, and to the writing process, but teachers should not feel guilty about using a significant part of the writing course to develop grammatical accuracy. Written feedback on writing is also called written corrective feedback and is known by the acronym WCF.

Although we focus a lot on feedback in this chapter, the main purpose of extensive writing is to develop skill in writing, and so, as in extensive listening and viewing, extensive reading, and informal conversation and problem-solving speaking, the emphasis should be on quantity of language use. In other words, do lots of it.

### What are the learning goals of extensive writing?

Extensive writing with feedback has two major goals. The major goal of extensive writing is developing the skill at getting the message across in a written form and becoming familiar with a relevant range of written genres. The major goal of feedback on extensive writing involves learning the accurate productive written use of language features (Table 16.1).

Writing also involves getting on top of the writing process (see Nation & Macalister, 2021, Chapter 8). This includes how to gather and organize ideas, how to turn ideas into text, how to review and edit what you have written, how to consider your reasons for writing, and how to take account of the reader that you are writing for.

Taking account of the secondary goals of extensive writing will involve the teacher providing some formal instruction for the learners, through feedback, training, and discussion.

**TABLE 16.1** The goals of extensive writing

| Goals | Specific focuses |
|---|---|
| Language | *Making accurate written productive use of vocabulary, multiword units, and grammar* |
|  | Learning topic-related vocabulary, multiword units, and grammar |
| Ideas | Learning how to manage the writing process |
| Skills | Communicating through writing |
| Text | Developing knowledge of formal and informal written genres |

*Note*: The major goals are in *italics*.

## How does feedback on extensive writing help learning?

In essence, extensive writing helps develop the writing skill through quantity of practice. It also helps develop accuracy in language use through deliberate attention to feedback on the writing, which is a quality of attention factor.

*Motivation:* If learners keep graphs of their errors per 100 words, then the improvement shown on the graph can enhance motivation. If teachers also respond to writing in terms of the message conveyed in the writing, this can help learners see writing as a useful skill to develop. Zhang and Hyland (2022) found that using a range of different kinds of feedback increased learners' engagement with the feedback.

*Focus:* Having to write develops the skill of writing. Feedback provides opportunity for a deliberate focus on language errors and a deliberate focus on aspects of the writing process, including setting goals, awareness of the reader, gathering ideas, organizing ideas, and reflecting on what has been written.

*Quantity:* Extensive writing provides large quantities of opportunity to practise writing. If the teacher has an awareness and a plan of the areas of written language use that need improving, then the teacher can give repeated and informed attention to those areas.

*Quality:* Feedback on writing, which is a part of assessment for learning, can help shape goals and learners' understanding of goals, clarify success criteria, develop understanding of the writing process, support on-going learning, train learners in the use of feedback, set further learning goals, and develop self-monitoring (Lee, 2017).

Technology-based feedback will work best if the learners develop skill in evaluating the feedback. That is, they are critical of the feedback they get, and they are aware of the weaknesses of technology-based feedback.

If teachers are not native speakers of English, then providing accurate feedback on grammatical errors can be challenging, particularly where the errors are not rule-based. This argues for a selective focus on rule-based correction where the feedback is likely to be accurate and is closely related to grammatical knowledge. It is not unusual for teachers who are not native speakers to have better explicit knowledge of English grammar than native-speaking teachers.

## What are the requirements of extensive writing?

### How can you support extensive writing?

Extensive writing involves doing large quantities of writing. This writing should be the productive equivalent of extensive reading in that it should involve tasks that are largely within the learners' capabilities, but which provide an opportunity to learn how to write, to learn how to do different kinds of writing, and to learn, enrich, and strengthen control of language features.

Chapter 2 outlined a system of tasks for supporting language learning. The tasks include experience tasks, shared tasks, guided tasks, and independent tasks. The aim of experience, shared and guided tasks is to help learners develop the capability of doing independent tasks. Table 16.2 lists a range of possibilities drawing on these different kinds of tasks. Hyland (2003) uses the term *scaffolding* to include pre-teaching of language features, analysis and manipulation of models, controlled composition (text completion and substitution), and guided composition (information transfer and medium transfer).

Lee (2017, pp. 16–19) suggests the use of feedback forms, which can include detailed descriptions, rating scales, and sections for personalized feedback.

Peer feedback can have several benefits for the learners giving the feedback and those receiving it. The major issue with peer feedback is with the quality of the feedback, and learners' perceptions of the quality of the feedback. To some extent, this issue can be overcome with training in providing feedback (Min, 2005).

**TABLE 16.2** Supporting extensive writing

| Kind of support | Activities |
| --- | --- |
| Before writing | Making the following writing an experience task |
| | Practising parts of the writing process |
| | Learning self-checking procedures for common spelling and grammar points |
| | Doing analysis of texts – reading like a writer |
| | Using responding to reading as a basis for writing |
| | Doing brainstorming and semantic mapping to gather and discuss ideas |
| | Filling in an information transfer table (see Chapter 17) |
| While writing | Guided writing |
| | Writing using frames and outlines |
| | Doing situational composition where the audience, content, and writing goals are clearly specified in the writing topic |
| | Shared writing |
| | Doing pair or group composition |
| | Learning from peer feedback |
| After writing | Experience |
| | Reflecting and commenting on your own writing |
| | Guided |
| | Learning from written feedback |
| | Shared |
| | Conferencing with the teacher |
| | Getting feedback on portfolios (several pieces of writing by the same writer) |
| | Getting peer feedback |

## What texts can be used for extensive writing?

There have been several attempts to identify different kinds of texts, using grammatical features, ideas content (topic types), and genre. Biber (1989) identified ten kinds of texts based on the co-occurrence of grammatical features, and each text type included a number of different genres. Table 16.3 outlines a range of possibilities for written work that a teacher or learner could sample from. The value of Biber's analysis for a writing teacher is that making sure that learners

TABLE 16.3 Types of written texts organized according to text types and genre

| Biber's text type and (purpose) | Possible written purposes | Genres |
|---|---|---|
| (1) Intimate interpersonal interaction (maintain personal relationships) | | Emails, Internet chat, Cell-phone texting |
| (2) Informational interaction (convey personal information) | | Personal letters, Postcards, Toasts |
| (3) 'Scientific' exposition (convey technical information) | Instruction Explanation | Recipes, Instructions, Memos PhD and Masters dissertations, Academic essays, Note-taking |
| (4) Learned exposition (convey less technical information) | Report Explanation Procedure | Academic articles, Official documents, Press reviews, Popular lore (popular magazines), Academic project work, Abstracts, Timed examination answers, Summaries, Research proposals, Film and book reviews, Responses to reading, Journal entries |
| (5) Imaginative narrative (entertain, but some inform) | Narrative | Stories, Prepared speeches |
| (6) General narrative exposition (a very wide range of purposes) | Recount Description | Letters, Incident reports, Songs, Poems, Press editorials, Newspaper stories, Religion, Biographies, Brochures, Catalogue entries, Reading logs, Filling forms[[Tab]] Advertising jingles, Jokes |
| (7) Situated reportage (reporting events in progress) | | |
| (8) Involved persuasion (argue and persuade) | Exposition | Persuasive essays, Professional letters, Editorials, Sermons |

are doing writing across several of Biber's text types will ensure that the learners have to deal with a good range of important grammatical features. Relating Biber's text types to genres ensures that learners are covering a relevant range of writing purposes.

## How much time should be given to extensive writing in a general language course?

Around half of the meaning-focused output strand should involve extensive writing. That is, around one-eighth of the time in a language course. Writing deserves time in a language course partly because it is often the way that language learning and other learning is assessed and the way that study in subject matter areas is assessed. Language users differ greatly in the amount of writing that they do, and increasingly writing involves typing skills. When planning a writing course, it is important to consider the kinds of writing and amounts of writing that learners need to do outside the course.

Because of its deliberate nature, writing can be a very useful means for developing accuracy in language use, particularly grammatical accuracy.

The time given to feedback on written work should be counted in the language-focused learning strand and would make up a very small proportion of the learning time in that strand. Unfortunately, the time that the teacher puts into giving feedback on writing will be much greater than the time most learners will spend considering the feedback.

## What are the requirements for learning from written feedback?

In this chapter, the focus is on feedback to promote learning. This kind of feedback has been called *Assessment for Learning* (AfL) and is a part of formative assessment.

As Hyland (2022, p. 79) points out, learning from feedback is one of the most contentious areas in foreign language instruction.

> My thesis is that grammar correction has no place in writing courses and should be abandoned. The reasons are: (a) research evidence shows that grammar correction is ineffective; (b) this lack of effectiveness is exactly what should be expected, given the nature of the correction process and the nature of language learning; (c) grammar correction has significant harmful effects; and (d) the various arguments offered for continuing it all lack merit.
> *(Truscott, 1996, p. 328)*

Truscott's suggestion is to replace the time spent on feedback with more writing. Although there has been considerable debate over the effectiveness of written feedback on writing (Ferris, 1999; Harwood, 2022; Truscott, 1996, 2007; Yu, Geng, Liu, & Zheng, 2021), the main issue for the teacher should be how we can make feedback work. For feedback to work, there needs to be good quality feedback and a willingness and capability in the learner to make use of this feedback.

Learning from feedback involves the principles described in Chapter 4 – motivation, focus of attention, quantity of attention, and quality of attention, and the research findings on learning from feedback can usually be explained by reference to these principles. Table 16.4 is organized around these four major factors affecting learning.

The initial focus on errors should be on errors that are likely to occur often. The most important are errors of subject-verb agreement, past tense-present tense, pronoun usage, article usage with countable and uncountable nouns, verb groups, and finite verbs and conjunctions. Each of these errors can be related to systematic checking rules (see Appendix 1), and each learner can keep a record of their progress towards mastery of these very common grammatical features. The negative effect of noting errors is that learners can become super-cautious in their writing and may not be prepared to take risks in what they write. To avoid this, feedback on errors needs to be balanced with positive feedback on content, expression, and organization.

A part of classroom time needs to be spent on learning self-correction procedures (Appendix 1). The mini-syllabus for this involves (1) the teacher explaining and modelling a procedure, (2) the learners practising it in pairs, (3) the learners applying the procedure to their own work, and (4) the teacher checking and monitoring learners' use of each procedure.

Ideally, each learner needs to have personal writing goals that are worked out with the help of the teacher. Some learners may prefer to concentrate on the content of their writing with the idea that the formal aspects of their writing will improve as they get more practice in writing. Others may prefer to have a staged set of error correction goals that directly relate to their current grammatical proficiency. Learners should play a major role in deciding what they want from feedback and have plenty of opportunities to reconsider their decisions. A straightforward way to do this is to get learners to do their writing in class time. While the learners are writing, the teacher calls on learners one-by-one to come for consultation with the teacher, bringing with them their recently marked piece of writing. This time is used to clarify any issues with the feedback, to check learners' understanding of self-correction procedures, and to negotiate learning goals. Class size will affect the use of this system of individual consultation. If class size is around 30 learners or less, then each learner can have an individual consultation once every two weeks during the writing class. If class sizes are larger, this may mean a consultation once a month. The value of having at least some of the extensive writing done in class time is that the writing is done, the writing is done under non-distracting conditions, and there is time for individual consultation.

**TABLE 16.4** How do you give effective formative feedback?

| Aspect | Application |
| --- | --- |
| *Motivation* | |
| Use feedback to motivate and involve learners. | Note positive features in the writing. Negotiate and set clear and achievable accuracy goals. Provide individual consultation. |
| *Focus of attention* | |
| Use methods of providing feedback that make feedback easier for the teacher to do, and are clear and constructive for the learners. | Use feedback symbols on the written work. Use feedback forms. Relate feedback to training in self-checking, analysis of models, rating scales, and principles of learning. |
| Include a wider focus than just grammatical errors. | Provide feedback on positive features of the writing. Provide feedback on vocabulary, content, genre, organization, style. |
| Balance selective feedback (focused) with occasional comprehensive feedback (unfocused). | Provide training in dealing with comprehensive feedback, including learners working out error density, error types, and learning strategies. |
| Help learners to take control of their own learning. | Negotiate immediate and long-term learning goals and feedback focus. Provide substantial repeated training in self-checking procedures. |
| Feedback for improvement should typically not be accompanied by grades (Lee, 2017 p. 20), because the grade distracts attention from the comments. | Separate writing for assessment from writing for learning. Use errors per 100 words graphs so that each learner has a clear record of improvement. |
| *Quantity of attention* | |
| Use feedback that helps learners (1) focus on the error, (2) spend time considering the correct form, and (3) find the correct form in a memorable way. | Use feedback symbols that support self-correction and the use of self-checking procedures. Provide correct answers when self-correction is not possible. |
| Provide spoken and written commentary on the overall text and on persistent issues in accuracy, organization, content, and style. | Balance negative comments with positive comments. Ensure that conferencing involves negotiation with the learner so that the learner is involved, understands, and has explicit things to focus on. |

*(Continued)*

TABLE 16.4 (Continued)

| Aspect | Application |
|---|---|
| *Quality of attention* | |
| With feedback on grammar, focus on the most common errors that can involve rules, procedures, and strategies, making sure that learners understand and can apply the rules, procedures, and strategies related to them. | Provide explicit spelling and grammar instruction on doubling of consonants and final silent *e* (free versus checked vowels), subject-verb agreement, past tense-present tense, pronoun usage, article usage with countable and uncountable nouns, verb groups, and finite verbs and conjunctions. Make learners aware of the distinction between performance errors and other types of errors. |
| Consider a range of sources of feedback. | In addition to feedback from the teacher, provide opportunities for feedback from peers, and technology. Provide training in peer feedback, including the use of feedback sheets. |
| Focus on the learning that can occur from the feedback. | Provide descriptive and diagnostic feedback of both strengths and weaknesses. |

When errors per 100 words are recorded on a graph, the drop in errors at least partly as a result of written corrective feedback, training in self-checking, and teacher conferencing is very dramatic, with errors typically halving over a few months of the course and reducing to a third of the initial total by the end of the year. The initial rapid drop in errors occurs because the errors that are avoided are careless errors (performance errors), and frequent errors that can be avoided by learning and applying self-checking procedures.

Once errors reach around 3-4 errors per 100 words, improvement is slow because the errors tend to be word-based rather than rule-based. For example, errors involving agreement between subject and verb, and article usage are rule-based errors and self-checking procedures can largely eliminate them. Such errors may initially be very frequent and have the potential to occur in almost every sentence. On the other hand, errors involving the correct use of a preposition after a verb, "depend on" or "depend to", are not rule-based but involve learning about the behaviour of a particular verb. This learning is piecemeal and can come from memorization or substantial experience with both input and output in the foreign language.

### How can extensive writing with feedback be done well?

1. Learners should write each week and teachers should expect a certain quantity of writing each week. To make sure that the writing is done and is each learner's own work, the writing can be done in class time, with the teacher using the time to give individual feedback on previous writing.
2. The teacher should choose topics for writing that ensure that a range of different kinds of writing is done and that the kinds of writing relate to learners' language use needs.
3. A small amount of time before the writing can be used to help learners gather ideas, and organize the writing, and meet some useful words and phrases relevant to the topic (see Table 16.2 for suggestions). The time spent on this preparation should not take much time away from writing.
4. While learners write, they can use dictionaries, peers, and the teacher to help them with problems they face.
5. When the writing is done, learners should spend a few minutes checking the writing to get rid of careless errors.
6. The teacher marks the learners' work, giving feedback using a procedure that the learners understand and can benefit from. Table 16.4 has a range of useful suggestions.
7. The teacher returns the marked work to the learners and also gives some feedback to the whole class on common errors and on procedures to use when checking for errors.
8. The learners look at the feedback and make changes to their piece of writing to take account of the feedback.
9. On a different day, when the learners are engaged on their next piece of writing, the learners come to the teacher individually to show the changes they have made and to talk about how they can improve their writing in general.

In a writing course, learners should do lots of writing. Beyond marking, one of the major problems a teacher will face is making sure that most of the time in the writing course is spent actually doing writing.

### How can I check that extensive writing is working well?

As with extensive language use across the other three skills of listening, speaking, and reading, quantity of language use is the first thing to look for. How much writing are the learners doing and what variety of types of writing are they doing? It is very useful for a teacher to look at each learner's writing portfolio, that is, the collection of all the pieces of writing that they have done. This can help learners see what progress they have made.

It is worth looking at learners' skill in checking their own work, as a very large proportion of errors that learners make tend to be ones that they can correct by themselves.

As a way of helping set goals, learners can be encouraged to talk about their own writing – where they see their weaknesses and strengths, what they need to improve, and what they would like to write about.

## What are the variants of extensive writing?

One of the major issues in writing is plagiarism. All writing courses need to deal with this issue and should provide instruction in the nature of plagiarism and how to avoid it. Academic writing necessarily involves the use of sources, and the first step in avoiding plagiarism is acknowledging those sources through the use of quotation marks, citation signals, such as citing verbs, and formal referencing involving in-text citing of sources and a list of references. Plagiarism has cultural elements particularly those relating to the status of the written word and respect for teachers and scholars. One way to discourage plagiarism is to convince the learners of the value of doing lots of writing to improve their writing skill.

Situational composition is kind of guided composition which still allows the learners a lot of freedom in their writing. The writing topic is described in detail, providing background information about the content of the writing, who the writing is intended for and the communicative purpose of the writing. This background information helps with several parts of the writing process and in the description of the task provides language items that learners could use in their own writing. Situational composition is somewhat like problem-solving discussion (Chapter 9) and could follow on from a problem-solving discussion task. Here is an example.

> You received the following email from your friend John Thompson.
> I don't know if you have heard, but my wife Gillian is suffering from dementia and I am unable to take care of her by myself. As a result, I have had to put her into a nursing home where she can get full-time care. I feel really bad about this as through the many years of our marriage we looked after each other and were always together. I am feeling very down about it.
> Send an email to John expressing your sympathy and trying to cheer him up by recalling some of the happy times you spent with him and his wife.

Here is another example.

> One of your friends came to your house for a meal and really enjoyed one of the dishes that you prepared. They asked for the recipe. Your friend however is not a very good cook and so will need fairly detailed instructions to make sure they get it right. Be very systematic in giving the instructions.

## Are there digital applications of this technique?

The use of highly accurate voice-to-text programmes makes writing much easier for those who are not good at typing. Such programmes include *Dragon Naturally*

*Speaking*, the Windows Voice Recognition app, and Google's AI speech to text. For those who type, predictive text also supports extensive writing. There are also numerous touch-typing courses to improve typing skills. Ideally, learning to touch-type should be a part of normal primary education.

There has been a large amount of research on providing automated feedback on writing, largely focusing on grammatical accuracy. Microsoft Word has its in-built spelling and grammar checker, and *Grammarly* has increasingly been the focus of research. The problem with such checkers for learners of English as a foreign language is that they tend to correct without much opportunity for learners to engage with and learn from the errors. The goals of extensive writing in a language course are for learners to learn the language and to learn how to write. The production of an accurate final product is a good outcome but not the main learning goal. Some academic institutions, focusing on content learning, suggest that learners use a combination of automated checking and self-checking on academic assignments so that inaccuracies in the text are removed so that they do not detract from assessment of the content. However, if learners are to learn from feedback, the learning conditions of focus of attention, quantity of attention and quality of attention need to operate, and automated feedback on writing should be used with these conditions in mind.

## Revisiting and linking to other activities

Hirvela (2013) sees an important link between reading and writing in academic settings in that poor writing may be a sign of poor reading or the inability to learn from reading. There is considerable value in seeing writing as a way of improving reading, and seeing reading as a way of preparing learners for writing. Having learners respond to their reading by writing about what they have read makes learners think more deeply about their reading. Allowing them the opportunity to draw on their reading will improve their writing.

## What does research say about the effectiveness of feedback on extensive writing?

Although there has been substantial debate about the effectiveness of corrective feedback, the research shows that if done well, it can be effective (Bitchener, 2021; Hyland & Hyland, 2006a, 2006b). Learners expect to get such feedback and typically value it. As well as pointing out errors, feedback should include praise, particularly where the praise clearly indicates the reasons for the praise (Zhou, Yu & Wu, 2022).

There is a lot of research on how to intervene in the writing process, but little research on the effect of quantity of writing on the quality of writing. Researching the effect of quantity of writing is important, because if quantity of writing has a major effect on quality, teachers may be able to reduce the marking that they do and make a substantial part of the extensive writing programme involve writing without detailed feedback.

## Research questions

### Motivation principles (Engagement)

For learning to occur, there needs to be a willingness to focus on what needs to be learned, and to give it quantity and quality of attention.

1  *Motivation: The degree of engagement with the task affects the likelihood of learning occurring.* How can learners be encouraged to pay close attention to feedback?
2  *Self-efficacy: Our confidence in our own skills of learning affects our success in learning.*

### Focus principles (Usefulness)

Learning requires giving attention to what needs to be learned.

3  *Focus: We learn what we focus on, and in addition, our learning is more useful if it closely resembles the use that we need to make of what we learn (transfer-appropriate).* Does integrating writing with preparatory activities result in fewer errors? Does training in minimum requirements (see Appendix 1) result in a substantial reduction in related errors?
4  *Accuracy: Our learning is more efficient if the information we are focusing on is complete, accurate, and comprehensible.* How much can computerized checking and peer-checking result in error reduction in the final draft? How well does this transfer to subsequent writing?

### Quantity principles (Amount)

5  *Repetition: The more repetitions, the stronger the learning.* Does repeated writing on the same topic result in improvement in the accuracy and complexity of writing?
6  *Time-on-task: The greater and longer the attention, the stronger the learning.* Is writing quantity related to writing improvement?

### Quality principles (Connections)

Elaboration and analysis increase and strengthen connections between the item to be learned and other knowledge making it easier to access the item.

7 *Elaboration: This includes enriching the encoding of an item through variation.* What are the advantages of doing a range of different kinds of writing?
8 *Analysis: This involves relating the familiar parts to the unfamiliar whole.* Does training in self-checking procedures result in a substantial increase in accuracy of writing?

The most useful research on extensive writing with feedback would be on the effect of writing quantity on proficiency in writing. This could also involve looking at whether feedback is necessary for improvement.

# 17
# INFORMATION TRANSFER

The strength of information transfer as a learning technique lies in the requirement to change the same information from one form to another, which applies the principle of elaboration (see Chapter 4). In this chapter, note-taking is included as a form of information transfer because good note-taking involves a new encoding of the input. Semantic mapping can also be a kind of information transfer.

## What is information transfer?

An information transfer exercise involves the transfer or change of information from a linguistic form to a diagrammatic form, or from a diagrammatic form to a linguistic form. During the transfer, the information remains substantially the same but the form of the information changes. In a receptive information transfer exercise, learners change spoken or written information into a diagram, chart, or picture. By making this change, the learners show that they have understood the information and that their understanding is deep enough to adapt it in some way. Here is a simple example. The learners listen to a description of a flowering plant while looking at a diagram. While listening, the learners label parts of the diagram. This is an information transfer exercise because the information about the plant is presented in a linguistic form and then the same information is put into a diagrammatic or semi-diagrammatic form (Palmer, 1982).

Information transfer is essentially a guided technique (see Chapter 2) in that part of the work needed to complete the task is already provided by the teacher in the form of the diagram. Information transfer is suited to the various kinds of group work (see Chapter 3) in that it can involve co-operating group work where learners help each other to complete the diagram or produce the output from the diagram, superior-inferior group work where one learner in the group provides the input for the other learners, and split information group work where different learners have diagrams with different pieces of information filled in that they must describe to others so that all end up with fully competed diagrams.

One excellent feature of the information transfer technique is that the nature of the exercise itself is a justification for its use. That is, information transfer is an excellent learning strategy because it requires learners to process deeply the information that they are dealing with and to deal with two types of encoding of that material (Craik & Lockhart, 1972; Paivio, 1971) which involves repetition.

Information transfer exercises can be used productively. That is, the learners look at a diagram and then use this as a basis for writing or speaking. This productive use often works best after the learners have had some experience of the receptive equivalents, because these can act as a model or example of the production required.

Here are some examples of receptive information transfer (Nation, 1988). The learners listen to a conversation between a landlady and a new boarder and label a plan of the rooms of the house using the information conveyed in the conversation. Similarly, the teacher talks about her family or an imaginary family, and the learners complete a family tree diagram. Palmer (1982) has an excellent list of other suggestions classified according to the type of diagram used. He uses the categories of maps and plans, grids and tables, diagrams and charts, diaries and calendars, and miscellaneous lists, forms, and coupons. The following suggestions add to Palmer's examples.

1 The learners listen to a report of a robbery and draw the robbers' route through the house on a diagram of the house.
2 The learners read descriptions of two languages and note their characteristics on a chart. The chart includes categories like script, use of stress, word-building processes.
3 The learners listen to a recorded conversation between a teacher and a parent and put grades and comments on a child's school report.

## What are the learning goals of information transfer?

Information transfer typically accompanies meaning-focused input or meaning-focused output activities, so the learning involved is largely incidental learning because the main focus is on the message. Table 17.1 presents the learning goals of information transfer.

The main goal of information transfer is to provide practice in meaning-focused use, particularly where this use involves taking notes (receptive) or

**TABLE 17.1** The goals of information transfer

| Goals | Specific focuses |
|---|---|
| Language | Learning new vocabulary and grammatical features |
|  | Strengthening and enriching partly known vocabulary and grammar through varied use |
| Ideas | Provide repetition of useful content |
| Skills | *Developing input or output skills including skill in notetaking or working from notes* |
| Text | Becoming familiar with a range of topic types and discourse patterns |

*Note: Italics* indicates the major goal.

producing from notes (productive). The incidental secondary goal is to provide an opportunity to repeat vocabulary, multiword units, and grammatical features in different ways, thus strengthening and enriching knowledge of them. These different ways include linguistic and diagrammatic presentation.

The information transfer diagrams used can provide explicit knowledge of useful ways of organizing content and text.

## How does information transfer help learning?

In essence, information transfer activities help language learning through quality of attention arising from the information appearing in both linguistic and diagrammatic forms. Information transfer activities involve incidental language learning because the focus is on the information involved rather than the language features.

*Motivation:* Information transfer activities often involve real-life tables and diagrams such as timetables, maps, plans, shopping lists, and diagrams of electronic devices. This can enhance motivation. The visual element of information transfer provides support for the linguistic element making it easier to understand or produce.

*Focus:* Information transfer involves a strong focus on the message, so any language focus is largely incidental.

*Quantity:* During information transfer, the information appears in two forms, linguistic and diagrammatic, and so there is a small amount of repetition. If this is accompanied by feedback or checking of the result of the information transfer, then this gives further repetition. Because the activity requires information to be transferred from one form to another, this encourages sustained attention.

*Quality:* The information in information transfer diagrams eventually appears in both linguistic and diagrammatic forms, thus involving elaboration. The move from linguistic to diagrammatic representation also requires decision-making which is a kind of analysis.

## What are the requirements of information transfer?

### How can you prepare for information transfer?

The major preparation for information transfer is deciding on the type of diagram that will be used. Palmer's (1982) article has a large number of very useful suggestions, and the examples he provides show that the topic of the input or output suggests the kind of diagram that might be used.

In addition to diagrams suggested by the topic, there are diagrams that reflect the type of information (topic types), and diagrams that reflect text organization. Preparation for the use of such diagrams involves understanding the patterns and organization that lie behind such diagrams. There has been considerable study of text organization, particularly at the level of the paragraph or a small group of paragraphs (Hoey, 1983; Zuck & Zuck, 1984). For example, a description of the parts of a laser can be input to an information transfer diagram based on the physical structure topic type. This topic type involves four kinds of information, namely the parts, where the parts are located in relation to each other, the features or characteristics of the parts, and their functions.

To make it easier for learners to see the patterns involved in the text, the first parts of the information transfer chart can already be filled in.

| *Part* | *Location* | *Features* | *Function* |
|---|---|---|---|
| Rod | | | |
| Cylinder | | | |
| Outer covering | | | |

This same physical structure pattern can be used with a text on the description of an ant colony, the administrative structure of a university, and the various pages, title page, etc. that go to make up a book. The learning from this use of the information transfer exercise can be of three types: (1) developing familiarity with language items used in the text, (2) understanding of the content of the text as a result of having to process it deeply, and (3) awareness of the physical structure pattern so that it can be applied to other texts. This third type of learning is of course the most generalizable and so of most interest to the teacher. Other patterns include the problem\solution\evaluation pattern (Hoey, 1983), forecasting (prediction\time\source\basis\range\reassessment\modification) (Zuck & Zuck, 1984), process, characteristics, theory, principle, instruction, state/situation, adaptation (Johns & Davies, 1983). Rhetorical patterns, such as comparison and contrast, exemplification, and elimination of alternatives can also be used as a basis for information transfer activities.

This focus of attention on the discourse of the text can be the basis for the use of a self-questioning strategy which allows learners to create their own information transfer diagrams (Franken, 1987). The questions that learners should ask themselves when reading (or preparing to write) a physical structure text would be,

What are the parts?  Where are they?  What are they like? What do they do?

We have seen how the physical structure topic type can apply to a variety of texts, but the same information transfer diagram could be used with all physical structure texts.

Similarly, when working with a text which involves the process topic type, learners can ask themselves the following questions.

What are the steps and changes? What causes the change at each step? What are the results of the steps?

The same or very similar questions can be asked about a text on soap making, the life cycle of a butterfly, enrolling in a university, or assembling cars. A suitable process topic-type diagram might look like this.

| Stage (Change) | Material & structure | Location | Time | Instrument & action |
| --- | --- | --- | --- | --- |
| | | | | |

If information transfer exercises are based on categories that apply to a large number of texts or situations, then the learners can turn these categories into questions that they use to create their own information transfer diagrams. This makes the technique very powerful, as it gives learners more control over their learning procedures.

*What texts can be used for information transfer?*

Information transfer is most suited to non-fiction texts, but it is not limited to such texts. Most non-fiction texts can be related to some kind of generalizable pattern of information or text organization. However, fiction texts can make use of story-grammar.

*How much time should be given to information transfer in a general language course?*

Information transfer provides support for communicative activities such as extensive listening, extensive reading, prepared speaking, pair speaking, note-taking, and writing. So, it does not make sense to try to say what proportion of the four strands it should occupy. It is enough to say that it has uses across the four skills of listening, speaking, reading, and writing, and should be used when learners need support in language reception or production.

### How can information transfer be done well?

Receptive information transfer involves listening to or reading a text and filling in an information transfer diagram. In most information transfer activities, the information transfer diagram is supplied by the teacher. At advanced levels, learners may need to decide what kind of diagram they will use.

1. One starting point for receptive information transfer is a text. This is particularly true if the input for the activity is a reading text. So, the first step in such a case is to find a suitable text. If the input is spoken and the teacher is confident enough to rely on their own skill at speaking from notes, then the starting point can be a completed diagram. The teacher uses the diagram as notes for the production of the spoken input.
2. The learners are given an incomplete or partly completed diagram that they must complete as they read or listen to the input.
3. If the learners are new to information transfer, they can listen to the spoken input more than once, or they can work with a partner as they read the written input.
4. Before they get feedback on their success in filling in the diagram, learners can form small groups to compare their completed diagrams and to discuss the parts where they filled in the diagram differently.
5. The teacher shows the completed diagram and discusses any points of disagreement with the learners. If necessary, this can be an opportunity to revisit the input.
6. If the information transfer diagram is based on a topic type or some other kind of generalizable pattern, the teacher should spend time pointing out how the same diagram could be used with different kinds of input. It helps if each generalizable diagram is given a descriptive name, such as the physical structure diagram or the state/situation diagram, so that it is easy to refer to when it is needed again.
7. Repetition and retrieval is greatly increased if the receptive outcome of information transfer is used for a productive information transfer activity (spoken or written) on another day. The procedure thus involves (1) listening or reading the input and filling in the information transfer diagram, (2) discussing and getting feedback on the results, (3) using the completed information transfer diagram to do a piece of writing or speaking. This procedure turns the information transfer activity into a linked skills technique (Chapter 21).

Learners should understand the value of using information transfer diagrams, particularly how they help in the learning of subject matter content through re-coding the information.

### How can I check that an information transfer activity is working well?

The successful completion of an information transfer diagram can be a sign that the activity is working well. Failure to complete the diagram can happen because the activity is not well designed or because the learner was not given enough support.

### What are the variants of information transfer?

As Palmer's (1982) many examples show, information transfer diagrams can take on a wide variety of forms. An information transfer diagram provides support for both comprehending input and providing output.

Note-taking can be seen as a kind of receptive information transfer activity, in that good note-taking involves recoding the input in a form that is revealing and memorable. Note-taking can be seen as filling two functions. One function is storage, where the information is recorded in some way so that it is available for later attention. The other function is encoding. Encoding is a way of making the information stick in memory. Encoding is a form of elaboration (see Chapter 4). An extreme way of looking at the encoding function of note-taking is consider that at the end of a lecture, the notes that the learners took during the lecture could be thrown away, because they have already filled their function of making the content of the lecture memorable and revealing.

What could good notes look like? One form of note-taking is to use headings and sub-headings and numbered organized lists as the encoded form. If the notes were held at some distance from someone who did not hear the lecture, by looking at the shape of the outline of the notes, they could say, "It seems that the lecture had three main points. The first point was the one that was developed the most, with six sub-points." and so on.

Another form of note-taking is to create a semantic map, with a central point containing the topic of the lecture and branching arms for each of the main points and further sub-arms for details about the points. The result would be a unique diagram that represented a re-shaping of the information in the lecture. At the end of the lecture, the note-taker may wish to re-draw the diagram to better represent their understanding and interpretation of the lecture.

Learners need training in note-taking and need to have plenty of opportunity to discuss their notes and others' notes to see the range of options that they can draw on to make the best use of the encoding function of note-taking.

*How can information transfer be used at all levels of proficiency?* At the elementary level, receptive information transfer can involve simply labelling diagrams, drawing on plans, or adding words to lists or tables. At the intermediate level, learners can begin using generalizable diagrams and begin learning about topic types. Advanced-level learners need to get into the encoding function of note-taking.

*How can information transfer be used in large classes?* Information transfer activities can be a part of a wide range of activities across the four skills of listening, speaking, reading, and writing. Receptive information transfer activities result in a completed information transfer diagram and filling in such diagrams is not affected by class size. Written productive information transfer can be a part of extensive writing activities and these largely involve individual work, and so they can easily be done in large classes or out of class. Spoken productive information transfer activities can be done as group work in large classes, but the noise factor may play a role in limiting their use.

### Are there digital applications of this technique?

Information transfer diagrams can be created through the use of technology, and this can result in very attractive and memorable information transfer diagrams. Where the completion of the information transfer diagram has a set correct answer, the use of digital technology can be used as a way of providing feedback.

### Revisiting and linking to other activities

Information transfer activities are a very useful way of revisiting reading texts in a course book to get varied repetition. In such activities, they can be used receptively where the learners fill in an information transfer diagram using information from the reading text. Then a few days later, the same completed information transfer diagram can be used productively when learners talk or write about the reading passage using the information in the information transfer diagram.

### What does research say about the effectiveness of information transfer?

The research on dual coding (Paivio, 1971) emphasizes the positive effect of processing information in two different ways, linguistically and non-linguistically. In terms of the principles described in Chapter 4, information transfer increases quality of attention through elaboration, the elaboration being the relating of the linguistic and pictorial mediums. This relationship also affects the quantity of attention in that attention needs to be given to the material as input and also as output.

The possible negative effect of information transfer occurs when too much attention and time is given to the non-linguistic representation, because this takes time away from attention to the linguistic form and it is this form which is the goal of language learning.

## Research questions

### Motivation principles (Engagement)

For learning to occur, there needs to be a willingness to focus on what needs to be learned, and to give it quantity and quality of attention.

1. *Motivation: The degree of engagement with the task affects the likelihood of learning occurring.* Is filling information transfer diagrams like completing a puzzle?
2. *Self-efficacy: Our confidence in our own skills of learning affects our success in learning.* What factors make filling an information transfer diagram easier?

### Focus principles (Usefulness)

Learning requires giving attention to what needs to be learned.

3. *Focus: We learn what we focus on, and in addition, our learning is more useful if it closely resembles the use that we need to make of what we learn (transfer-appropriate).* Does the transfer-appropriateness of an information transfer diagram make the activity more engaging? Is the language entered into an information transfer diagram more likely to be learned than other language in the input to the activity?
4. *Accuracy: Our learning is more efficient if the information we are focusing on is complete, accurate, and comprehensible.* Are information transfer activities which require verbatim reproduction of information better for learning than those requiring varied reproduction?

### Quantity principles (Amount)

5. *Repetition: The more repetitions, the stronger the learning.* How large a part does repetition (input and output) play in the effect of information transfer on learning? How can repetition be maximized in an information transfer activity?
6. *Time-on-task: The greater and longer the attention, the stronger the learning.* Do information transfer activities increase the amount of attention that learners give to input compared to comprehension questions?

## Quality principles (Connections)

Elaboration and analysis increase and strengthen connections between the item to be learned and other knowledge making it easier to access the item.

7 *Elaboration: This includes enriching the encoding of an item through variation.* Is there a scale of non-linguistic representation and does this scale reflect differences in the effect on learning? That is, are some types of non-linguistic representation more effective than others? Is this because they involve more or less linguistic information?
8 *Analysis: This involves relating the familiar parts to the unfamiliar whole.* Does using the same information transfer diagram, such as the diagram for a particular topic type, reduce the effect of the diagram on remembering the information because it is not unique?

There needs to be a careful wide-ranging review of relevant research on the effects of non-linguistic encoding on language learning. This could include the effects of semantic mapping, reading accompanied by pictures, language learning from viewing, the keyword technique, and information transfer. It is likely that the same principles of learning are involved in all these kinds of activities and a careful review may be able to find common features that contribute to language learning. In several ways, this review would be an examination of the principle of elaboration.

# 18
# GUIDED WRITING

The four skills of listening, speaking, reading, and writing each have three major learning components. They have a language-focused learning component that gives deliberate attention to the particular skill and the language features involved in it. In the case of writing, this is guided writing. They have a meaning-focused input or meaning-focused output component, such as extensive reading or extensive writing, and they have fluency development component, which in the case of writing is ten-minute writing.

## What is guided writing?

Guided writing can take many forms, depending on what kind of support is given and what part of the writing process is focused on. In this chapter, we take a narrow focus and focus on mechanical (handwriting) and grammatical support. This, thus, excludes most kinds of picture composition where the focus is on content. It also excludes many intermediate and advanced guided writing activities that focus on the organization of text, and the use of technical vocabulary and multiword units. Guided writing, of the kind described in this chapter, is largely an elementary and low intermediate-level activity, for learners who know much less than 2,000-word families (CEFR Levels A1 & A2) and who would struggle with extensive writing.

Guided writing is clearly a guided activity. In such activities (see Chapter 2), part of the work in the activity is already done by the teacher or course designer, so the learner only has to focus on a part of the task of writing. In the most basic guided writing task, the learner has to copy a short passage. This gives the learner practice in forming the letters and words. Guided writing can sometimes

DOI: 10.4324/9781003496151-23

involve shared activities where learners work together to produce a single piece of writing. Here is a list of some possible guided writing activities ranked in order of difficulty.

> Copy the text.
> Write the text from dictation.
> Copy a text making small changes to it.
> Fill the blanks in the text with these words and phrases.
> Fill the blanks in the text with your own words and phrases.
> Copy a text making some substantial changes to it.
> Do a dicto-gloss (Wajnryb, 1989) which involves group work where learners listen to a text and work together to write the text from memory.

The classic, unfortunately neglected, guided writing text is *Ananse Tales* by Dykstra, Port, and Port (1966) (see also Dykstra, 1964; Dykstra & Paulston, 1967). This is now out-of-print, but Appendix 3 of *Teaching ESL/EFL reading and writing* (2nd ed.) by Nation and Macalister (2021) contains a list of the 57 graded changes that learners were required to make to the texts (about Ananse the spider) in the guided writing course. Here is a sampling to show the extent of the changes.

> 1 Copy the text.
> 2 Rewrite the text with word substitution (*basket* for *gourd*).
> 3 Rewrite with pronoun change (*Ananse the spider* with *Ananse's wife*).
> 4 Rewrite with plural change.
> ...
>
> 7 Rewrite changing *every day* to *yesterday* (tense change).
> 8 Rewrite in the future and also change to the plural.
> ...
>
> 24 Rewrite joining the following sentences by *and* or *but*.
> ...
>
> 29 Rewrite adding prepositional phrases after five of the following words.
> ...
>
> 42 Rewrite adding time clauses to any six sentences.
> 43 Rewrite adding concessive clauses (clauses beginning with *although, even though*) before or after the following sentences.
> ...

55 Rewrite supplying a suitable middle to the passage using five or six sentences.
56 Rewrite the passage in your own words without looking at the model.
57 Create a folk tale of your own. You should use between 50 and 100 words in your tale.

Each of the texts required changes at three or four levels. However, the learners would begin at Level 1 Copy the text, and when they had done that on two or three passages that had that requirement, they would then look for a passage with the Level 2 requirement, Rewrite with the given word substitution. When they made no errors with that, they then moved to Level 3, and so on. Most of the changes require consideration of the content of the story, so they are far from being just a mechanical exercise.

Here is an example of one of the 44 texts in the course.

---

**How Wisdom Spread Among the Tribes (Part I)**

[1] Ananse, the spider, managed to collect all the world's knowledge in one spot. [2] He placed it in a gourd and then decided to climb a tree and hang the gourd there so that he might keep all the wisdom on earth for himself. [3] When Ananse reached the largest tree in the forest, he took some string and tied it to the gourd. [4] Next he hung the gourd in front of him, and set himself to climb the tree. [5] However, he was unable at first to do so. [6] His son, who was only a small child, suggested that he put the gourd on his back, but Ananse only laughed and called him a foolish boy.

1 Copy.
2 Rewrite the entire passage changing the word gourd to basket each time it appears.
3 Rewrite the entire passage changing *Ananse, the spider*, to *Ananse's wife*. Remember to change the pronouns.

---

Those who have used the course or variants of it spoke of how the learners enjoyed doing it and especially the learners' high degree of success in making the changes, and the feeling of satisfaction that learners had in progressing through the language features involved in the changes.

Guided writing tasks such as these would be the very opposite of what teachers of young learners of English as a first language would wish to use, and rightly so. For such learners who already have a strong oral command of the language, they need to use writing to express the ideas that are important to them, even though their spelling and ways of expressing their ideas are far from what they will soon be using. However, for learners of English as a foreign language with a small vocabulary and very shaky control of the grammar of English, a guided writing course provides a clear achievable series of steps that cover much of the knowledge needed to write a grammatically accurate paragraph. It also makes the teacher's task of checking work very straightforward, especially if the teacher is also not a native speaker of English.

When the learners have a good basic control of the mechanics of writing, spelling, and grammar, they can then do more extensive and original writing.

## What are the learning goals of guided writing?

Where learners' first language does not involve the same script as the foreign language, writing at the elementary level can be a real challenge, and guidance and practice are needed in tasks as basic as forming the letters of the language and writing words (Table 18.1).

The major learning goal of guided writing is being able to turn familiar ideas into written form with a high level of accuracy. This involves the more general goal of turning receptive knowledge (listening and reading) into productive knowledge. This is not as straightforward as it seems as there is much to be learned to bridge the gap between reading and writing. Guided writing should also develop the learners' skill in writing the letters and words of the language, as well as spelling the words correctly.

## How does guided writing help learning?

Guided writing helps learning by reducing the difficulty of the task of writing to a relatively small aspect of the task, typically producing written forms and writing grammatically correct sentences and paragraphs. It takes away the need for the learner to consider what to write about, how to organize the ideas and text, and how to make it comprehensible and engaging for the reader. The learner has to focus on getting the written forms and grammar right. In essence, guided writing helps learning through quantity of deliberate and accurate language use.

*Motivation:* Guided writing tasks are usually well supported so that the learner has a very high possibility of doing the writing well. Guided writing has modest formal goals and these transfer well to use out-of-class.

**TABLE 18.1** The goals of guided writing

| Goals | Specific focuses |
| --- | --- |
| Language | *Producing accurate written sentences and paragraphs using known language* |
|  | Turning receptive knowledge into productive knowledge |
| Ideas |  |
| Skills | Developing fluency in writing letters and words |
| Text |  |

*Note:* The major goal is in *italics*.

*Focus:* The focus in guided writing is a deliberate focus on the written form of words and on grammar. It has a strong accuracy focus, and learners should expect to do most guided writing activities without many errors.

*Quantity:* Guided writing tasks do not typically involve a lot of writing in each session, but it should be done often. There is certainly value in coming back to the same piece of writing and doing it again more quickly.

*Quality:* The main quality element in guided writing is variation in that the learners may be required to use the same grammatical constructions in a variety of ways.

## What are the requirements of guided writing?

### How can you prepare for guided writing?

A good guided writing course allows learners to work at their own level and to proceed at their own pace, and so there should be a range of writing options available. Although the *Ananse Tales* course has 57 levels, a guided writing course probably needs only five or six, beginning with copying, then moving to dictation, then making supported small changes to a text, then making less supported larger changes, and finally class and group composition.

### What texts can be used for guided writing?

Guided writing topics and texts should relate to the kinds of writing that learners will need to do. Increasingly, this involves computer-based communication. It is not easy to decide what kinds of texts to use. If the learners are studying content courses in English, then writing for content assessment, such as assignments or exams, is very important. If learners are not assessed on content matter in English, then writing is likely to be closely related to interests and hobbies (recipes, instructions, making lists, leaving notes for others to read, labelling), form-filling and buying online, social networking (emails, texts, chat postings), work (writing a curriculum vitae), and study (note-taking, summarizing).

### How much time should be given to guided writing in a general language course?

Guided writing fits into the language-focused learning strand of a course. It shares the time in this strand with hearing and pronunciation practice, the memorization parts of informal conversation, intensive reading, feedback on writing, using word cards, substitution tables, and learner training. Guided writing is most often used at the elementary stages of language learning until learners can do more extensive writing. It should occupy around one-fifth of the time in the language-focused learning strand at the elementary stages of proficiency. This is around one-twentieth of the total course time.

### How can guided writing be done well?

Guided writing largely depends on getting it right, and so graded writing activities are needed. Because guided writing should be largely an individual or small group activity to cater for learners' differing proficiency levels, there needs to be some quick procedure for deciding what level of guidance a learner needs. The steps in using guided writing activities are straightforward.

1. The learner is directed to a guided writing activity at the right level for them.
2. The learner does the writing activity. If it involves making changes to parts of a text, the changes should be underlined or highlighted.
3. The teacher looks quickly at the changes and gives feedback on them. Most often the changes will be correct, so the teacher needs to praise the accurate work. The teacher will find the job easier and the learners will learn more from the feedback if the teacher uses a marking system that indicates the type of error (subject-verb agreement, article usage, verb form usage, conjunctions, etc.), and there is periodic training in how to self-correct the most common kinds of errors (see Chapter 16 and Appendix 1).
4. Each learner keeps their pieces of writing together in chronological order as a record of their progress.
5. If the teacher has a well-organized set of guided writing tasks, then learners can note their progress through these tasks on a checklist of the tasks.

### How can I check that a guided writing activity is working well?

Guided writing deliberately focuses on accuracy, and so learners should be completing guided writing tasks with few if any errors.

Because guided writing activities run the risk of being mechanical exercises where little thought is given to the content and goals of the activity, it is worth observing how the learners do the activities. This can help the teacher decide if they need to be changed in some way, or if they are achieving their goals in a satisfactory way.

### What are the variants of guided writing?

Substitution tables (Chapter 19) can involve guided writing at the sentence level. However, in this chapter, the focus is on writing at the paragraph level and higher. Productive information transfer (Chapter 17) fits comfortably within guided writing.

Blackboard composition (Radford, 1969) (involving the whole class) and group composition are forms of guided writing where the learners (and teacher) work together to produce a written text. These co-operative tasks are on the border of guided writing and extensive writing.

*How can guided writing be used at all levels of proficiency?*

Guided writing activities as described in this chapter are intended for the elementary level. There are guided writing activities for more advanced levels where the guidance is focused on genre and content.

### Are there digital applications of this technique?

The most basic guided writing activities, such as copying, dictation, and writing with small changes are well suited to an app.

The issue of handwriting needs careful thought as there is value in being able to form letters and words, both as a language-learning aid and a life skill. Related to this, there is the issue of writing using voice recognition. Voice recognition has now reached a high level of accuracy and is very efficient. The effects on pronunciation are worth researching, but voice recognition technology is likely to reduce the need to learn to touch-type and write.

### Revisiting and linking to other activities

The *Ananse Tales* course has repetition built into it in that the same task is repeated on several different texts, and each text has around three tasks at different levels, meaning that it is highly likely to be re-visited several times.

Guided writing can be based on previously studied material, and should work particularly well if there is a sequence of linked skills work going from reading to speaking to writing, all based on the same text.

### What does research say about the effectiveness of guided writing?

There has been research on sentence-level activities, such as blank-filling (Webb, Yanagisawa & Uchihara, 2020) and sentence combining (Walter, Dockrell & Connelly, 2021), and research on group activities such as dicto-comp (Chun & Aubrey, 2023; Jacobs & Small, 2003). However, there is a lack of research on grammar-focused paragraph-level guided composition.

### Research questions

Many of these questions focus on the *Ananse Tales* type of guided writing.

*Motivation principles (Engagement)*

For learning to occur, there needs to be a willingness to focus on what needs to be learned, and to give it quantity and quality of attention.

1 *Motivation: The degree of engagement with the task affects the likelihood of learning occurring.* What are learners' attitudes to guided writing? Does success in guided writing encourage learners to do more guided writing? How do learners feel about writing out the whole passage when there is only a small amount of change to the passage?
2 *Self-efficacy: Our confidence in our own skills of learning affects our success in learning.* Does the *Ananse Tales* scheme of grammatical difficulty correspond to the difficulty learners experience with the various tasks?

### Focus principles (Usefulness)

Learning requires giving attention to what needs to be learned.

3 *Focus: We learn what we focus on, and in addition, our learning is more useful if it closely resembles the use that we need to make of what we learn (transfer-appropriate).* What guided writing activities are the most effective? How well does practice in guided writing transfer to free writing? Do the *Ananse Tales* tasks make learners engage with the whole text or just with the parts involved in changes?
4 *Accuracy: Our learning is more efficient if the information we are focusing on is complete, accurate, and comprehensible.* How effective is self-marking or peer-marking in guided writing activities? Does the explicit teaching of grammar have positive effects on the quality of guided writing?

### Quantity principles (Amount)

5 *Repetition: The more repetitions, the stronger the learning.* Does the repetition of the same grammar-based changes in guided writing result in improvement in the quality of the changes made?
6 *Time-on-task: The greater and longer the attention, the stronger the learning.* How long does it take to do an *Ananse Tales* task? Does writing out the whole passage result in more learning than just writing the changes?

### Quality principles (Connections)

Elaboration and analysis increase and strengthen connections between the item to be learned and other knowledge making it easier to access the item.

7 *Elaboration: This includes enriching the encoding of an item through variation.* Does re-writing the same passage several times with different changes affect learning from the passage?

8 *Analysis:* This involves relating the familiar parts to the unfamiliar whole. Does the strong grammar focus in the *Ananse Tales* guided writing result in deliberate knowledge of grammatical features? Do such activities increase skill in self-checking written work?

Any research on sustained guided writing beyond the sentence level would be valuable. The most useful research would examine the effect of guided writing on freer writing.

# 19
# SUBSTITUTION TABLES

The classic article on substitution tables is George (1965). His article on substitution tables made use of his pioneering corpus work on verb form frequency (George, 1963), and was the forerunner of his book containing 101 ready-to-use substitution tables (George, 1967). The various verb constructions in the tables in the book reflected the findings of his verb frequency count, in that the more frequent constructions appeared in several tables while the less frequent constructions appeared less frequently in the tables. The frequency of the main verb construction in each table was indicated using a four-level signalling system. The tables contain around 1,200 of the 2,000 most useful word families of English. Free digital copies of the book and articles are available at H. V. George publications | School of Linguistics and Applied Language Studies | Victoria University of Wellington (wgtn.ac.nz). In 1916, one of the pioneers of modern foreign language teaching, Harold E. Palmer, published a book called *Colloquial English,* Part 1, *100 Substitution Tables* (W. Heffer & Son, Cambridge), and George's title is a respectful acknowledgement of that, with the 101 indicating some improvements.

The use of substitution tables was also called pattern practice and simple substitution tables were a central part of many oral-aural language courses, including language laboratory work, in the middle of the twentieth century, for example *English 900*.

## What is a substitution table?

Figure 19.1 is an example of a simple substitution table (Table 3) taken from H. V. George's book. Brackets indicate that the item is optional. Note that the full stop has a column of its own.

|  |  | cry |  |
|  |  | be afraid |  |
|  |  | be sad |  |
|  |  | worry |  |
|  |  | be alarmed |  |
|  |  | be scared |  |
| (Please) | don't | go there |  |
| (Now) | let's not | walk past them | . |
| (Now please) |  | say that |  |
|  |  | take any notice |  |
|  |  | be angry |  |
|  |  | do that |  |
|  |  | boast about it |  |
|  |  | be greedy |  |
|  |  | be unkind |  |
|  |  | get rude |  |
|  |  | laugh at them |  |
|  |  | be cruel to them |  |
|  |  | be unfair |  |

**FIGURE 19.1** A substitution table based around the negative imperative pattern (George, 1967).

| How many | | | ? | | |
| What | | require | | | |
| Which one | do you | want | | | |
| When | | need | | | |
| Why | | | it | ? | |
| How often | | | that | | |
| What | | | them | for | ? |

**FIGURE 19.2** Table 10 on question forms from George (1967).

A substitution table allows learners to see several sentences based on the same useful grammatical pattern, and allows them to make many correct sentences using this pattern. Substitution tables can be used for written work or oral work. The use of substitution tables fits into the language-focused learning strand of a course because it involves deliberate attention to language features. It is a guided technique, because the parts of the sentences are already provided for the learners, requiring them only to combine them to make sentences. Substitution tables can be used in independent individual work, pair, and group work, or with the class working with the teacher. There is a video on the use of substitution tables on Paul Nation's resources page.

Figure 19.2 is a small but complicated table (Table 10 in George, 1967). Note that the horizontal lines in column 1 restrict what can be chosen in columns 4–6.

In the last line of the table, the line above *What* indicates that it needs to be used with *for*.

## What are the learning goals of substitution tables?

A substitution table is used to gain an awareness of sentence patterns and the range of substitutions that can be made in those patterns (Table 19.1).

The major learning goal when using substitution tables is to learn the word order and possible substitutions of the most frequent and regular sentence patterns. Substitution tables may also involve learning some useful vocabulary and multiword units.

## How do substitution tables help learning?

In essence, substitution tables help language learning through quantity and quality of deliberate attention to the patterned components of sentences.

*Motivation:* Substitution tables provide the opportunity to make a very large number of correct sentences. They thus set learners a task where they are highly likely to succeed. The sentences involved in the substitution tables are ones that learners are likely to need in their use of English and this clear relevance can be a motivating factor.

*Focus:* Although the focus is on producing correct sentences, the layout of the substitution table makes it clear that sentence patterns and the slots within them are a major focus.

*Quantity:* Each table can provide a large amount of practice with each pattern. That is, each table involves an enormous number of examples of the same pattern. Moreover, the same substitution tables can be returned to several times in order to get to a good level of fluency with the pattern.

*Quality:* The major quality principle at work in the use of substitution tables is analysis, namely developing awareness of the parts of the sentence pattern. The columns in the table indicate the main parts of the sentence pattern, and the items in each column show what can fit into parts of the pattern. For example, Figure 19.3 shows the verb+*to*+stem, verb+stem+*ing* and verb+object patterns based on the verbs *like, hate,* and *love.*

After practising the sentences in the table, the learners should have some conscious awareness of the patterns involved and should have memorized a variety of useful phrases that can be used in these patterns and in other places.

**TABLE 19.1** The goals of learning from substitution tables

| Goals | Specific focuses |
|---|---|
| Language | *Learning the most useful and productive sentence patterns of English* |
|  | Learning some useful vocabulary and multiword units |
| Ideas |  |
| Skills | Developing accuracy in spoken and written language use |
| Text |  |

*Note:* The major goal is in italics.

| I<br>We<br>They | love<br>hate<br>like<br>don't like | to boast<br>to sing<br>to work<br>to get up early<br>to stay in bed late<br>to go to the cinema<br>to go round the market<br>to read<br>to solve puzzles<br>to camp out<br>ice cream<br>sweets<br>fruit<br>boasting<br>singing<br>working<br>getting up early<br>staying in bed late<br>going to the cinema<br>going round the market<br>reading<br>solving puzzles<br>camping out |
|---|---|---|

FIGURE 19.3  Substitution table 18 from George (1967).

The typical follow-up to work with a particular table can involve learners using the pattern to make their own sentences that describe their own likes and dislikes – *I like eating chocolate, I like to play computer games* – or those of their classmates. Substitution tables thus take learners beyond the single isolated sentence and into seeing a sentence as a pattern where substitutions can be made to make new sentences. Substitution tables thus illustrate both the syntagmatic and paradigmatic aspects of language knowledge and use.

Many learners expect formal grammar to be a part of their language learning course, and substitution tables provide an opportunity for the discussion of grammatical features to be linked to useful sentences and sentence patterns. George's *Teachers' and Advanced Students' Guide* to his 101 substitution tables provides commentary on each of the tables. The commentary on table 18 (see Figure 19.3), for example, includes a discussion of Simple Present Neutral in regards to feelings, the high frequency of the verb+*to*+stem construction and the lesser frequency of verb+stem+*ing*, and the nominal and verbal aspects of *to*+stem and stem+*ing*. Both the substitution tables and the Guide are available free from H. V. George's web page.

## What are the requirements of substitution tables?

The major requirement is ready-made substitution tables. Simple substitution tables can be quickly made but there are lots of dangers in constructing tables because they may result in some strange unanticipated sentences. Fortunately,

George's (1967) book contains a large number (101) of useful, well-tested tables within a largely controlled vocabulary.

### How much time should be given to substitution tables in a general language course?

Using substitution tables fits into the language-focused learning strand of a course where it competes for time with other activities that deliberately focus on language. Less than one-sixteenth of the total course time should involve substitution tables, and it is probably enough to spend 20 minutes or so on one every one or two weeks.

### How can substitution tables be used well?

To do spoken practice with the substitution table, the teacher writes the table on the board and then gets the learners to repeat some sentences from the table. When the learners are familiar with the idea of a substitution table, the teacher then says a sentence and then points to a word or phrase in one of the columns. The learners then have to say the sentence substituting the word or phrase in the original sentence. The teacher then points to another word in the same column and the learners once again say the sentence making the substitution. The substitution activity can be varied in many ways.

1. The teacher points to a word and then points to an individual learner who repeats the sentence making the substitution. The teacher then points to a different word and to a different learner.
2. The teacher goes through the items in a column in a predictable order. Then the teacher points at items in the same column in an unpredictable order.
3. The teacher speeds up the activity.
4. The teacher rubs out some of the words and phrases in the substitution table but still points to the empty space where they were when getting the learners to repeat. This challenges the learners to remember what was in the spaces.
5. The teacher gets the learners to think of their own substitution which is not in the table.

Substitution tables can also be used for homework by getting the learners to write out some sentences from the table and to add two or three that follow the same pattern but have a substitution provided by the learner.

### How can I check that a substitution table activity is working well?

Substitution tables should involve accurate production, so errors that occur during the use of substitution tables are likely to be a sign of careless use. If learners are able to create some of their own substitutions, then the pattern in the table has been well understood.

### What are the variants of substitution tables?

The most simple substitution table is one where there is a single sentence and there is substitution in only one part of the sentence. This kind of table does not require preparation and is useful when dealing with a particular error that a learner has made.

### Are there digital applications of this technique?

There are no current digital applications based on substitution tables, but there should be. Because substitution tables involve already prepared material, an app could provide a spoken version of the chosen sentences to listen to and then to copy. The technique of the gradually disappearing table is also well suited to an app. This technique involves the table gradually being rubbed off the whiteboard while learners complete the substitutions from memory.

### Revisiting and linking to other activities

The effective use of substitution tables requires coming back to the same tables several times at increasingly spaced intervals in order to reach a high degree of automaticity with the sentences in the tables. Each revisiting can be made interesting and challenging by increasing the speed and by going beyond the table to draw on learners' own life experience, using the pattern in the table.

Substitution tables can be used as remedial work. A learner who makes a mistake in their writing or speaking can be directed to a particular relevant table and then can practice producing correct sentences in their problem area.

### What does research say about the effectiveness of substitution tables?

There is no research directly focusing on the use of substitution tables as a means of learning language. However, the use of substitution tables fits well with Skill Acquisition Theory (DeKeyser, 2015) to explain the learning of language.

> The basic claim of Skill Acquisition Theory is that the learning of a wide variety of skills shows a remarkable similarity in development from initial representation of knowledge through initial changes in behavior to eventual fluent, spontaneous, largely effortless, and highly skilled behaviour, and that this set of phenomena can be accounted for by a set of basic principles common to the acquisition of all skills.
>
> *(p. 94)*

According to Skill Acquisition Theory, learning proceeds through three stages which have been given a variety of names but here we will use declarative (knowing about something), procedural (acting on or using knowledge), and automatic (fluent, spontaneous use). These three stages roughly correspond to presentation, practice, and production, although *production* is not a helpful term when explaining the development of receptive knowledge. Developing automaticity requires a great deal of practice and is related to the power law which maps improvement with cumulative but diminishing returns. The movement through these three stages represents changes in the quality of knowledge and knowledge retrieval. That is, the improvement is not just speeding up but represents changes in the ways knowledge is structured and stored.

If we apply this to substitution tables, then becoming familiar with a particular table and the grammar that lies behind it represents declarative knowledge. In Skill Acquisition Theory, this declarative knowledge is valuable and contributes to later learning. As the learners do some practice with the table, they move to the level of procedural knowledge. As a result of considerable spaced, repeated, further practice including going beyond the table, they can move to the automatic level where the pattern is a part of their fluent use of the language.

Procedural knowledge can be very specific, so receptive knowledge does not transfer readily to productive knowledge, and written knowledge may not transfer readily to spoken knowledge or vice versa. If substitution tables are used to improve speaking, then they should be practised orally. If they are used to improve writing, then they should involve written practice.

DeKeyser (2015) stresses that Skill Acquisition Theory does not explain all aspects of foreign language learning and that it is compatible with several other explanations of how language is learned, such as implicit learning.

> Skill Acquisition Theory ... focuses on how explicit learning (which is often the only realistic possibility for specific learning problems because of time constraints or logistic issues) can, via proceduralization and automatization of explicitly learned knowledge, lead to knowledge that is functionally equivalent to implicit knowledge.
>
> *(p. 106)*

## Research questions

### *Motivation principles (Engagement)*

For learning to occur, there needs to be a willingness to focus on what needs to be learned, and to give it quantity and quality of attention.

1 *Motivation: The degree of engagement with the task affects the likelihood of learning occurring.* Do learners like using substitution tables? Do the suggested variations in the way substitution tables are used maintain interest in using substitution tables? (see the section on using substitution tables well).

2 *Self-efficacy: Our confidence in our own skills of learning affects our success in learning.* How successful are learners in making their own original substitutions in a substitution table?

*Focus principles (Usefulness)*

Learning requires giving attention to what needs to be learned.

3 *Focus: We learn what we focus on, and in addition, our learning is more useful if it closely resembles the use that we need to make of what we learn (transfer-appropriate).* What factors lie behind persistent grammatical error? What deliberate attention helps the learning of grammar? What knowledge is gained from working on substitution tables? What learning from substitution tables transfers outside the activity?
4 *Accuracy: Our learning is more efficient if the information we are focusing on is complete, accurate, and comprehensible.* Do learners make errors when using substitution tables? What are the causes of these errors? Do the substitutions interfere with each other?

*Quantity principles (Amount)*

5 *Repetition: The more repetitions, the stronger the learning.* Does coming back to the same substitution table several times result in substantially more learning from the table? How many re-visitings are optimal for learning?
6 *Time-on-task: The greater and longer the attention, the stronger the learning.* How much time should be spent on a substitution table? Does rubbing out parts of the table result in stronger learning?

*Quality principles (Connections)*

Elaboration and analysis increase and strengthen connections between the item to be learned and other knowledge making it easier to access the item.

7 *Elaboration: This includes enriching the encoding of an item through variation.* Is getting learners to suggest their substitutions an effective part of using a substitution table?
8 *Analysis: This involves relating the familiar parts to the unfamiliar whole.* Do learners infer grammatical rules for using a substitution table? Should the use of a substitution table be accompanied by explicit grammatical analysis and commentary? (see the Teachers' Book for *101 Substitution Tables*).

Any research on substitution tables would be valuable. The most useful research would focus on the effect of substitution tables on grammatical accuracy in speaking.

# 20
# 10-MINUTE WRITING

Instead of using the heading *10-minute writing*, this chapter could be called *Timed writing* because there is nothing special about the time limit of 10 minutes, except that it provides a reasonable length of time for learners write a useful amount under time pressure without the activity being too exhausting. The chapter could also be called *Repeated writing* because for each of the four skills of listening, speaking, reading, and writing, there is proven value in repeating easy tasks so that they become more fluent. However, as is argued below, writing on different easy topics as in 10-minute writing uses a path to fluency that involves getting fluent with the small parts of the writing process, forming the letters that make up words, writing commonly used words, and writing familiar phrases. So, on this chapter we will look at 10-minute writing, with the understanding that repeated easy writing is also a useful addition to a writing fluency development programme.

### What is 10-minute writing?

10-minute writing is a fluency development technique that involves the learners trying to write as much as they can on a very familiar topic within a set time limit. The activity is scored by each learner counting the number of words (tokens) written and entering the result on their graph. Their goal should be to write more words each time.

Because 10-minute writing fits into the fluency development strand of a course, it needs to meet the five criteria for a fluency development activity.

1   10-minute writing involves familiar language and ideas. It is easy.
2   10-minute writing should involve the accurate use of the language.

DOI: 10.4324/9781003496151-25

3 10-minute writing involves pressure to go faster because the number of words written in 10 minutes is recorded on a graph.
4 10-minute writing is meaning-focused. It is not marked for accuracy, and any response that the teacher makes to the piece of writing is related to its content not its language features.
5 10-minute writing involves quantity of practice. The learners write for 10 minutes.

Like most fluency development techniques, 10-minute writing is an experience task where the learners bring a lot of previous knowledge to the task. It is an individual activity where each learner works independently. The weak point in 10-minute writing is the uncertain nature of accuracy. With writing, this factor is not so critical in that there are many aspects of writing such as the formation of the letters of words, the spelling of words and use of set phrases that will get useful practice even if the level of the control of grammar is not that great.

## What are the learning goals of 10-minute writing?

10-minute writing involves becoming fluent in the production of written text. This is a very important skill, especially where assessment is carried out using writing under timed conditions. 10-minute writing also helps in turning receptive knowledge of language items into productive knowledge. Table 20.1 presents the learning goals of 10-minute writing.

The major learning goal of 10-minute writing is developing fluency in writing. Fluency activities also strengthen knowledge of known and partly known words through meeting or using them in varied contexts. This elaboration of knowledge includes turning receptive knowledge into productive use.

## How does 10-minute writing help learning?

There needs to be part of a writing course where the writing is not assessed for accuracy, but there is the opportunity to develop fluency. If attention was

**TABLE 20.1** The goals of 10-minute writing

| Goals | Specific focuses |
|---|---|
| Language | Strengthening and enriching partly known vocabulary and grammar |
|  | Moving receptive knowledge of words phrases and sentences into productive use |
| Ideas |  |
| Skills | *Being able to write with fluency* |
| Text |  |

*Note*: The major goal is in *italics*.

given to accuracy in 10-minute writing, this would result in the slowing down of production and the loss of the fluency goal. In the use of all the four language skills of listening, speaking, reading, and writing, there needs to be a meaning-focused strand pushing the boundaries of knowledge, a strand of deliberate learning through study of the skill and its parts, and a strand for getting really good at using what is well known, the fluency strand. 10-minute writing is a fluency activity for writing. In essence, 10-minute writing helps language learning through quantity of easy practice with the skill of writing.

*Motivation:* Writing involves handwriting and typing, and these two forms of writing are essential, and it is not difficult for learners to see the value of both. It is easy to set staged goals for writing and typing that are easily achievable. When learners are more proficient, the challenge of timed exams can increase the motivation to be able to write quickly.

*Focus:* The focus is on the speedy production of written language to express familiar ideas.

*Quantity:* 10-minute writing is like speed reading in that, initially, the increases in fluency come from becoming fluent with the small parts of the language use process, that is the letters, letter combinations, and words. That is, increases in fluency in reading and writing come from increasing speed of letter recognition in reading or letter formation in writing, and becoming fluent with the use of very high-frequency words, such as the function words like *the*, *of*, and *and*, and content words such as *like*, *answer*, and *child*. Increases in speaking speed on the other hand come initially from the memorization of stretches of language, namely phrases, clauses, and sentences, such as those found in the survival vocabulary. The fluency increases in both cases rely on repetition, but for spoken language, the repetition is initially of large units, while for written language, it is repetition of the smaller units. While these can be seen as two different paths to fluency, they both rely on repetition for fluency development.

*Quality:* There is a change in the size of the unit of processing as fluency in writing develops, as words are treated as whole units and later multiword units are treated as units. The change in the size of the unit is a kind of elaboration as single words are connected with the phrases and sentences they occur in.

## What are the requirements of 10-minute writing?

Fluency development involves making the best use of what is already known. The major issue with fluency development techniques is that they need to provide practice with largely accurate language, otherwise the learners are practising errors. The research on another fluency development technique, 4/3/2, shows that speeded practice does not result in error reduction. The 4/3/2 research also shows that repetition is helpful for fluency development. These two findings suggest that 10-minute writing might have the most favourable results if the writing is prepared for in various ways, and if there is opportunity to do the same piece of writing several times.

### How can you prepare for 10-minute writing?

10-minute writing can be based on topics previously covered in class, and it can be based on writing where the writer has already received feedback. One of the values of 10-minute writing is in preparation for written exams which have a time limit and where some of the questions can be largely predicted. By writing a prepared answer several times, more can be written within the same time period with the chance of getting a better grade because more facts are included. However, 10-minute writing has language learning goals that go beyond this.

### How much time should be given to 10-minute writing in a general language course?

10-minute writing fits into the fluency development strand and writing fluency should make up one-quarter of this strand. If 10-minute writing is seen more broadly as timed or repeated writing, then 10-minute writing should occupy one-sixteenth of the total course time. If there are other writing fluency development activities, then the time for 10-minute writing will be less.

### How can 10-minute writing be done well?

The challenge to write faster should be a clear goal of 10-minute writing. The teacher should look at each learner's writing speed graph, noting whether the speed is going up or not and commenting on it in a supportive way.

10-minute writing could occasionally involve repeated writing, that is, rewriting what was done in the last session of 10-minute writing. It would be a good idea for the learner to look over the previous piece of writing first to consider where improvements could be made.

1. For the first session of 10-minute writing, the teacher needs to explain the rules and goal of 10-minute writing. The rules are simply to write as much as you can in the set time, and don't worry about errors. The best learner is the one who writes the most. The writing is strictly timed so that comparisons of the amount written at different times makes sense.
2. Each learner should have a 10-minute writing graph, with the number of words written on the vertical axis, and the title of the piece of writing on the horizontal axis.
3. The teacher can suggest a topic, or the learners can choose their own topic. Before they begin writing, the learners must have chosen a topic so that part

of the 10 minutes is not wasted searching for a topic. 10-minute writing is likely to be more effective if the topics being written about are truly easy for the learner. Making the writing easier can involve expanding on the same topic on successive pieces of writing. This will reduce the number of different words involved and provide a few more opportunities for repetition of vocabulary.

4 Before doing 10-minute writing on a given topic, learners could talk about the topic in pairs or small groups to stimulate ideas and the relevant words and phrases. The ways of supporting experience tasks described in Chapter 2 are all ways of making the task easier, and possibly reducing errors.

5 When the 10 minutes are up, the teacher says "Stop writing!" and the learners then count the number of words they have written. The safest way to do this is to count 20 words and then make a slash mark / after the 20th word and then count the next 20 and so on. The learners can quickly check their counting by seeing if the distance between the slash marks is roughly the same.

6 The learners then enter the number of words written on their graph.

7 The teacher can read some of the pieces of writing if the learners are willing, but the teacher should make no comments about accuracy but should comment positively on the content, saying things like "That was interesting. Write more about that next time.", or "Next time explain more about that."

8 Because 10-minute writing has not been extensively researched, it is worth the teacher looking at the various pieces of writing by the same learner to see how quickly the quantity of writing increases, whether errors become fewer, and whether the writing involves more complex sentences.

As in 4/3/2 and 3/3/3 (see Chapter 12), we want learners to become fluent in using language accurately. This means that some 10-minute writing activities should involve copying, rewriting, writing with some previous focus on accuracy, and having one or two accuracy goals when doing the writing, such as subject-verb agreement or article usage.

### How can I check that a 10-minute writing activity is working well?

Because 10-minute writing is a fluency development activity, then an increase in the amount written (as shown on the learners' graphs) is a good measure of success. Fluency activities should also involve accuracy of use, so looking over learners' 10-minute writing can indicate if they contain too many errors. The response to too many errors should not be an emphasis on accuracy but should involve preparation for the activity so that the learners are using language that they know well. This preparation can involve a more careful choice of topic, reading before writing, and basing the writing on material already covered in earlier lessons.

## What are the variants of 10-minute writing?

Linked skills activities (see Chapter 21) consist of three activities all focusing on the same topic. Typically, the third activity in the series is likely to be a fluency development activity because the previous two activities have prepared for it. If this third activity is a writing activity, then this could contribute to writing fluency. If one of the preceding activities is also a productive activity, that is, it involves speaking or writing, then this will provide greater support for the third activity contributing to writing fluency.

Repeated writing involves doing the same piece of writing again with the aim of doing it faster and better. Repeated writing activities are most likely to involve verbatim repetition, and verbatim repetition is most likely to help fluency development. A variant of 4/3/2 can be used with 10-minute writing where the learners write the same text three times, perhaps with a time schedule of 10/9/8. The three pieces of writing need not be done on the same day, and the learners could read their previous piece, looking out for any errors, before writing it again.

It is possible to organize writing activities where learners write to each other with different learners playing different roles. Some of these roles could involve writing the same kind of letter several times to different people.

Writing fluency is not limited to handwriting. A very useful part of a language course would be developing skills in typing in the foreign language. Writing would then involve two kinds of fluency development, fluency in typing, and fluency in composing. Each of these two kinds of fluency would strongly affect each other, and early practice in typing fluency should involve copy-typing very easy foreign language texts so that the emphasis could be on typing rather than composing.

### How can 10-minute writing be done at all levels of proficiency?

At elementary levels of proficiency, 10-minute writing can simply involve copying. The technique of delayed copying (Hill, 1969) could be used, but it needs to be checked that this does not slow down. In delayed copying (see Chapter 6 on dictation), the learner looks at a phrase in a text holds it in memory and then looks away and writes it. The goal is to hold as long a phrase as possible. The time allowed for 10-minute writing can be changed to suit the skills of the learners.

For high intermediate and advanced learners, 10-minute writing can become repeated writing as carefully prepared answers to possible exam questions are written and rewritten at speed, with the goal of writing as much as possible in the set time.

### Are there digital applications of this technique?

10-minute writing is well suited to computerization as computers can count the number of words written and put results on a graph. Computers can also measure the accuracy and speed of copying. There are various typing tutor programmes that focus on the speed and accuracy of typing, and these are useful preparation for computer-based 10-minute writing.

### Revisiting and linking to other activities

10-minute writing should be linked to other activities where possible, because this is likely to make the 10-minute writing easier and more accurate. Writing on the same topic again will have strong effects on fluency through repetition. In Chapter 21, we look at the linked skills activity where the same topic is focused on three times, one immediately after the other, but each time using a different one of the four language skills of listening, speaking, reading, and writing. In this sequence of three skills, the third step is typically an opportunity for fluency development because of the support provided by the previous two steps. It is useful to see 10-minute writing as part of a sequence of focusing on the same topic, with the 10-minute writing coming at or near the end of the sequence. So, the first meeting with a particular topic could come through reading. Then, a few days later, the learners talk about what they previously read. Then, a few more days later, it becomes the topic for 10-minute writing.

### What does research say about the effectiveness of 10-minute writing?

Unsurprisingly, Chenoweth and Hayes (2001) found that fluency development in writing increases as proficiency develops. Research on the 10-minute writing technique confirms the findings of research on the 4/3/2 technique, namely that fluency-directed activity brings about improvement in fluency but not usually in accuracy and complexity (Nguyen, 2015). Nguyen's research used 7-minute writing rather than 10-minute writing because her learners struggled to write for 10 minutes. While there were some accuracy and complexity improvements, they were not consistent or striking. As with 4/3/2, some kind of preparation or intervention may be needed to improve accuracy while focusing on fluency.

### Research questions

#### *Motivation principles (Engagement)*

For learning to occur there needs to be a willingness to focus on what needs to be learned, and to give it quantity and quality of attention.

1 *Motivation: The degree of engagement with the task affects the likelihood of learning occurring.* What do learners think about 10-minute writing? Do they value it?
2 *Self-efficacy: Our confidence in our own skills of learning affects our success in learning.* Do some learners find the time pressure of 10-minute writing upsetting? Are learners willing to do 10-minute writing without being concerned about errors?

*Focus principles (Usefulness)*

Learning requires giving attention to what needs to be learned.

3 *Focus: We learn what we focus on, and in addition, our learning is more useful if it closely resembles the use that we need to make of what we learn (transfer-appropriate).* What range of increases in speed occur as a result of 10-minute writing? Does speed continue to increase throughout a course? Do accuracy and complexity increase throughout a course? Do increases in speed during 10-minute writing transfer to other kinds of writing?
4 *Accuracy: Our learning is more efficient if the information we are focusing on is complete, accurate, and comprehensible.* Do accuracy interventions, such as trying to avoid one particular kind of error, slow down fluency development? What kinds of accuracy interventions have positive effects on accuracy? Do these interventions affect fluency?

Does narrow 10-minute writing where learners stick to one topic area result in fewer errors and greater fluency than varied 10-minute writing?

*Quantity principles (Amount)*

5 *Repetition: The more repetitions, the stronger the learning.* Does repeated writing result in faster fluency development than 10-minute writing?
6 *Time-on-task: The greater and longer the attention, the stronger the learning.* Is 10 minutes per session a suitable time for developing writing fluency? Should a time limit be based on likely quantity of writing done?

*Quality principles (Connections)*

Elaboration and analysis increase and strengthen connections between the item to be learned and other knowledge making it easier to access the item.

7 *Elaboration: This includes enriching the encoding of an item through variation.* Does 10-minute writing involve recall of multiword units?

8 *Analysis:* This involves relating the familiar parts to the unfamiliar whole. Do learners self-correct during 10-minute writing?

Research on fluency development in other skills will suggest useful questions to answer when researching 10-minute writing.

Any research on 10-minute writing would be useful. The most useful research would focus on the effects of 10-minute writing on fluency in writing with a consideration for writing accuracy.

# PART 5
# General purpose

# 21
# LINKED SKILLS ACTIVITIES

Linked skills activities are really three techniques joined together using the same material. They typically involve a mixture of individual work, group work, and whole class work.

## What are linked skills activities?

In a linked skills activity, the learners work on the same material through three successive skills. For example, (1) they read the material, (2) then they listen to it, and (3) then they write about it. There are many such combinations. The last activity in each series becomes a fluency development activity because of the previous practice in the other two skills.

Linked skills activities fit into the three meaning-focused strands of meaning-focused input, meaning-focused output, and fluency development. The third part of the activity is usually a fluency development activity because of the support provided by the previous two parts. Some parts may involve group work, and the later two parts are highly likely to be experience tasks because of the preceding part(s).

Linked skills activities have many benefits, and these benefits are typical of those where a single topic or subject is focused on for a considerable period of time, as in content-based learning. One of the major benefits for a teacher is that they generally require very little work to prepare and organize, but they get a lot of work from the learners. They can also provide very useful conditions for language and content learning. Let us look first at how linked skills activities can be made, and how to judge whether a linked skills activity has been well made or not.

## What are the learning goals of linked skill activities?

Linked skills activities present opportunities for many different kinds of learning across the four skills of listening, speaking, reading, and writing. However, it is possible to prioritize the learning goals and Table 21.1 tries to do that.

The major learning goal of linked skills activities is developing fluency in language use across the four skills of listening, speaking, reading, and writing. However, the language learning goals of strengthening and enriching partly known language features and learning some new language features are also very important learning goals for linked skills activities, and we will look at ways of monitoring the activities to see that this learning is likely to occur.

## How do linked skill activities help learning?

Linked skills activities are rich in opportunities for learning. This is because the material is treated quite differently through the use of at least three different language skills. Varied repetition is a major learning factor in such activities. In essence, linked skills activities help language learning through quantity and quality of message-focused language use. Both quantity and quality of attention come from the three steps involved. Most of the learning will be incidental learning, but there is opportunity for deliberate learning through interaction, guessing from context, and feedback.

*Motivation:* Linked skills activities typically engage the learners because there is a strong focus on an interesting topic area and the work is clearly manageable because of the knowledge built up during the sequence of activities.

*Focus:* Linked skills activities focus on the message and so most learning will be incidental learning. Linked skills activities do not involve language-focused learning, but a variant of linked skills activities would involve a deliberate learning step as one of the three parts to the procedure.

**TABLE 21.1** The goals of linked skills activities

| Goals | Specific focuses |
|---|---|
| Language | Strengthening and enriching partly known vocabulary and grammar |
| | Moving receptive knowledge of words phrases and sentences into productive use |
| | Meeting and using a small amount of unfamiliar topic-related vocabulary and multiword units |
| Ideas | |
| Skills | *Developing fluency in language use across the four skills* |
| Text | |

*Note:* The major goal is in *italics*.

*Quantity:* Linked skills activities involve repetition, spaced retrieval, varied meetings, and varied use. In a well-designed linked skills activity, the same topic-related vocabulary will occur in all three steps.

*Quality:* Linked skills activities involve both receptive and productive use and use across at least three different language skills.

## What are the requirements of linked skills activities?

### How can you prepare for linked skills activities?

Linked skills activities involve finding a good topic and usually a good text to base the activity on. The teacher then needs to work out the three steps and carefully consider the sequence of the steps, so that the final step covers the learning goal of the activity. These points are all considered in following sections of this chapter.

### How much time should be given to linked skills activities in a general language course?

Linked skills activities include the three strands of meaning-focused input, meaning-focused output, and fluency development. Because they set up such useful conditions for learning, particularly through varied repetition, it is worthwhile scheduling them as regular activities, perhaps occurring once every two weeks. Because of their necessarily complex nature, each covering three or four skills and three strands, it is difficult to give a particular proportion of course time. However, they could make up around an eighth of the total fluency development time and about an eighth of meaning-focused input and meaning-focused output time, making a total proportion of less than one-eighth (one-eighth of three-quarters) of total course time.

## How can linked skills activities be designed and done well?

Let us take a typical piece of material which may be used when making linked skills activities – a reading passage with accompanying questions. The examples are based on a text on food handling safety to avoid food poisoning.

The activities are described in Table 21.2, which should be read horizontally. It contains five sets of linked skills activities. Each row is one linked skills series of three activities. The item on the left is the first activity in the series, which is then followed by the one in the middle, and then by the one on the right. Theoretically, there are 24 possible linked skills sequences (four choices from listening, speaking, reading, and writing for the first activity, a choice from three

**TABLE 21.2** Five sets of linked skills activities

| | First activity | Second activity | Third activity |
|---|---|---|---|
| 1 | Read the questions without seeing the text and try to guess the answers (Read) | Listen to the text and check and correct your answers (Listen) | Talk about the differences between your guesses and the right answers (Speak) |
| 2 | Read the text (Read) | Listen to the questions and write answers to them (Listen/Write) | Write guidelines for storing food safely (Write) |
| 3 | Write guidelines for storing food safely using your own experience and background knowledge (Write) | Talk about your guidelines with another learner (Speak) | Read the text and answer the questions (Read) |
| 4 | Listen to the text being read to you by the teacher taking notes if you wish (Listen) | Write what you can remember about the text (Write) | Do a 4/3/2 activity on the content of the passage (Speak) |
| 5 | Talk to a partner about what you know about good food storage procedures (Speak) | Read the text and answer the questions (Read) | Either prepare and deliver a talk to your partner about (1) good food storage procedures OR (2) the danger of not handling food carefully (Speak) |

for the second activity, and a choice for two for the third activity) if no skills are repeated in the series. Note, however, that there can also be a lot of variety in the nature of actual activity. That is, there are many kinds of speaking activities for example, so 24 is clearly an underestimate.

So, in the first linked skills series, learners read the questions by themselves and try to choose the correct multiple-choice answers. Then they hear the text being read to them by the teacher while they look at the questions and their answers, correcting them when necessary. In the third step, they talk to a partner about their guesses and the correct answers and report orally to the whole class on the most difficult questions. The last activity in the series is a fluency activity because the previous work has made this final activity easy.

Note in the fifth linked skills series that the sequence is Speak-Read-Speak. In the last step the learners work in pairs, one learner delivering talk 1 about food storage and the other learner giving talk 2 about dangers. Linked skills activities need not use three different skills but can repeat a skill aiming for a higher performance in the second use of the same skill.

Note that it is possible to mix and match some of the individual activities in Table 21.2 to make a new series.

How can we judge which series of activities is likely to be the most effective? We will look at this from the perspective of vocabulary learning, and also from the perspective of the relative difficulty of the activities in the series.

1. Ideally, all three activities in the series should draw very strongly on the same piece of content material. This will ensure that the activities become easier as learners proceed through the series and that the same vocabulary and grammatical structures are repeated during the series.
2. Essentially, the three activities should make use of the same language items, particularly vocabulary and multiword units. The recurrence of the vocabulary will help learning through the opportunity for repeated retrieval and hopefully creative use of the vocabulary.
3. The first activity in the series should be reasonably easy for the learners to do. The following activity will be helped by the one(s) before it.
4. Typically, the last activity in a series of three is highly likely to be a fluency development activity, because at this point the material that learners are working with is very easy because they have now worked with it at least two times. That is, they should be well in control of the content of the material and of the language used to express this content. The challenge to them is to use this now familiar content and language through a skill (listening, speaking, reading, or writing) which has previously been unpractised with this material. If the teacher does have a fluency goal for this final activity in the series of three, or wants the activity to be done particularly well, the teacher should look at the final activity to see if it is a receptive skill (listening or reading) or a productive skill (speaking or writing). If it is a productive skill, then it is probably important that one of the two preceding activities in the series also involves productive use of the language. So if the final activity is a writing activity, it may be useful to make sure that one of the two preceding activities is a speaking activity, or vice versa. This is because productive skills (speaking and writing) are usually much more challenging than receptive skills, particularly from a vocabulary perspective. Having practised the material with a productive skill once makes it much easier to use it again productively in the next or later activity in the series. Thus, in Table 21.2, the fifth linked skills series beginning with speaking is likely to be very effective in preparing for the final activity in the series. Similarly, series 4, where the productive skill of writing is followed by the productive skill of speaking, is likely to enable better performance of the speaking activity than if both of the preceding activities had been receptive activities.

## How can I check that a linked skills activity is working well?

The following things are worth looking for when linked skills activities are being used.

1. Is exactly the same topic being focused on in each of the three steps of the linked skills activity?
2. Are the learners coping well with the activities, especially in the last two steps of the series?
3. Do the same language items keep recurring in each of the three activities?
4. Are the learners retrieving the target vocabulary in activities 2 and 3 in the series rather than repeating them from the input sheet?
5. Do activities 2 and 3 involve creative use of the vocabulary from activity 1?
6. Are the learners handling the content of the activity more confidently in the later steps?
7. Are the learners interacting well with each other in some steps of the activity? Are they explaining the meanings of words to each other? Are they clarifying ideas clearly to each other?
8. Do the learners seem to enjoy doing the activity?

The activities which are the last two steps in a linked skill series are highly likely to be experience tasks. That is, they are activities where learners bring a lot of background knowledge to the activity. The early steps of the series of linked skills activities can create and strengthen this knowledge. Because of this, typically the last activities in a linked skill series are likely to have many of the features of a fluency development task. That is, the task is very easy to do and learners can do it at a faster than usual speed. For this reason, it is important that it is not just used as a throwaway activity (for example, for homework write …), but is given the time and attention that it deserves.

### Further examples

Here is a more detailed example of a linked skills activity. (1) The teacher writes a topic on the blackboard, for example, *Washing your hands*. The learners then form small groups of three or four people to share what they know about this topic and to predict three ideas that the following reading text might contain. (2) After a few minutes of this, the teacher then hands out the reading text which discusses research on the way in which people can best wash their hands. The learners read the text quietly or do paired reading where two learners sit together to read a single copy of the text, and after each paragraph they check that they have understood what they have read and clarify any problems.

(3) Then the learners have to write a set of instructions that will go above wash basins in the school, advising people on the most effective way of washing their hands. This is a linked skills activity because the same topic *Washing your hands* is focused on across the three different skills of speaking, reading, and writing.

It is usually easy to design such linked skills activities around a reading text. Note that the reading text could be involved in the first activity, the second activity, or the third activity in the series. Here is another linked skills activity based around the same topic. (1) The teacher gives the learners a list of actions that can be involved in washing your hands.

Wet your hands thoroughly
Use plenty of soap
Dry your hands carefully
Rub your hands together
Let a lot of water run over your hands
Shake your hands thoroughly before drying them
Put soap on your hands, wash them, put soap on them again and wash them again

The learners work individually and read the list carefully, putting the actions in order from the most important for cleanliness to the least important. (2) The learners then form small groups and compare their ranking with the others in the group. The group decides on a common ranking. (3) The learners then get the reading text and see if their ranking agrees with the ideas presented in the text.

Table 21.3 contains several more examples of linked skills activities. As you can see, such activities are very easy to design especially if there is a reading passage to use as a part of the activity. Such activities require very little work from the teacher but provide a good range of meaning-focused input and meaning-focused output for the learners. When reading Table 21.3, look across each row for the three steps in the activity.

A good linked skills activity keeps attention focused on the same ideas and language through the three steps, begins with a manageable activity, and has a productive step at steps 1 or 2 if step 3 is a productive activity.

Linked skills activities are largely meaning-focused input and meaning-focused output activities, although the last activity in a well-planned series is likely to be a fluency development activity. There is also good reason for language-focused learning to be one of the activities in a linked skills activity.

**TABLE 21.3** Examples of four linked skills activities

| Step one | Step two | Step three |
|---|---|---|
| Read the text and list the three most important ideas. | Form groups of four learners and compare your ideas and reach an agreement on the three most important ideas. | Write a summary of the text including the three most important ideas. |
| The teacher writes a topic on the board and each learner thinks of one idea they know about that topic and writes it down. | Each learner then tells their idea to the teacher who writes the ideas on the board, organizing them under headings where possible. | The learners then read a text on the same topic noting any ideas that were not on the board. |
| The learners listen to a talk. They can then ask questions about it to get a good understanding. | The learners then read a text on the same topic. | They write what they think are the three most important ideas in the text. |
| The teacher prepares ten comprehension questions on a text. On the board the teacher writes the numbers from 1 to 10 and next to each number writes one or two keywords from the question or answer. Working by themselves, the learners read the text and using the keywords try to predict what the questions and their answers will be. | The learners then form pairs to compare what their predictions of the questions and answers are and to improve their predictions. | The teacher then asks learners for their predictions, tells them the question, and asks the learners for the answer. This is an amusing activity especially if one or two of the keywords are actually the answers to the teacher's questions. |

## What are the variants of linked skills activities?

There are other activities which share some of the features of linked skills and that set up similar learning conditions. These include:

Quantity of input activities like extensive reading and content-based instruction.
Repetition activities like repeated reading and Say it!
Procedures such as the pyramid procedure.
Focused activities like narrow reading, narrow listening, and narrow writing.

The description of linked skills activities in this chapter has not included a language-focused learning step in the sequence of activities. This is because in most courses, there is already too much time given to language-focused learning and not enough to message-focused communicative activity. However, because the major goal of linked skills activities is fluency development, it is worth considering making one of the two early steps in the sequence have a language-focused learning focus. An alternative would be to have four steps instead of three with one of the early ones language-focused learning. The aim of the language-focused learning step would be to ensure a good level of accuracy and perhaps grammatical and lexical complexity in the final step of the sequence. This language-focused learning step could involve dictation of a text, peer feedback perhaps using the pyramid procedure, digital checking of written text, class-based interaction with the teacher, or listening critically to a recording of a previous step.

### *How can linked skills activities be done at all levels of proficiency?*

The experience approach to learning to read is a kind of linked skills activity. In this approach, the learner draws a picture, then tells the teacher about the picture while the teacher writes exactly what the learner says under the picture. The learner then reads the written text while showing the picture to others including their parents. While this activity intentionally involves verbatim repetition, it is not difficult to make adjustments that bring in varied repetition. These adjustments could include retelling without notes or a script, allowing listeners to question the speaker, and adding role play.

For advanced learners, linked skills activities can involve working from several sources rather than a single source, that is several different texts or a mixture of spoken and written texts.

### *How can linked skills activities be used for self-directed learning?*

In several ways, linked skills activities are like project work or theme-based learning, where the same topic is dealt with in a variety of ways. The advantage of such work is that the vocabulary load of sticking with the same topic is substantially reduced compared to covering two or three unrelated topics (Sutarsyah, Nation & Kennedy, 1994). The other major advantage is the build-up of background knowledge which makes it possible to give less attention to content and more attention to accuracy. With some careful thought, it is possible to design linked skills activities that suit self-directed learning, for example, (1) reading a text quietly and carefully, (2) reading it aloud and recording it to listen to critically, and re-recording it aiming at the best recording, and (3) writing a written summary of the text, or giving a brief spoken summary of the text online to a fellow learner or native speaker.

### Are there digital applications of this technique?

It would be great have a web site that has copyright-free reading passages accompanied by ready-to-use suggestions for linked skills activities.

There are some web sites that have material that is well suited to the development of linked skills activities. The *our world in data* web site is particularly useful.

### Revisiting and linking with other activities

Linked skills activities already involve repetition, but there is clearly an advantage in basing a linked skills activity on a text or topic already covered in the course, and coming back to the same linked skills topic several weeks later.

### What does research say about linked skills activities?

Three step linked skills activities are largely unresearched.

Ellis (2018), distinguishes three different kinds of rehearsal:

1 procedural repetition, where the same procedure is used with different content,
2 content repetition, where a different procedure is used with the same content,
3 task repetition, where the same task is repeated with the same procedure and content.

Content repetition comes closest to what is involved in linked skills, but the differences in procedure in linked skills is probably much greater than what was envisioned as a different procedure.

Two step linked skills activities are reasonably common, where, for example, learners write a summary of what they have just read, or give an oral report on their reading, or do group brainstorming about a topic before reading about it.

### Research questions

#### *Motivation principles (Engagement)*

For learning to occur, there needs to be a willingness to focus on what needs to be learned, and to give it quantity and quality of attention.

1 *Motivation: The degree of engagement with the task affects the likelihood of learning occurring.* Do learners enjoy doing linked skills tasks? How many steps in a linked skills task can learners tolerate?
2 *Self-efficacy: Our confidence in our own skills of learning affects our success in learning.* Do learners see linked skills tasks as easy to do? Do learners feel more confident about their likely success in a linked skills task as they progress through the steps?

*Focus principles (Usefulness)*

Learning requires giving attention to what needs to be learned.

3 *Focus: We learn what we focus on, and in addition, our learning is more useful if it closely resembles the use that we need to make of what we learn (transfer-appropriate).* What are the benefits of linked skills activities? Do all the three skills used in a linked skills task result in learning? Do the second and third steps in a linked skills activity show a higher level of performance than there would be without the previous step(s)? Is the learning from the third step greater than the learning from the previous steps? Does the strong focus on content have negative effects on language learning? Does including a language-focused learning step result in better performance in the final step and more transfer outside the task?
4 *Accuracy: Our learning is more efficient if the information we are focusing on is complete, accurate, and comprehensible.* Is there evidence of self-correction and peer correction during linked skills tasks?

*Quantity principles (Amount)*

5 *Repetition: The more repetitions, the stronger the learning.* What amount of repetition occurs across the three steps of a linked skills activity? How can this repetition be maximized? Is the repetition in linked skills activities directly related to the learning that occurs? What are the advantages and disadvantages of doing the three parts of a linked skills activity immediately one after the other compared with spacing each of the three parts by a day or more?
6 *Time-on-task: The greater and longer the attention, the stronger the learning.* Is the amount of attention given to a language feature in the second or third step less than the attention given if there were no previous steps?

*Quality principles (Connections)*

Elaboration and analysis increase and strengthen connections between the item to be learned and other knowledge making it easier to access the item.

7 *Elaboration: This includes enriching the encoding of an item through variation.* Do the different steps in a linked skills task result in varied use of vocabulary? To what extent does the use of a different skill result in varied use compared with the effect of different sub-task?
8 *Analysis: This involves relating the familiar parts to the unfamiliar whole.* Do several members of the same word family occur among the target vocabulary

in linked skills activities? Do learners see the connection between the word family members? Are there many analysable multiword units among the target vocabulary of the linked skills activity? Are learners able to analyse their multiword units?

Any research on linked skills activities would be welcome. Complex techniques such as prepared talks, linked skills, and project work are likely to provide a wide variety of opportunities for learning. Detailed case studies of such activities could show if factors such as deliberate attention, repetition, varied use, and self and peer correction occur often enough to have positive effects on learning. Such case studies would also be likely to provide useful guidelines for the effective design of such activities. This kind of research could then lead on to more controlled studies of learning from such activities. The case studies should come first so that research on the effects of such activities involves well-designed activities that are most likely to support learning.

# 22
# PROJECTS

### What are projects?

Projects are extended pieces of work on a single topic, drawing on data-gathering and research from a variety of sources, and resulting in a substantial written report and an oral report. They are also called project work (Fried-Booth, 1982) and issue logs (Watson, 2004). They can be done as group work with each group producing a written and spoken report, or they can be done as individual work. In this chapter, we look at projects as individual work. Projects very quickly become experience tasks as learners gain more knowledge about the subject area they have chosen to research. Project work is well suited to multimedia presentations, but it is important to make sure that they involve lots of language use. All four strands are involved in projects, with the major focus being on meaning-focused output. Projects have many similarities with linked skills activities (Chapter 21), the major differences being that project work extends over several weeks and has more substantial input and outcomes.

### What are the learning goals of projects?

Projects involve a mixture of incidental learning and deliberate learning, but largely involve incidental learning through varied meetings and use (Table 22.1).

The major language learning goal of projects is becoming more proficient in language use through focusing on a single topic for a substantial period of time.

For learners at most levels, projects help develop study and research skills. These skills include gathering and integrating data from various sources, evaluating the quality of data, avoiding plagiarism by acknowledging sources and

TABLE 22.1 The goals of projects

| Goals | Specific focuses |
| --- | --- |
| Language | Learning new topic-related language items through varied meetings and varied use |
|  | Strengthening knowledge of partly known language items |
| Ideas | Developing research skills including using multiple sources and avoiding plagiarism |
| Skills | *Developing proficiency in the four skills of listening, speaking, reading, and writing* |
| Text | Learning how to research and structure oral and written presentations |

*Note:* The major goal is in *italics*.

signalling direct quotation, making oral presentations, and writing a formal assignment for assessment.

## How do projects help learning?

Projects involve purposeful language use. The topic of each project should be chosen by the learner because it interests them and relates to their future use of the language. Although the outcomes of the project are an oral report and a written report, there should be several intermediate steps along the way that provide opportunities for deliberate learning, feedback, and reflection. In essence, projects help language learning through quantity and quality of message-focused language use. Both quantity and quality of attention come from the various steps involved in project work (gathering data, sharing data, presenting data in spoken and written forms, getting feedback). Most of the learning will be incidental learning but there is opportunity for deliberate learning through dictionary look-up, guessing from context, and feedback.

*Motivation:* The choice of an interesting and relevant topic will help engagement in projects. When work on a project begins, it seems like a very challenging task, but the narrow focus soon makes the work seem more achievable.

*Focus:* Language learning during a project is largely incidental because the learners' focus is on information. The demands of oral and written presentation, however, direct the learners' deliberate attention to accuracy in output.

*Quantity:* The narrow focus of project work means that the reading involved is narrow reading, and the other skills of listening, speaking, and writing are similarly narrow. The same content material is dealt with across the four skills providing plenty of repetition. The written assessment requirement and the public oral presentation encourage repeated practice and attention to feedback.

*Quality:* Quality of attention to language features is enriched by meeting and using the same language items across the four skills, and by the varied linguistic contexts of these meetings and uses.

## What are the requirements of projects?

### How can you prepare for projects?

The various steps in a project provide an opportunity for the teacher to supply small pieces of useful input about the nature of research questions, how to gather data, the importance of keeping a record of the sources of the data, how to avoid plagiarism, how to make a list of references, how to format an assignment, how to give feedback on others' work, and the criteria for the assessment of the written assignment. Where possible, this information should also be available in a clear written form for learners to refer to when they need it.

### What topics can be used for projects?

The choice of topic should be guided by learner interest and relevance to later use of the language. Each learner in the class should be working on a different topic. Some assignments could be in the same topic area but should involve different research questions.

Projects should involve research questions and not just be topics, such as *pollution, global warming,* or *electric cars* which do not require a particular question to be answered. Having a research question forces learners to collect and examine their data from a particular viewpoint, and thus process it more deeply and thoughtfully. Having a research question and understanding what a research question does prepares learners for future research. Most research questions are likely to be reviews of data, but if appropriate, they could involve small-scale experiments, surveys, or corpus-based work. Here are some examples of research questions which can be used as models for the learners to use when writing their own research question.

How much of global warming is the result of human activity and how much is natural?
Do electric cars reduce pollution?
Do farmers get paid a fair price for their produce?
Do learners need teachers?
Is crime increasing?
Are mobile phones good for you?
Is it worth owning your own house or apartment?
Why do many young people not vote?

Is distance learning as good as learning in a classroom?
What has been the most effective change in reducing road deaths?

### How much time should be given to projects in a general language course?

Projects fit into all four strands, and the time spent on them contributes to extensive listening, prepared talks, extensive reading, and writing with feedback. Similarly, they contribute to fluency in each of the four skills. Much of the work involved in projects could be out-of-class work, but such work is counted when looking at a balance across the four strands. During a school term or semester, it would be reasonable for project work to occupy a couple of hours per week for the whole semester.

### How can projects be done well?

The worst kind of project work is where some of the learners do most of their work on the project in the week before the written report is due. The solution to deal with this is to break the project into four or five clearly defined steps, with each step involving monitoring by the teacher and other learners.

1. The learners each decide on a topic that they are going to research. Each learner should write a short paragraph describing their topic and the reasons for choosing that topic. Ideally, the paragraph should contain a research question. These paragraphs can be discussed in small support groups of three or four people, with each learner providing helpful suggestions for the topic coverage and sources of data.
2. The learners begin gathering information on their topic, taking notes, and building up a list of properly formatted references. The format of the references is checked against models provided by the teacher.
3. Every two weeks or so, the support groups meet, and each learner reports to the others in the small group on their progress. Each group gives a brief written progress report to the teacher after each meeting.
4. Each learner writes the first draft of a formal assignment using the conventions of assignment writing, including headings and sub-headings, a research question, a list of references, and a well-signalled organization of the information. Each person's assignment is reviewed by one other person in the support group using a checklist supplied by the teacher (see below).
5. The oral presentation is a prepared talk (Chapter 10). It should be practised several times before it is presented to the class or a large section of the class. The oral presentation should be quite short (around ten minutes) and should not involve reading the assignment aloud. It should be a quite different kind

of presentation from the assignment, with a small number of main points, informal language, plenty of examples, a handout or a PowerPoint display, and the opportunity for the listeners to ask questions.
6 The written assignment is submitted to the teacher after a web-based check and a check by one other learner in the group. The teacher provides feedback on both language and content. The teacher also provides a grade.

Projects focus on content, but there needs to be some focus on the language as well. At the various steps, there is opportunity for peer feedback and teacher feedback on language accuracy and complexity. The learners should also be encouraged to put unfamiliar words and multiword units on to word cards for deliberate learning.

*A possible checklist for commenting on another learner's written draft at step 4*

---
Are there spelling, vocabulary, and grammatical errors?
Are there enough headings and are the headings helpful and relevant?
Is the assignment easy to understand?
Does the assignment answer the research question?
Has the writer used a wide range of sources?
Is the format of the reference list correct?

---

The learner using the checklist should also indicate particular points that may need changing.

*How can I check that project work is working well?*

The following questions can guide teacher observation of learner activity during project work.

Are the learners using the L2 in their peer discussions and feedback?
Are learners reading each other's drafts carefully and seeking clarification and giving helpful feedback?
Is group monitoring of data gathering effective in that it encourages learners to keep working on the project?
Are there too many steps or not enough steps?
Is there a lot of useful repetition of the relevant language for the activity?
Are there signs of new language learning during the project?
Are the learners excited about their project?

## What are the variants of projects?

Mini-projects with many of the components of larger projects can be used as a way to introduce learners to project work or where there is not a lot of time available for project work. Such mini-projects may be completed within a week or two.

*How can projects be used at all levels of proficiency?* The steps for projects described above are for learners at upper-secondary school, or in pre-university classes. However, even lower-proficiency learners can do a kind of project work that involves multiple sources and different kinds of presentation. With young learners, instead of research questions, the topics can be more descriptive. The data gathering can involve drawing and labelling pictures, copying pieces of text, reading non-fiction graded readers, and ask and answer sessions where learners answer prepared questions about their topic.

## Are there digital applications of this technique?

The internet is a useful source of information for projects. Unfortunately, the internet provides opportunities for plagiarism and the use of artificial intelligence to write assignments. The steps suggested for projects attempt to provide step-by-step monitoring, but basically it will be the attitudes of the learners which determine how much original work goes into the assignments and how much the learners benefit from project work. This should be made clear to the learners and their co-operation needs to be sought to make sure that project work is done properly. It is worth reflecting on the factors that bring about change (Macalister & Nation, 2020, Chapter 12) and how these can be used to encourage learners to take projects seriously. Put simply, successfully encouraging change involves using rules, reason, and involvement. Rules are included in the steps for projects and involve checking by peers, checking by the teacher, and assessment. Reason involves making the learners aware of the learning goals of projects and how the activity and the various steps help language learning and the development of study skills. Involvement includes giving the learners a real say in what is done and how it should be carried out, so that they take responsibility for the project work and feel that it belongs to them. These three ways of rules, reason, and involvement help each other, but ideally involvement should be the most effective way of making sure that learners use internet resources in a responsible way. Kato, Spring, and Mori (2023) describe project-work to make a homepage as a part of computer-mediated distance learning.

## Revisiting and linking to other activities

Projects already involve a lot of different skills and repetition of content. Nonetheless, it would be useful for fluency development to follow-up a project with a 4/3/2 activity several weeks later, or with a written fluency development activity such as ten-minute writing, in order to maximize the fluency benefits of project work.

## What does research say about the effectiveness of projects?

Projects are a kind of content-based instruction (also called learning through the curriculum, or content and language integrated learning), where the focus is on the subject matter (the content) and most of the language learning is incidental. However, the four strands apply to content-based instruction in the same way that they apply to other types of language courses. That is, as well as a content-based focus there also needs to be a language-focused learning focus where some deliberate attention is given to language learning (Langman, 2003).

There is a journal called the *Journal of Immersion and Content-based Language Education* which publishes research and theory on content-based instruction.

## Research questions

### Motivation principles (Engagement)

For learning to occur, there needs to be a willingness to focus on what needs to be learned, and to give it quantity and quality of attention.

1 *Motivation: The degree of engagement with the task affects the likelihood of learning occurring.* Do projects become self-motivating? That is, do learners quickly become increasingly interested in a project? What factors affect this interest? Do projects affect motivation to use the language? Are learners proud of their completed projects?
2 *Self-efficacy: Our confidence in our own skills of learning affects our success in learning.* Do projects need to be planned to suit individual learner capabilities or do learners find their own suitable level of work?

### Focus principles (Usefulness)

Learning requires giving attention to what needs to be learned.

3 *Focus: We learn what we focus on, and in addition, our learning is more useful if it closely resembles the use that we need to make of what we learn (transfer-appropriate).* Does project work involve a useful combination of a focus on communication and a focus on language features? What kinds of language focus occur during project work?

4 *Accuracy: Our learning is more efficient if the information we are focusing on is complete, accurate, and comprehensible.* Does project work encourage unwanted verbatim copying of material? How can this be avoided? Is the framing of an original research question an effective way of reducing copying?

### Quantity principles (Amount)

5 *Repetition: The more repetitions, the stronger the learning.* Is there substantial repetition of topic-based vocabulary and multiword units during a project? Does this affect learning of these items?
6 *Time-on-task: The greater and longer the attention, the stronger the learning.* Are projects best done as individual activities or should they involve substantial amounts of pair or group work?

### Quality principles (Connections)

Elaboration and analysis increase and strengthen connections between the item to be learned and other knowledge making it easier to access the item.

7 *Elaboration: This includes enriching the encoding of an item through variation.* Does having the outcomes of a spoken presentation and a written assignment result in varied use of target vocabulary? Does project work result in strong and substantial knowledge of academic and technical vocabulary?
8 *Analysis: This involves relating the familiar parts to the unfamiliar whole.* Is the target vocabulary met and used in varied forms (various family members) during project work? Does project work increase knowledge of word parts?

As has been noted above, projects are a small version of content-based instruction. There needs to be a careful review of the research and theory of content-based instruction in its various forms that focuses on the guidelines that it provides for the more limited technique of project work. See the end of Chapter 21 on linked skills for further research on projects.

# 23
# VOCABULARY FLASH CARDS

The most effective way to quickly learn a lot of vocabulary is to put the most useful words on to small cards or into a flash card programme along with their first language translations and to study them for short periods of time spread over several weeks. This technique fits into the language-focused learning strand and involves independent learning. It is a guided technique because it explicitly provides everything that needs to be learned. Only the learning needs to be done. Using flash cards can be classified as a vocabulary learning strategy, and it can incorporate two other strategies, the word part strategy and the keyword technique.

Flash card learning is often criticized, largely because it is decontextualized learning which does not involve communication. It is also suggested that it does not work, resulting in poor learning and quick forgetting. These criticisms are not supported by research findings, largely because over 120 years of research on paired associate learning and word card learning has repeatedly shown that it is efficient, effective, long-lasting, and results in the kind of knowledge needed for normal language use. For a survey of this research, see Nation (2022, Chapter 11).

Vocabulary learning can occur across the four strands of meaning-focused input, meaning-focused output, language-focused learning, and fluency development. Flash card learning is part of the language-focused learning strand and is simply one of a complementary range of ways in which vocabulary can be learned. Any course which excludes flash card learning is limiting the ways of learning and will not be as effective as a course that includes it.

DOI: 10.4324/9781003496151-29

### What is the flash card strategy?

The flash card strategy involves putting useful words or multiword units and their translations in the first language into a flash card app or onto hard copy word cards. On hard copy cards, the word is written on one side and its translation on the other side. The learner then goes through the cards looking at the word form and trying to recall its translation. The learner goes through cards at various times several hours, days, or weeks apart until the translations are easily recalled. Once the vocabulary has been learned receptively in this way, the cards should be turned over for productive learning, with the learner looking at the first language translation and trying to recall the word form. The flash card strategy involves rote learning.

### What is the learning goal of the flash card strategy?

The flash card strategy has a single simple goal (as Table 23.1 shows), quickly learning the word forms and meanings of a large number of words and multiword units. The justifications for this strategy are that it is highly effective and highly efficient and results in both explicit and implicit knowledge. Implicit knowledge is the kind of subconscious knowledge needed for normal language use.

### How does the flash card strategy help vocabulary learning?

In essence, flash cards help vocabulary learning because they provide a large quantity of accurate attention (deliberate, spaced repetition) to transferable vocabulary knowledge. The weakness of flash cards is that there is low quality of attention in that the repeated meetings are not varied. However, it is possible to add analysis of word parts and use of the keyword technique to increase the quality of attention.

*Motivation:* The main motivator of the flash card strategy is its success. Wilkinson (2020) found that getting peers to test each other on their word cards was a good motivator, but that several learners lacked the motivation to learn from word cards. Such learning probably needs to be started as an in-class activity.

TABLE 23.1 The goal of the flash card strategy

| Goals | Specific focuses |
| --- | --- |
| Language<br>Ideas<br>Skills<br>Text | *Deliberately learning vocabulary and multiword units* |

*Note:* The major goal is in *italics*.

*Focus:* The focus is on the accurate deliberate learning of large amounts of decontextualized vocabulary, namely learning the written and spoken forms of the word and connecting it with its first language translation.

*Quantity:* The essence of flash card learning is repetition and spaced retrieval. That is, the cards should be used often in relatively short sessions rather than in one or two long study sessions. The word should be on one side of a card and the meaning on the other so that there is the opportunity to recall (retrieve) the meaning when looking at the form rather than always seeing them both together.

*Quality:* The main quality component of flash card learning is retrieval. However, for words that prove difficult to retain, the word part strategy (analysis) or the keyword technique (elaboration) can be used.

## Requirements of the flash card strategy

An important part of the flash card strategy is choosing what words to learn. There are well-designed word lists available to sequence the learning of vocabulary in the most cost-effective way (see, for example, the BNC/COCA lists on Paul Nation's resources pages). The Vocabulary Levels Tests available on Paul Nation's resources pages can be used to work out what word list to work on, or learners can simply look at the lists in frequency order picking out words to learn. Alternatively, learners can choose unknown words met in their reading or listening, preferably checking their frequency. There is an app that allows quick checking called Word Family Finder designed by Laurence Anthony that quickly shows what 1,000-word frequency level a particular word occurs in along with its family members.

Learners need some training in flash card use and this should involve becoming familiar with the ideas of word frequency, retrieval, spaced repetition, and receptive and productive learning. They should also be introduced to the word part strategy, the idea of word families, and the keyword technique.

Learners should be encouraged to persist with word card learning. This can be done by getting learners to regularly test each other in class on their word cards, keeping records of the amount of words learned, and having learners report on their word card learning to their classmates. A class vocabulary box (Coxhead, 2004) of shared cards can be used for in-class work.

## How can the flash cards strategy be used well?

The following description of the strategy is based on using hard-copy word cards rather than a flash card app, in order to spell out the main steps involved. This description is largely taken from Nation (2008). Understanding these steps will allow informed use of flash card programmes.

1 The learner makes some small cards about 4 cm by 2 cm from ordinary photocopying or printing paper. These are small enough to be easily carried

around in a pocket or handbag and are light and not bulky, so two or three packs of 50 cards in each pack could be easily carried. The cards are held together by a rubber band.
2 The learner writes a useful word, phrase, or sentence on one side and its translation into the first language on the other. Translation is usually the most effective way of learning the meaning of a word.
3 The learner then goes through the pack, looking at each foreign word or phrase and trying to recall what was written on the other side. If the translation cannot be recalled, then the card is turned over to see what was written there.
4 Words which were easy to recall are placed on the bottom of the pack. Those that had to be turned over are slipped somewhere into the middle so that they can be looked at again soon.
5 After going through the pack once or twice, it is put away, ready to be looked at again in about half an hour.
6 The cards in the pack are looked at again at increasingly spaced intervals of time – half an hour later, later that day, the next day, two days later, a week later, a month later, and so on.
7 The cards should be shuffled occasionally so that they appear in a different order.
8 Words that are difficult to remember can be transferred to a new pack. Special techniques like the keyword technique and the word part analysis strategy can be applied to these words.
9 When the words have been learned receptively (look at the foreign word, recall its meaning), then the cards are turned over and the words are learned productively (look at the L1 word and recall the foreign word).
10 If some words are particularly difficult to learn, break them into word parts if possible, or use the keyword technique to help them stick in memory. Writing the word or saying the word can also help the word form stay in memory. If a new word is learned in a multiword unit containing an already known word, this can help retention.

A flash card app takes care of several of these steps.

## Relating the flash card strategy to other learning

It is useful to relate vocabulary size to proficiency levels, because this clarifies the amount of vocabulary learning needed to reach various levels. The CEFR (Council of Europe Framework of Reference for languages) levels describes six proficiency levels, with the lowest level being A1 and the highest, C2. In Table 23.2, there is an attempt to relate the CEFR levels to vocabulary sizes

**TABLE 23.2** The CEFR levels with suggested vocabulary and word family levels

| Level | CEFR descriptors | Suggested vocabulary size | Suggested word family size |
|---|---|---|---|
| C2 | Mastery | 7,000–9,000 words and beyond | Level 6 and beyond |
| C1 | Advanced | 5,000–6,000 words Oxford 5,000 (B2–C1) See introduction to OALD 10th edition p.x. | Level 5 |
| B2 | Vantage | 4,000 words (2,000–3,000 high-frequency words plus 1,000–2,000 relevant technical vocabulary) Oxford 3,000 (B2) | Level 4 |
| B1 | Threshold | 2,000–3,000 most frequent high-frequency words | Level 3 |
| A2 | Waystage | The most frequent 1,000-word families | Level 3 partial (inflections plus un-, -ly, -er, -th) |
| A1 | Breakthrough | The minimum could be the 120 words and phrases from the survival vocabulary[a] with the upper limit around 500 flemmas | Flemma + -ly |

[a] Nation and Crabbe (1991).

and word family sizes, that is, how many word families a learner knows and the affixes which would be likely to occur in these families. A flemma is a word and its closely related inflected forms, where the same flemma can include different parts of speech. A word family is a word and its closely related inflected and derived forms.

A in column 1 can be classified as Elementary, B as Intermediate, and C as Advanced. Columns 1 and 2 are CEFR descriptions. The full CEFR descriptions can be found on the web. Column 3 (Suggested vocabulary size) is based on the BNC/COCA word families and versions of it. These are freely available from Paul Nation's resources pages. The suggested word family size in column 4 is based on Bauer and Nation's (1993) *Word families* article (available under Publications on Paul Nation's resources web site).

## Variants of the flash card strategy

Vocabulary notebooks are sometimes recommended as a way of learning new words. However, vocabulary notebooks do not encourage retrieval, because the word and its translation are next to each other.

There are two strategies that can be used with the flash card strategy – the keyword technique and the word card strategy.

## The keyword technique

The keyword technique is primarily a way of making a strong link between the form of an unknown word and its meaning. It involves two steps after the learner has met the unknown word and has found or been provided with its meaning. The first step is to think of a first language word (the keyword) which sounds like the beginning or all of the unknown word. The second step is for the learner to think of a visual image where the meaning of the unknown word and the meaning of the keyword is combined. Here is an example.

If an Indonesian learner wants to learn the English word *parrot*, the learner could use the keyword *parit* which is the Indonesian word for "ditch". The learner then thinks of an image involving a parrot and a ditch.

The technique is more clearly seen as a four-part process.

| 1 | 2 | 3 | 4 |
|---|---|---|---|
| The unknown word | → The first language keyword | → A mental image combining the meaning of the unknown word and the meaning of the keyword | → The meaning of the unknown word |

Here are some examples. The keywords have been chosen from a variety of languages including English. For languages like Chinese with a very limited syllable structure, it may also be useful to choose keywords not only from the first language but from known words in the second language.

| fund | → *fun* (Thai) meaning "teeth" | → Imagine a fund of money being eaten by a set of teeth | → a supply of money for a special purpose |
| candid | → can The English word meaning a container | → Imagine a can with a label that honestly shows its contents | → honest and truthful |
| core | → *hor* (Serbo-Croat) meaning "choir" | → Think of a choir standing on the core of an apple | → the most important or central part |

Step 2 provides a word form link between the unknown word and the keyword. Step 3 provides a meaning link between the keyword and the meaning of the unknown word. Thus, the whole sequence provides a link from the form of the unknown word to its meaning.

The unknown word, because of its formal similarity to the keyword, prompts recall of the keyword. The keyword prompts recall of the image combining the keyword meaning and the meaning of the unknown word. This image prompts recall of the meaning of the unknown word and completes the set of links between the form of the unknown word and its meaning.

Instead of an image at step 3, some experimenters have used a sentence which describes what the image might be, for example, "There is a pin in the pintu". The keyword technique can be used with ready-made keywords and images as in the examples above. This is generally recommended for younger learners and seems to work as well as self-created keywords and images.

## Using word parts

The word part strategy involves breaking complex words into known parts and relating the meaning of the whole word to the meanings of the parts. Use of this strategy involves learning the meaning of the most useful word parts and the meaning of a few useful stems. Nation and Bauer (2023) provide lists of the most useful affixes and plenty of graded examples for practice in cutting words into their parts. See Paul Nation's resources pages under Word parts for ready-to-use material. Bauer and Nation (2020) provide detailed information on the various affixes.

## How can the flash card strategy be used at all levels of proficiency?

Flash cards can be used at all levels of proficiency but are probably not appropriate for very young learners.

## Are there digital applications of this strategy?

Vocabulary flash cards are also called word cards, and the strategy is ideally suited to being programmed into an app. Unfortunately, the programming is often done by programmers who have not carefully read the research on deliberate vocabulary learning and paired associate learning, and so the research is not as well applied as it could be. In an attempt to deal with this, Nakata (2011) wrote a very useful article critiquing flash card programmes and providing a well-supported list of guidelines for designing such apps. Some of the better flash card programmes are *Anki*, *iKnow*, and *Quizlet*.

## What does research say about the flash card strategy?

There is a very long history of research on paired associate learning and the use of the word card strategy for learning foreign language vocabulary. The research is dealt with in detail in Nation (2022, Chapter 11) and Nakata (2020). It shows very consistent results. Flash card vocabulary learning is effective, efficient, and has long-lasting effects. Research has shown that it simultaneously results in both explicit and implicit knowledge (Elgort, 2011), meaning that as well as providing conscious knowledge of the word and its meaning, it also provides subconscious knowledge of the kind needed for normal language use. Words and multiword units that are deliberately learned using flash cards are readily available for use in reading and the other language skills provided both the spoken and written forms are learned both receptively and productively using flash cards.

Wilkinson (2020) found that getting learners to make their own cards helped learning, but it was more efficient and effective to have ready-made cards. Learners preferred ready-made cards.

**Research questions**

There is an enormous amount of research on paired associate learning and on learning foreign language vocabulary from word cards. There is a lack of research on how this learning relates to language use.

*Motivation principles (Engagement)*

For learning to occur, there needs to be a willingness to focus on what needs to be learned, and to give it quantity and quality of attention.

1 *Motivation: The degree of engagement with the task affects the likelihood of learning occurring.* How can learners be encouraged to use a flash card app or word cards?
2 *Self-efficacy: Our confidence in our own skills of learning affects our success in learning.* Do some learners experience difficulty in learning from word cards?

*Focus principles (Usefulness)*

Learning requires giving attention to what needs to be learned.

3 *Focus: We learn what we focus on, and in addition, our learning is more useful if it closely resembles the use that we need to make of what we learn (transfer-appropriate).* Does eye-tracking during reading show that words learned on flash cards are readily available for reading? Does using word cards for productive learning (see L1 translation, retrieve L2 word) result in faster retrieval during reading? Should learners study word cards containing the vocabulary of a graded reader before reading the reader or should they make word cards during their reading?
4 *Accuracy: Our learning is more efficient if the information we are focusing on is complete, accurate, and comprehensible.* What errors occur if learners make their own word cards?

*Quantity principles (Amount)*

5  *Repetition: The more repetitions, the stronger the learning.* Is it worthwhile coming back to the same word cards after a year or more to ensure that previous learning is not lost?
6  *Time-on-task: The greater and longer the attention, the stronger the learning.* Does retrieval speed increase during flash card learning? Is this increase reflected in fluency increases in reading? Does redistributing words to different learning sets result in more time being spent on each word and thus result in stronger learning?

*Quality principles (Connections)*

Elaboration and analysis increase and strengthen connections between the item to be learned and other knowledge making it easier to access the item.

7  *Elaboration: This includes enriching the encoding of an item through variation.* Does varying different word family members as the cue word result in stronger learning than always using the same family member in a flash card programme?
8  *Analysis: This involves relating the familiar parts to the unfamiliar whole.* Should word cards indicate the word parts of the word being learned?

There is a very large amount of research on how to do flash card learning and the guidelines for such learning are well established. It is good that these guidelines continue to be explored and checked, but the most needed research on flash card learning of vocabulary is on the effect of such learning on normal reading. That is, how readily does the knowledge gained from flash card learning transfer to normal language use? It seems likely that eye-tracking studies will play a major role in such research.

# 24
# LEARNER TRAINING

It is certainly stretching the idea of a teaching technique to call learner training a technique. Nonetheless, it certainly does what other teaching techniques do, and that is it helps learners learn a language. Singling it out as a technique has the good effect of stressing its importance.

Most learners do not apply good principles to the learning that they do, and many teachers are not aware of findings of the enormous amount of research on how to learn. Training learners in how to learn can change people's lives. Most people are not aware of how they can dramatically improve their learning by understanding some well-proven learning principles. One of the most important things that a teacher can do is to show learners how to learn.

## What is learner training?

Learner training involves learning well-established principles of learning and consciously applying those principles to the learning task. In this book, we focus on eight principles. There are some other principles that relate to course design. These include the principle of the four strands which is covered in Chapter 1, the cost/benefit principle which relates to choosing the most useful language features to learn, and the autonomy principle that is covered in this chapter. For a more extended discussion of principles, see Chapter 4 of Macalister and Nation (2020) *Language Curriculum Design*.

## What are the learning goals of learner training?

Learner training helps learners take control of their own learning through understanding what must be done in order for language items to stay in their memory.

This understanding involves ideas (the principles of learning) and the application of these ideas to learning activities. In this book, the principles are used to analyse activities to see how they work, but the goal is much wider than that. Learners should be able to apply the principles to any learning task they are engaged in and these learning tasks go beyond the learning of a language.

As Table 24.1 shows, the major learning goal of learner training is conscious knowledge of the principles of learning and learning how to apply them. This training could be carried out in the second language, but there are very good reasons for this training to be done in the learners' first language. Using the first language would save time, would ensure that the instruction is more likely to be understood by everyone, and would allow the learners to interactively engage with the principles and their application.

### How does learner training help learning?

Many of the activities that are done in the classroom are done with the learners and too often the teacher not really understanding why they are being done. This can result in them being done in a way that defeats their purpose. By far, the most persistent and serious example of this is where the material in the lesson is dealt with but is never returned to again, meaning that it is not likely to be learned and available for use. This why a substantial section of Chapter 4 of this book focused on repetition, and why every technique chapter has a section on revisiting the same material. Learner training results in informed learners who know why they are doing the various activities they are required to do and what they need to do to make sure that they learn from those activities.

Learning how to learn is itself a learning task, and so now we will look at how the principles of learning apply to learning and applying the principles themselves.

*Motivation:* Analysing activities has immediate benefits for learning. If the analysis is done in a practical way on activities that the learners often use, the analysis has obvious transfer value. The challenge to the teacher is to make the analysis comprehensible, engaging, and relevant.

**TABLE 24.1** The goals of learner training

| *Goals* | *Specific focuses* |
| --- | --- |
| Language | |
| Ideas | *Learning the meta-cognitive knowledge and skills to apply the principles of learning* |
| Skills | |
| Text | |

*Note*: The major goal is in *italics*.

*Focus:* Learner training involves a deliberate focus on well-proven ways of learning. The knowledge involved is not complicated and is highly effective. It is worth presenting the principles as items to be memorized because they are well proven and effective.

*Quantity:* As with all learning, spending time on what is to be learned and coming back many times to what should be learned is a major factor in successful learning. During learner training, the learners should repeatedly practice analysing activities and repeatedly reflect on how to improve learning. Focusing on one principle at a time is a useful way of making sure that each principle gets a sustained focus of attention.

*Quality:* Analysing teaching and learning activities is an elaborative process with each analysis enriching knowledge of the underlying principle.

## What are the requirements of learner training?

### How can you prepare for learner training?

Teachers need to have a clear understanding of the principles of learning. One of the major purposes of this book is to show how a small number of very important principles are at work, or should be at work, in the most useful language teaching techniques. So, reading this book is useful preparation. The activities for analysis by the learners can be taken from this book, and it is useful to think of four or five examples outside language learning that could also be used as examples of the principles at work. These could include learning people's names, remembering historical facts, memorizing a recipe, memorizing a poem or song, or learning the road code as preparation for getting a driving licence. The principles apply well beyond the classroom.

### How much time should be given to learner training in a general language course?

Learner training fits into the language-focused learning strand of a course, because it involves deliberate attention to the nature of learning. It should only make up a small proportion of this strand because although it is important, it only requires the learning of small number of principles and spaced and varied practice in the application of these principles. In total, this should not take up about more than an hour of course time over a year.

### How can learner training be done well?

The important requirements of learner training are that the principles are well understood, and are often practised and referred to when other learning techniques are being used. In every one of the 20 teaching technique chapters of this book, the section entitled **How does __ help learning?** explicitly shows how the principles apply to that particular technique.

The most useful way to approach the principles of learning described in Chapter 4 of this book is to go directly to their applications as shown in column 2 of Table 24.2.

There is such a large number of applications that it is necessary to prioritize the most widely applicable and useful ones, so that these can be the focus of initial training. Top of the list is using repeated spaced retrieval. This application is the most robust finding of well over 100 years of memory research and the one most researched. Note the three very important parts of repetition, spacing, and retrieval. Second on the list, and also strongly supported by research, is use deliberate learning. Third, where learning does not stick, use some trick to make it stick, such as by analysing what you are learning, or by visualizing it or linking it to something memorable. Fourth, the more time you spend studying or using something, the more likely you are to learn it. This is called the time-on-task principle.

These four general applications are an excellent starting point for learner training. The training can follow these steps. We will apply the steps to the first recommended general application, using repeated spaced retrieval, using the particular application of word card or flash card learning (see Chapter 23).

1 The teacher should describe a particular application (word cards) and then show how it applies the idea of repeated spaced retrieval.
2 The learners should then make four or five word cards and practise using them.
3 The teacher warns the learners that they will be asked to show how to make and use word cards while explaining to the teacher and others what they are doing. Research on self-regulated learning shows the value of getting learners to think aloud while they analyse their learning (Flavell, 1976). This checks that the learners really understand the application and provides another repetition of the particular application.
4 The teacher sets the learners the task of making a few more word cards at home, and then the next day, gets them once again to demonstrate using the cards while explaining what they are doing.
5 On another day, the teacher says that there is a short dialogue in the course book that should be memorized, and asks the learners to work in pairs to come up with three suggestions regarding how this could be done using the idea of repeated spaced retrieval. For example, one suggestion could be look at it today and then look at it again tomorrow. This applies repetition and spacing. The learners make their suggestions, and the teacher and learners comment on them. (Answer: Look at the dialogue, close your eyes or close

TABLE 24.2 Principles and their applications for language learning

| Principle | Application in techniques |
| --- | --- |
| 1 Motivation | Learn obviously useful language items |
| | Set challenging but achievable goals |
| | Use puzzle-like and test-like tasks |
| | Record successful learning using graphs |
| 2 Self-efficacy | Use vocabulary control in listening and reading materials |
| | Do pre-study training to make sure you are successful |
| | Work with small numbers of items to learn |
| 3 Focus | Give deliberate attention to what you want to learn |
| | Understand what is involved in knowing what you want to learn |
| | Have a clear learning goal |
| 4 Accuracy | Don't use trial-and-error, use study and test |
| | Make sure that what you are learning is correct, so use dictionaries or glossaries |
| | Make sure you understand what you are learning, so use the L1 if necessary |
| 5 Repetition | Use peer testing |
| | Use related tasks |
| | Encourage quantity of graded reading and listening |
| | Encourage opportunities for negotiation of meaning |
| | Revisit the same material several times |
| 6 Time-on-task | Use spaced retrieval |
| | Use self-testing |
| | Spend time on using the language and on studying what you want to learn |
| | Use larger numbers of items as skill in learning increases |
| 7 Elaboration | Visualize examples of use |
| | Find members of the same word family |
| | Learn words with their known collocations |
| | Do plenty of extensive reading to see examples of use |
| | Focus on both written and spoken forms |
| | Say or write the words |
| | Try to use what you are learning |
| | Use pictures of the meaning as well as translations |
| | Do both receptive and productive learning |
| 8 Analysis | Look for the core meaning of various senses of words |
| | Use memory tricks such as the Keyword technique |
| | Learn word parts |
| | Do multiword unit analysis and analysis of grammatical patterns |
| | Use analogy or patterning of form, meaning, and use. For example, for vocabulary, look at spelling regularities and irregularities, look for a core meaning among various uses, look for similarities among collocates |

the book and try to retrieve the dialogue from your memory. Come back to the dialogue on at least five different occasions. Practice it with a partner at least five times in one session).
6 On another day, the teacher gets the learners to think about how extensive reading involves repetition, spacing, and retrieval, and how further repetition and retrieval could be added to the activity (Answer: By making word cards when unfamiliar words are met in reading).
7 By now, the learners should be familiar with the idea of repeated spaced retrieval. Every so often, when the learners are about to do an activity, such as dictation, information transfer, or any other activity, such as the ones in this book, the teacher gets the learners to think about whether and how the activity makes use of repeated spaced retrieval, and how the activity could be improved by including repeated spaced retrieval.

The same activity, using word cards or flash cards, can be analysed again, this time looking at a different general application, such as using memory tricks, using deliberate attention, or spending time on the cards such as with peer testing.

### *How can I check that learner training is working well?*

Learner training involves the application of metacognitive knowledge, so a good way to see how well learner training is working is to get learners talking about how to learn. First, the learners should understand the principle they are working with and have a short way of referring to it. Occasionally, the teacher should ask learners to explain a particular principle and how it helps learning. Second, the learners should be able to analyse an activity to describe what principles are at work in it. This analysis provides a good opportunity for the teacher to see how well the learners can apply the principles. An extension of this is to ask the learners how they would go about learning to write well or improving their pronunciation, or to learn some subject matter content, such as a mathematical formula or historical facts.

### What are the variants of learner training?

There are several ways of approaching the learning of the principles of learning. In the approach suggested above, the actual principles as described in Chapter 4 are seen as something to be dealt with near the end of the learning process rather than at the beginning. The approach suggested above starts with just one general application and then looks at how it applies to one technique. Gradually, the general application is extended to the analysis of other techniques and then later on another general application is introduced.

Another approach would be to start with the principles and then move to applications. This could be overwhelming for some learners, but it may appeal to some adults.

The learner training could be carried out using the L1, and if the teacher is a fluent L1 speaker this is probably the most effective way.

There is a free book called *What do you need to know to learn a foreign language?* on Paul Nation's resources pages under Publications. It has been translated into several languages to make it more accessible for learners of English. It covers the basic principles of language learning.

### How can learner training be used at all levels of proficiency?

Even very young learners can be taught the value of repetition, spacing, and retrieval; however, learner training is likely to be most effective with older learners, at secondary school level or beyond.

### Are there digital applications of this technique?

Learning through the internet and computer-based interaction involve the same learning principles as any other kind of learning. The internet expands the possibilities for learning and interaction but it does not involve different principles of learning.

It would be useful to have an online training course on how to learn a foreign language.

### Revisiting and linking to other activities

Before learners do an activity, it is useful to occasionally remind them how the activity helps learning. This should be accompanied by how they should do the activity so that they have the best chance of learning from it.

### What does research say about the effectiveness of learner training?

Learner training fits within the broad framework of the self-regulation of learning (self-regulated learning). The self-regulation of learning has been defined as "the degree to which students are metacognitively, motivationally, and behaviourally active participants in their own learning process" (Schunk & Zimmerman, 2011, p. 4). The degree to which learners self-regulate (self-direct) their learning is a good predictor of later success in learning (Butler, 2015).

Butler notes that the early research on self-regulated learning by Flavell (1976) showed that it is useful to distinguish three aspects, knowledge about, reflection on, and regulation of one's cognitive activities. That is, knowing how to learn is not enough. Learners need to reflect on their own learning and to see how their new knowledge about learning relates to their learning. They then have to apply their new knowledge about learning to the task in hand. The steps suggested in this chapter include these three aspects.

Research shows that beliefs about learning do not match with the research findings (Bjork, Dunlosky & Kornell, 2013), and so there is value in learners getting to understand well-proven principles of learning.

## Research questions

### Motivation principles (Engagement)

For learning to occur there needs to be a willingness to focus on what needs to be learned, and to give it quantity and quality of attention.

1 *Motivation: The degree of engagement with the task affects the likelihood of learning occurring.* Do learners value training in how to learn? Does including information about how to learn in course books make the course books more attractive to teachers?
2 *Self-efficacy: Our confidence in our own skills of learning affects our success in learning.* Does learner training have substantial effects on feelings of self-efficacy?

### Focus principles (Usefulness)

Learning requires giving attention to what needs to be learned.

3 *Focus: We learn what we focus on, and in addition, our learning is more useful if it closely resembles the use that we need to make of what we learn (transfer-appropriate).* Do learners find that the principles of learning agree with their own experience? Does this affect acceptance of the principles? Does training in how to learn result in more effective self-regulated learning?
4 *Accuracy: Our learning is more efficient if the information we are focusing on is complete, accurate, and comprehensible.* What level of understanding is needed to apply the principles?

### Quantity principles (Amount)

5 *Repetition: The more repetitions, the stronger the learning.* Is learner training best done intensively or spread over a period of time?
6 *Time-on-task: The greater and longer the attention, the stronger the learning.* How much training is needed to get learners to be able to apply the principles of learning to their own learning?

## Quality principles (Connections)

Elaboration and analysis increase and strengthen connections between the item to be learned and other knowledge making it easier to access the item.

7 *Elaboration: This includes enriching the encoding of an item through variation.* Does wide variation of applications work better than focusing on a narrow range of applications?
8 *Analysis: This involves relating the familiar parts to the unfamiliar whole.* Is it best to practice one principle at a time or to draw on all of them?

A thorough and careful review of the existing theory and research on learner training is needed with a focus on guidelines for learner training in language learning. Most of the existing theory and research involved will be with native speakers and will go beyond language learning, but will still be a useful source of guidelines. Without such a review, investigations of learner training in learning another language are likely to be re-discovering what has already been discovered. The next important focus would be on the effects of learner training on language proficiency.

# PART 6
# Research

# 25
# RESEARCHING LANGUAGE TEACHING TECHNIQUES

### Researching the four strands

The principle of the four strands is not easy to research and relies upon several assumptions, the main assumption being that the four strands should be of roughly equal size. This assumption is a very useful assumption because it provides us with a principled way of allocating time in a language course, both at the level of the strand and at the level of the technique.

One implication that comes from the principle of the four strands is that three-quarters of the time in a course should be spent using the language – using language at the boundaries of learners' knowledge in the two meaning-focused strands, and using language that is already known to develop fluency in the fluency development strand. Using the language to learn the language is at the core of the communicative approach to language teaching, but it relies on another idea that several researchers seem reluctant to accept (Long, 2020). This idea is that in order for the meaning-focused strands and the fluency development strand to work, learners need to use language-controlled material. This idea was the reason that Michael West and others created word lists and graded readers based on word lists for learners of English as a foreign language in the 1920s and on into the 1950s. Work with corpora and texts of various kinds has provided plenty of evidence of the heavy vocabulary burden of unsimplified material written for native speakers of English, even that written for young native speakers. Nevertheless, there is the often unstated feeling that "authentic" unsimplified material must be better, and as a result there is a reluctance to make extensive use of language-controlled material. This is unfortunate, because unless learners make extensive use of language-controlled material, particularly graded

DOI: 10.4324/9781003496151-32

readers, learning language through language use cannot be a substantial part of elementary and low intermediate-level language courses.

## Research on learning through language use

There is a lack of research on the time-on-task principle in foreign language learning, namely research that relates quantity of language use to language learning. One of the most important studies in this area is the research by Beglar, Hunt, and Kite (2012). In this study, the researchers looked at the effect of extensive reading on fluency development in a year-long extensive reading programme. The most striking finding was that the greatest gains in reading fluency did not happen with the learners who read the most, but happened with the learners who read the most vocabulary-controlled material. This is a good example of the focus principle as well as the time-on-task principle. You do not get fluent by reading difficult material slowly. You become fluent by reading material that allows you to read fluently.

We need research on each of the four skills of listening, speaking, reading, and writing that looks at the effect of quantity of language use on language proficiency. This research needs to involve language-controlled material and learners at a range of proficiency levels. It also needs to involve a range of language-proficiency measures including word part knowledge, vocabulary knowledge, knowledge of multiword units, grammar knowledge, listening and reading comprehension, spoken and written production, and fluency. Such research is very important because it is directly relevant to three-quarters of the time spent in a well-balanced language course. A lot of research on second language acquisition examines the effects of interventions which change the nature of normal language use. This is revealing and useful, but there is still a lack of research on the effect of substantial normal language use at the right levels for the learners involved. This lack is not so great in extensive reading (Nation & Waring, 2020), but even there, there are few studies longer than a few weeks.

It seems obvious that the more you use the language, the better you will become at using it. However, as the Beglar, Hunt, and Kite (2012) study shows, this use needs to be genuine language use, not a long struggle with material that is way beyond learners' current level.

## Research on language-focused learning

The techniques described in this book which fit into the language-focused learning strand of a course are an interesting collection. Each language skill has its own language-focused learning techniques. Some, namely intensive reading, writing with feedback, and project work involve a supported struggle with difficult material. Others involve an isolated focus on aspects of the language that need to be learned. These include dictation, hearing and pronunciation practice, guided writing, substitution tables, and vocabulary flash cards. Hearing and pronunciation practice and vocabulary flash cards are well researched, but there is no research on dictation, guided writing, and substitution tables when they are used as foreign language learning techniques. Part of the reason for this lack of research may be that these techniques may be seen as outdated. An assumption that lies behind their inclusion in this book is that each language skill should have its own language-focused learning techniques. That is, there should be a place in the learning of each skill where there is a deliberate focus on some aspects of the skill, because such a focus will deal with problems in the use of the skill, and will speed up the learning of the skill. This may be a faulty assumption, and there are those who argue that feedback on writing is a waste of time. It is thus important that we look closely at the unproven language-focused learning techniques, particularly dictation, guided writing, and substitution tables, to see what effect they have, and whether this effect could be more readily achieved by some other language-focused learning technique or simply by quantity of language use.

There is plenty of evidence that there should be a language-focused learning strand in a language course. We need more research to show what should be in that strand.

## Principles and research questions with references to previous studies

Through this book, we have used the set of principles described in Chapter 4 to suggest questions for research. In this section, we use the same principles and questions and add references to published studies that show a way of investigating particular questions. These could be a useful starting point for anyone wishing to design research.

It is important to consider a range of ways of answering the questions. One of the classic case studies of language teaching techniques is Hosenfeld's (1976) investigation using think-alouds of learners doing some guided activities such as blank-filling. Her study showed that the way the learners did the activities defeated the learning goals of the activities. Single-subject case studies provide valuable insights into what actually happens.

There are factors such as repetition and retrieval that contribute to learning. Several techniques such as the pyramid procedure, dictation, prepared talks, 4/3/2, linked skills, and projects involve steps where the same material is repeated. Careful observation of such activities can reveal whether this repetition actually occurs, whether it involves items that need to be learned, and whether these repetitions set up good conditions for learning. In addition, such observation can suggest ways of improving the technique so that better learning conditions occur. For example, in bridging the gap between the written version of a prepared talk and the final spoken presentation, what kinds of support best preserve the accuracy of the talk?

It is well worth looking at learners' understandings of the goals of learning activities and how activities should be done well. It is likely that a good understanding of activities results in improvement in the use of those activities.

Let us now look again at possible questions.

### Motivation principles (Engagement)

For learning to occur, there needs to be a willingness to focus on what needs to be learned, and to give it quantity and quality of attention.

1 *Motivation: The degree of engagement with the task affects the likelihood of learning occurring.* Do learners want to do this task? (Banister, 2023). Do they think that this should be a regular activity in their course? Do they enjoy it when they do it? (Tsang, 2023). Does their enjoyment when doing the task increase their willingness to do similar tasks? What factors encourage the learners to do the task – choice of content, the challenge of the task, obvious value outside the course, pair or group work, signs of progress (a graph, a record of work done, success in the task?) (Sato & Ballinger, 2016; Zhou, Yu & Wu, 2022).
2 *Self-efficacy: Our confidence in our own skills of learning affects our success in learning.* What difficulties do learners encounter during the task? What support helps them to be successful? (Bitchener, 2021; Hyland & Hyland, 2006a, 2006b). Which support is the most effective? Does vocabulary control increase self-efficacy? Do learners successfully complete the task? (Kato, Spring & Mori, 2023).

### Focus principles (Usefulness)

Learning requires giving attention to what needs to be learned.

3 *Focus: We learn what we focus on, and in addition, our learning is more useful if it closely resembles the use that we need to make of what we learn (transfer-appropriate).* What do learners focus on during the task? (Barcroft, 2006, 2015; Thai & Boers, 2016). Do some aspects of the task result in unwanted focuses? (Boers, Warren, Grimshaw & Siyanova-Chanturia, 2017; Chang & Millett, 2014, 2016). Do learners improve in doing the task during repeated performance of the task? (Macalister, 2014; Tran, 2012). What do learners learn from doing the task? (Lee, Jang & Plonsky, 2015; Thomson &

Derwing, 2015; Wilkinson, 2020). Does learning transfer outside the task to different material? (De Jong & Perfetti, 2011; Tran, 2012). Does doing the task result in improvement in related tasks and skills? (Bismoko & Nation, 1974; Tran, 2012). What are the most useful topics to cover? (Nation & Crabbe, 1991).

4 *Accuracy: Our learning is more efficient if the information we are focusing on is complete, accurate, and comprehensible.* Is the language used during the task largely accurate? (Strong & Boers, 2019). Do learners successfully complete the task with a minimum of error and mis-comprehension? (Beglar, Hunt & Kite, 2012). How do learners cope with errors and unknown language items during the task? (Newton, 2013). What support reduces the chances of error? (Ellis, 2009; Montero-Perez, Den Noortgate & Desmet, 2013; Peters, Heynen & Puimège, 2016; Uchihara, Webb & Trofimovich, 2021). Which support works best?

*Quantity principles (Amount)*

5 *Repetition: The more repetitions, the stronger the learning.* Does the task involve plenty of repetition? (Uchihara, Webb & Yanagisawa, 2019; Waring & Takaki, 2003). Does a corpus analysis of the activity show lots of opportunities for learning? What kinds of repetition occur during the task and across later uses of the task? How much repetition is needed to get substantial learning from this task? (Waring & Takaki, 2003). How can repetition be increased? What spacing of repetition works best? Does redoing the same task several days later increase learning? What patterns of improvement occur during repeated use of the task? (Chung & Nation, 2006). Is some intervention needed to bring about improvement during repeated use of the task? Is repetition and the kind of repetition directly related to learning? Are learners willing to do repeated tasks? What kinds of changes are needed to keep a repeated task interesting? What effect does a narrow content focus have on repetition and the difficulty of the task? What are the effects of repetition on accuracy, complexity, and fluency? What changes to the task are needed to get a wider range of learning from the task? (Ellis, 2009).

6 *Time-on-task: The greater and longer the attention, the stronger the learning.* Does the task involve lots of attention to what needs to be learned? (Folse, 2006; Hill & Laufer, 2003). Is there a direct relationship between time-on-task and learning? How much time needs to be spent on the task to result in substantial learning? What factors in the design of the task affect the time spent on the task? What other factors affect the time spent on the task? What factors take time away from the goals of the task? How can we deal with these factors? Do observers learn as well as active participants?

## Quality principles (Connections)

Elaboration and analysis increase and strengthen connections between the item to be learned and other knowledge making it easier to access the item.

7 *Elaboration: This includes enriching the encoding of an item through variation.* What are the different types of quality of attention? What kinds of quality most affect learning? (Bitchener, 2021; Paribakht & Wesche, 1996; Wesche & Paribakht, 2000). How can we investigate the quality of the time spent on the task? What kinds of varied repetition occur during the task? (Joe, 1995). How is this repetition best classified and counted? What are the most useful scales to reveal the extent of variation of vocabulary in language use across the four skills? (Joe, 1998). Are separate scales needed for word form, word meaning, and word use? Is the frequency of various kinds and levels of variation directly related to learning? What kinds of feedback most affect learning? (Newton, 2013). Does the task involve language-related episodes that help language learning? (McDonough & Sunitham, 2009). Does this activity strengthen knowledge of previously met words? (Pigada & Schmitt, 2006).

8 *Analysis: This involves relating the familiar parts to the unfamiliar whole.* Language analysis works at all levels of language – the components of sounds, the sounds that make up words, sound-spelling correspondences, spelling patterns and rules, word parts, parts of multiword units, parts of speech, grammatical constructions, topic-type components, rhetorical analysis, and discourse analysis. Do several members of the same word family occur among the target vocabulary in the activity? Do learners see the connection between the word family members? (Wei, 2015). What kinds of language analysis occur in the task? Is feedback involving grammatical analysis more effective than correction? (Bitchener, 2021). Does language analysis result in improvement in language use? Does language analysis occur during incidental learning?

Many of the studies referred to above are experimental studies involving a control group and experimental group and a range of careful controls. Anyone who is considering doing such a study should look at meta-analyses of studies in their chosen area. Meta-analyses set up criteria for the inclusion of a study in the meta-analysis. These criteria are ways of assessing the quality of the studies and they provide a very useful guide when designing new research. Meta-analyses referred to in this book include Johnson et al. (1981), Webb, Yanagisawa, and Uchihara (2020), Montero Perez, van den Noortgate, and Desmet, (2013), Johnson and Tabari (2022), Krashen (2007), Nakanishi (2015), and Swanborn and de Glopper (1999).

# APPENDIX 1

## A feedback system for writing and self-checking procedures

Giving feedback on writing provides another opportunity for giving attention to grammar. It is a good idea to have a system for signalling grammatical errors in writing. The system should be reasonably simple with only about seven or eight signals, so that the learners can quickly remember it and know what to do when they see each signal. The following table contains an example of such a system. The letter on the left goes in the margin of the piece of writing and the mark goes in the text.

### A marking system for grammatical errors

| Sign in the margin | Meaning of the sign | Mark in the text |
|---|---|---|
| A | Article usage. Incorrect usage of countable or uncountable nouns. | The noun is underlined. |
| J | Joining word (Conjunctions). A conjunction is missing or there are too many conjunctions. | Crossing out or an insertion mark. |
| Agr | Agreement. The subject and the verb or the pronoun and noun or the determiner and noun are not in agreement with each other. | The two items that should agree each have a box around them and the two boxes are joined. |
| Sp | Spelling. | A diagonal line through the spelling error. |
| V | Verb group. The items in the verb group do not fit with each other. | The two items that should agree have a circle around them and the two circles are joined. |
| VF | Verb form. The wrong form of the verb (stem, -ing, -ed) is used. | The error is circled. |

*(Continued)*

(Continued)

| | | |
|---|---|---|
| NS | Not a sentence. An essential element of a sentence (subject, verb) is missing. | An insertion mark. |
| P | Punctuation. A question mark or a full stop is missing. | The error is circled. |

Errors which relate to individual words, such as the pattern a verb takes, are dealt with on a word-by-word basis. In order to make use of such a system, the learners need to understand the grammar and self-checking procedures that lie behind the system. Here are some very useful procedures for frequently occurring errors.

### Checking countable and uncountable nouns

If an error occurs with countable or uncountable nouns, the learner looks at the particular noun in the piece of writing and asks the following questions: Is the noun countable or uncountable? If it is countable, do I mean one or more than one? If I mean one, does the singular noun have *a*, *the*, or a similar word (*each, every, this, that, one, his*) in front of it? If I mean more than one, is the noun in the plural form?

### Joining words

If an error occurs with joining words, ask the following questions: Where are the finite verbs? How many are there? Is there one less joining word compared to the number of finite verbs? That is, if there are two finite verbs, there should be only one joining word. If there are three finite verbs, there should be two joining words.

### Verb groups

If the error occurs with verb groups, then the learners need to check the application of verb group rules. This can be presented as a numbered system.

| 5 | 4 | 3 | 2 | 1 |
|---|---|---|---|---|
| can | have | is | is | stem |
| could | has | am | am | stem+ed |
| shall | had | are | are | stem+ing |
| should | having | was | was | |
| may | | were | were | |
| might | | be | be | |
| must | | been | being | |
| | | being | | |

Words in column 5 are followed by the verb stem (modals)
Words in column 4 are followed by non-finite stem+ed (perfect)
Words in column 3 are followed by stem+ing (continuous, progressive)
Words in column 2 are followed by non-finite stem+ed (passive)

## Finite and non-finite verbs

Intermediate and advanced learners can benefit from knowing about finite and non-finite verbs and how to recognize them. This is because finite verbs are involved in verb tense agreement, subject-verb agreement, and the use of conjunctions. Finite verbs are verbs that change their form if we change the time or person referred to. So, in the sentence *He wants to leave*, *wants* is finite because if we change *he* to *they*, we have to change *wants* to *want*. Similarly, if we change time referred to from present to past, then *wants* changes to *wanted*.

There are rules associated with finite verbs.

> Subjects and finite verbs must agree.
> Finite verbs in the same text agree with each other unless there is a clear reason to change.
> Sentences with two finite verbs need to contain a joining word.

These are rules that are sometimes broken but they are good enough to help learners with checking their own written work.

## Pronoun agreement

Pronouns need to agree with the word they refer to. This agreement can be agreement of number (singular or plural), and agreement of gender (male or female).

## Minimum requirements

One way of strongly encouraging learners to self-check their written work is to set minimum requirements for the submission of work to be marked. These minimum requirements must be met before a piece of work is marked. The list of minimum requirements must be short, well understood, and involve very frequent language features. They must also involve language features that the learners are capable of checking by themselves. A useful list could include spelling, subject-verb agreement, pronoun agreement, and the use of articles in front of singular countable nouns. If a learner's work contains two or more errors involving minimum requirements, it is returned to the learner for checking before it is eventually marked. Because the list of minimum requirements involves language features that occur in almost every sentence, it has the effect of greatly reducing careless errors in writing.

# REFERENCES

Adolphs, S., & Schmitt, N. (2003). Lexical coverage of spoken discourse. *Applied Linguistics, 24*(4), 425–438.
Al-Homoud, F., & Schmitt, N. (2009). Extensive reading in a challenging environment: A comparison of extensive and intensive reading approaches in Saudi Arabia. *Language Teaching Research, 13*(4), 383–401.
Allen, V. L. (Ed.) (1976). *Children as teachers*. Academic Press.
Aronson, E. et al. (1975). The jigsaw route to learning and liking. *Psychology Today, 8*(9), 43–50.
Ashton-Warner, S. (1963). *Teacher*. Simon and Schuster.
Banister, C. (2023). Exploring peer feedback processes and peer feedback meta-dialogues with learners of academic and business English. *Language Teaching Research, 27*(3), 746–764.
Barcroft, J. (2006). Can writing a word detract from learning it? More negative effects of forced output during vocabulary learning. *Second Language Research, 22*(4), 487–497.
Bauer, L. (2023). *English phonetics, phonology and spelling for the English language teacher*. Routledge.
Bauer, L., & Nation, I. S. P. (1993). Word families. *International Journal of Lexicography, 6*(4), 253–279.
Bauer, L., & Nation, I. S. P. (2020). *English morphology for the language teaching profession*. Routledge.
Beglar, D., Hunt, A., & Kite, Y. (2012). The effect of pleasure reading on Japanese university EFL learners' reading rates. *Language Learning, 62*(3), 665–703.
Bejarano, Y. (1987). A cooperative small-group methodology in the language classroom. *TESOL Quarterly, 21*(3), 483–504.
Bell, T. (2001). Extensive reading: Speed and comprehension. *The Reading Matrix, 1*(1), 1–13.
Biber, D. (1989). A typology of English texts. *Linguistics, 27*, 3–43.

Biber, D., & Conrad, S. (2009). *Register, genre, and style*. Cambridge University Press.
Bismoko, J., & Nation, I. S. P. (1974). English reading speed and the mothertongue or national language. *RELC Journal, 5*(1), 86–89.
Bitchener, J. (2021). Written corrective feedback. In H. Nassaji & E. Kartchava (Eds.), *The Cambridge handbook of corrective feedback in second language learning and teaching*, Cambridge Handbooks in Language and Linguistics (pp. 207–225). Cambridge University Press. https://doi.org/10.1017/9781108589789.011
Bjork, R. A., Dunlosky, J., & Kornell, N. (2013). Self-regulated learning: Beliefs, techniques, and illusions. *Annual Review of Psychology, 64*, 417–444.
Boers, F. (2014). A reappraisal of the 4/3/2 activity. *RELC Journal, 45*(3), 221–235.
Boers, F., & Thai, C. (2017). Repeating a monologue under increasing time pressure: A replication of Thai and Boers (2016). *The TESOLANZ Journal, 25*, 1–10.
Boers, F., Warren, P., Grimshaw, G., & Siyanova-Chanturia, A. (2017). On the benefits of multimodal annotations for vocabulary uptake from reading. *Computer Assisted Language Learning, 30*(7), 709–725.
Briere, E. J. (1967). Phonological testing reconsidered. *Language Learning, 17*(3&4), 163–171.
Brown, D., & Barnard, H. (1975). Dictation as a learning experience. *RELC Journal, 6*(2), 42–62.
Brown, G. (1978). Understanding spoken language. *TESOL Quarterly, 12*(3), 271–283.
Brown, G., Anderson, A., Shillcock, R., & Yule, G. (1984). *Teaching talk*. Cambridge University Press.
Brown, R., Waring, R., & Donkaewbua, S. (2008). Incidental vocabulary acquisition from reading, reading-while-listening, and listening to stories. *Reading in a Foreign Language, 20*(2), 136–163.
Brysbaert, M. (2019). How many words do we read per minute? A review and meta-analysis of reading rate. *Journal of Memory and Language, 109*, 104047.
Butler, D. L. (2015). Metacognition and self-regulation in learning. In D. Scott & E. Hargreaves (Eds.), *The SAGE handbook on learning* (pp. 291–309). SAGE Publications.
Bygate, M. (2018). *Learning language through task repetition*. John Benjamins.
Carver, R. P. (1994). Percentage of unknown vocabulary words in text as a function of the relative difficulty of the text: Implications for instruction. *Journal of Reading Behavior, 26*(4), 413–437.
Chang, A. C.-S., & Millett, S. (2013). Improving reading rates and comprehension through timed repeated reading. *Reading in a Foreign Language, 25*(2), 126–148.
Chang, A. C.-S., & Millett, S. (2014). The effect of extensive listening on developing L2 listening fluency: Some hard evidence. *ELT Journal, 68*(1), 31–39.
Chang, A. C.-S., & Millett, S. (2016). Developing L2 listening fluency through extended listening-focused activities. *RELC Journal, 47*(3), 349–362.
Chenoweth, A. N., & Hayes, R. J. (2001). Fluency in writing: Generating text in L1 and L2. *Written Communication, 18*(1), 80–98. https://doi.org/10.1177/0741088301018001004
Cho, K. S., & Krashen, S. (1993). Acquisition of vocabulary from the Sweet Valley High Kids series: Adult ESL acquisition. *Journal of Reading, 32*, 662–667.
Chun, L. T., & Aubrey, S. (2023). Using a modified dictogloss to improve English as a second language learners' use of genre-appropriate conventions and style. *RELC Journal, 54*(3), 817–827. https://doi.org/10.1177/00336882211045783.
Chung, M., & Nation, I. S. P. (2006). The effect of a speed reading course. *English Teaching, 61*(4), 181–204.

Claridge, G. (2005). Simplification in graded readers: Measuring the authenticity of graded texts. *Reading in a Foreign Language, 17*(2), 144–158.

Coxhead, A. (2004). Using a class vocabulary box: How, why, when, where and who. *Guidelines, 26*(2), 19–23.

Coxhead, A., & Walls, R. (2012). TED talks, vocabulary and listening for ESP. *TESOLANZ Journal, 20*, 55–67.

Craik, F. I. M., & Lockhart, R. S. (1972). Levels of processing: A framework for memory research. *Journal of Verbal Learning and Verbal Behavior, 11*, 671–684.

Cramer, S. (1975). Increasing reading speed in English or in the national language. *RELC Journal, 6*(2), 19–23.

Davies, N. F. (1982). Training fluency: An essential factor in language acquisition and use. *RELC Journal, 13*(1), 1–13.

deHaan, J., Reed, W. M., & Kuwada, K. (2010). The effect of interactivity with a music video game on second language vocabulary recall. *Language Learning & Technology, 14*(2), 79–94.

de Jong, N., & Perfetti, C. A. (2011). Fluency training in the ESL classroom: An experimental study of fluency development and proceduralization. *Language Learning, 61*(2), 533–568.

DeKeyser, R. (2015). Skill acquisition theory. In B. VanPatten & J. Williams (Eds.), *Theories in second language acquisition: An introduction* (pp. 94–112). Routledge.

De Morgado, N. F. (2009). Extensive reading: Students' performance and perception *The Reading Matrix, 9*(1), 31–43.

Derwing, T. M. (2017). The efficacy of pronunciation instruction. In O. Kang, R. I. Thomson, & J. Murphy (Eds.), *The Routledge handbook of contemporary English pronunciation* (pp. 320–334). Routledge.

Doughty, C., & Pica, T. (1986). "Information gap" tasks: Do they facilitate second language acquisition? *TESOL Quarterly, 20*(2), 305–325.

Dykstra, G. (1964). Eliciting language practice in writing. *ELT Journal, 19*(1), 23–26.

Dykstra, G., & Paulston, C. B. (1967). Guided composition. *ELT Journal, 21*(2), 136–141.

Dykstra, G., Port, R., & Port, A. (1966). *A course in controlled composition: Ananse tales*. Teachers College Press, Columbia University.

Elgort, I. (2011). Deliberate learning and vocabulary acquisition in a second language. *Language Learning, 61*(2), 367–413.

Elkins, R. J., Kalivoda, T. B., & Morain, G. (1972). Fusion of the four skills: A technique for facilitating communicative exchange. *Modern Language Journal, 56*(7), 426–429.

Elley, W. B. (1991). Acquiring literacy in a second language: The effect of book-based programs. *Language Learning, 41*(3), 375–411.

Elley, W. B., & Mangubhai, F. (1981). *The impact of a book flood in Fiji primary schools*. New Zealand Council for Educational Research.

Ellis, R. (2005). Principles of instructed language learning. *System, 33*, 209–224.

Ellis, R. (2009). The differential effects of three types of task planning on the fluency, complexity, and accuracy in L2 oral production. *Applied Linguistics, 30*(4), 474–509. https://doi.org/10.1093/applin/amp042

Ellis, R. (2018). *Reflections on task-based language teaching*. Multilingual Matters.

Ferris, D. (1999). The case for grammar correction in L2 writing classes: A response to Truscott (1996). *Journal of Second Language Writing, 8*, 1–10. https://doi.org/10.1016/S1060-3743(99)80110-6

Flavell, J. H. (1976). Metacognitive aspects of problem solving. In L. B. Resnick (Ed.), *The nature of intelligence* (pp. 231–235). Erlbaum.

Folse, K. (2004). Myths about teaching and learning second language vocabulary: What recent research says. *TESL Reporter, 37*(2), 1–13.

Foote, J. A. (2017). Ethics and the business of pronunciation instruction. In O. Kang, R. I. Thomson, & J. Murphy (Eds.), *The Routledge handbook of contemporary English pronunciation* (284–297). Routledge.

Franken, M. (1987). Self-questioning scales for improving academic writing. *Guidelines, 9*(1), 1–8.

Fried-Booth, D. (1982). Project work with advanced classes. *ELT Journal, 36*(2), 98–103.

George, H. V. (1963). A verb form frequency count. *ELT Journal, 18*(1), 31–37.

George, H. V. (1965). The substitution table. *ELT Journal, 20*(1), 41–48.

George, H. V. (1967). *101 substitution tables for students of English*. Cambridge University Press. (Students' book and Teachers' book). These two books are out of print but they can be found on the LALS resources web site by typing H. V. George.

Ghadirian, S. (2002). Providing controlled exposure to target vocabulary through the screening and arranging of texts. *Language Learning and Technology, 6*(1), 147–164.

Gibson, R. E. (1975). The strip story: A catalyst for communication. *TESOL Quarterly, 9*(2), l49l54.

Grant, L., & Nation, I. S. P. (2006). How many idioms are there in English? *ITL – International Journal of Applied Linguistics, 151*, 1–14.

Graves, M. F. (1986). Vocabulary learning and instruction. *Review of Research in Education, 13*, 49–89.

Guthrie, J. (2003). Concept-oriented reading instruction. In A. Sweet & C. Snow (Eds.), *Rethinking reading comprehension* (pp. 115–140). Guilford Press.

Harris, D. P. (1970). Report on an experimental group administered memory span test. *TESOL Quarterly, 4*(3), 203213.

Harwood, D. (2022). 'Teaching the writer to fish so they can fish for the rest of their lives': Lecturer, English language tutor, and student views on the educative role of proofreading. *English for Specific Purposes, 68*, 116–130. https://doi.org/10.1016/j.esp.2022.07.002

Hill, G. W. (1982). Group versus individual performance: Are N + 1 heads better than one? *Psychological Bulletin, 91*, 5l7539.

Hill, L. A. (1969). Delayed copying. *English Language Teaching Journal, 23*(3), 238239.

Hill, M., & Laufer, B. (2003). Type of task, time-on-task and electronic dictionaries in incidental vocabulary acquisition. *IRAL, 41*(2), 87–106.

Hirvela, A. (2013). *Connecting reading and writing in second language writing instruction*. University of Michigan Press.

Hoey, M. P. (1983). *On the surface of discourse*. Allen and Unwin.

Holmes, J., & Brown, D. F. (1976). Developing sociolinguistic competence in a second language. *TESOL Quarterly, 10*(4), 423431.

Honeyfield, J. (1977). Simplification. *TESOL Quarterly, 11*(4), 431–440.

Horst, M. (2005). Learning L2 vocabulary through extensive reading: A measurement study. *Canadian Modern Language Review, 61*(3), 355–382.

Hosenfeld, C. (1976). Learning about learning: Discovering our students' strategies. *Foreign Language Annals, 9*(2), 117–129.

Hu, M., & Nation, I. S. P. (2000). Vocabulary density and reading comprehension. *Reading in a Foreign Language, 13*(1), 403–430.

Huang, H. D. (2023). Examining the effect of digital storytelling on English speaking proficiency, willingness to communicate, and group cohesion. *TESOL Quarterly, 57*(1), 242–269.

Huffman, J. (2014). Reading rate gains during a one-semester extensive reading course. *Reading in a Foreign Language, 26*(2), 17–33.

Hwang, K., & Nation, P. (1989). Reducing the vocabulary load and encouraging vocabulary learning through reading newspapers. *Reading in a Foreign Language, 6*(1), 323–335.

Hyland, K. (2003). *Second language writing.* Cambridge University Press.

Hyland, K. (2004). *Genre and second language writing.* University of Michigan Press.

Hyland, K. (2022). *Teaching and researching writing* (4th Ed.). Routledge.

Hyland, K., & Hyland, F. (Eds.). (2006a). *Feedback in second language writing: Contexts and issues.* Cambridge University Press.

Hyland, K., & Hyland, F. (2006b). State-of-the-art-article: Feedback on second language students' writing. *Language Teaching, 39,* 83–101.

Ilson, R. (1962). The dictocomp: A specialized technique for controlling speech and writing in language learning. *Language Learning, 12*(4), 299301.

Jacobs, G. M., Power, M. A., & Loh, W. I. (2002). *The teacher's sourcebook for cooperative learning: Practical techniques, basic principles, and frequently asked questions.* Corwin Press.

Jacobs, G., & Small, J. (2003). Combining dictogloss and cooperative learning to promote language learning. *The Reading Matrix, 3*(1), 1–15.

Joe, A. (1995). Text-based tasks and incidental vocabulary learning. *Second Language Research, 11*(2), 149–158.

Joe, A. (1998). What effects do text-based tasks promoting generation have on incidental vocabulary acquisition? *Applied Linguistics, 19*(3), 357–377.

Joe, A., Nation, P., & Newton, J. (1996). Vocabulary learning and speaking activities. *English Teaching Forum, 34*(1), 2–7.

Johns, T., & Davies, F. (1983). Text as a vehicle for information: The classroom use of written texts in teaching reading in a foreign language. *Reading in a Foreign Language, 1*(1), 1–19.

Johnson, D. W. et al. (1981). Effects of cooperative, competitive, and individualistic goal structures on achievement: A metaanalysis. *Psychological Bulletin, 89,* 4762.

Johnson, M. D., & Tabari, M. A. (2022). Task planning and oral l2 production: A research synthesis and meta-analysis. *Applied Linguistics, 43*(6), 1143–1164. https://doi.org/10.1093/applin/amac026

Jones, D. (1918). *An outline of English phonetics.* Teubner.

Jordan, R. R. (1990). Pyramid discussions. *ELT Journal, 44*(1), 46–54.

Kato, F., Spring, R., & Mori, C. (2023). Incorporating project-based language learning into distance learning: Creating a homepage during computer-mediated learning sessions. *Language Teaching Research, 27*(3), 621–641.

Kessler, M., Ma, W., & Solheim, I. (2022). The effects of topic familiarity on text quality, complexity, accuracy, and fluency: A conceptual replication. *TESOL Quarterly, 56*(4), 1163–1190.

Krashen, S. (1985). *The input hypothesis: Issues and implications.* Longman.

Krashen, S. (2007). Extensive reading in English as foreign language by adolescents and young adults: A meta-analysis. *The International Journal of Foreign Language Teaching, 3*(2), 23–29.

Lado, R. (1965). Memory span as a factor in second language learning. *IRAL, 3*(2), 123129.

Lai, F. K. (1993). The effect of a summer reading course on reading and writing skills. *System, 21*(1), 87–100.

Lambert, C., Kormos, J., & Minn, D. (2017). Task repetition and second language speech processing. *Studies in Second Language Acquisition, 39*, 167–196.

Langman, J. (2003). The effects of ESL-trained content-area teachers: Reducing middle-school students to incidental language learners. *Prospect, 18*(1), 14–26.

Laufer, B. (1992). Reading in a foreign language: How does L2 lexical knowledge interact with the reader's general academic ability? *Journal of Research in Reading, 15*(2), 95–103.

Lee, I. (2017). *Classroom writing assessment and feedback in L2 school contexts.* Springer Nature Singapore Pte Ltd. https://doi.org/10.1007/978-981-10-3924-9

Lee, J., Jang, J., & Plonsky, L. (2015). The effectiveness of second language pronunciation instruction: A meta-analysis. *Applied Linguistics, 36*(3), 345–366.

Levis, J. M. (2016). Research into practice: How research appears in pronunciation materials. *Language Teaching, 49*, 423–437.

Levis, J. M., & Rehman, I. (2023). Pronunciation and technology. In E. Hinkel (Ed.), *Handbook of practical second language teaching and learning* (pp. 296–311). Routledge.

Loewen, S., & Wolff, D. (2016). Peer interaction in F2F and CMC contexts. In M. Sato & S. Ballinger (Eds.), *Peer interaction and second language learning: Pedagogical potential and research agenda* (pp. 163–184). John Benjamins.

Long, M. H. (2020). Optimal input for language learning: Genuine, simplified, elaborated, or modified elaborated? *Language Teaching, 53*, 169–182.

Long, M. H., & Porter, P. A. (1985). Group work, interlanguage talk, and second language acquisition. *TESOL Quarterly, 19*(2), 207228.

Lucker, G. W., Rosenfield, D., Sikes, J., & Aronson, E. (1976). Performance in the interdependent classroom: A field study. *American Educational Research Journal, 13*(2), 115123.

Macalister, J. (2010). Speed reading courses and their effect on reading authentic texts: A preliminary investigation. *Reading in a Foreign Language, 22*(1), 104–116.

Macalister, J. (2014). Developing speaking fluency with the 4/3/2 technique: An exploratory study. *The TESOLANZ Journal, 22*, 28–42.

Macalister, J., & Nation, I. S. P. (2020). *Language curriculum design* (2nd Ed.). Routledge.

Macalister, J., & Webb, S. (2019). Can L1 children's literature be used in the English language classroom? High frequency words in writing for children. *Reading in a Foreign Language, 31*(1), 62–80.

Maley, A., Duff, A., & Grellet, F. (1980). *The mind's eye.* Cambridge University Press.

Martinez, R., & Schmitt, N. (2012). A phrasal expressions list. *Applied Linguistics, 33*(3), 299–320.

Maurice, K. (1983). The fluency workshop. *TESOL Newsletter, 8 (August)*, p. 29. A revised version appeared in Baily, K., & Savage, L. (Eds.) (1994). *New ways in teaching speaking.* TESOL.

McCafferty, S. G., Jacobs, G. M., & DaSilva Iddings, A. C. (2006). *Cooperative learning and second language teaching.* Cambridge University Press.

McCarthy, C. J., Bauman, S., Choudhuri, D. D., Coker, A., Justice, C., Kraus, K. L., Luke, M., Rubel, D., & Shaw, L. (2022). Association for specialists in group work guiding principles for group work. *The Journal for Specialists in Group Work, 47*(1), 10–21. https://doi.org/10.1080/01933922.2021.1950882

McDonough, K., & Sunitham, W. (2009). Collaborative dialogue between Thai EFL learners during self-access computer activities. *TESOL Quarterly, 43*(2), 231–254.

McLean, S., & Rouault, G. (2017). The effectiveness and efficiency of extensive reading at developing reading rates. *System, 70*(1), 92–106.

McQuillan, J. (2019). Is children's literature as hard as scholarly articles about children's literature? A comment on Macalister and Webb (2019). *Reading in a Foreign Language, 31*(2), 302–304.

Miller, G. A. (1956). The magical number seven, plus or minus two: Some limits on our capacity for processing information. *Psychological Review, 63*(2), 81–97.

Millett, S. (2014). Quicklistens: Using what they already know. *Modern English Teacher, 23*(4), 64–65.

Min, H. T. (2005). Training students to become successful peer reviewers. *System, 33*(2), 293–308.

Mondria, J. A. (2003). The effects of inferring, verifying and memorising on the retention of L2 word meanings. *Studies in Second Language Acquisition, 25*(4), 473–499.

Montero Perez, M., van den Noortgate, W., & Desmet, P. (2013). Captioned video for L2 listening and vocabulary learning: A meta-analysis. *System, 41*, 720–739.

Nakanishi, T. (2015). A meta-analysis of extensive reading research. *TESOL Quarterly, 49*(1), 6–37.

Nakata, T. (2011). Computer-assisted second language vocabulary learning in a paired-associate paradigm: A critical investigation of flashcard software. *Computer Assisted Language Learning, 24*(1), 17–38.

Nakata, T. (2020). Learning words with flash cards and word cards. In S. Webb (Ed.), *The Routledge handbook of vocabulary studies* (pp. 304–319). Routledge.

Nation, I. S. P. (1976). Creating and adapting language teaching techniques. *RELC Journal, 7*(2), 1–15.

Nation, I. S. P. (1977). The combining arrangement: Some techniques. *Modern Language Journal, 61*(3), 89–94.

Nation, I. S. P. (1979). The curse of the comprehension question: Some alternatives. *Guidelines: RELC Journal Supplement, 2*, 85–103.

Nation, I. S. P. (1980). Graded interviews for communicative practice. *English Teaching Forum, 18*(4), 26–29.

Nation, I. S. P. (1985). Opportunities for learning through the communication approach. In B. K. Das (Ed.), *Communicative language teaching* (pp. 120129). RELC.

Nation, I. S. P. (1988). Using techniques well: Information transfer. *Guidelines, 10*(1), 17–23.

Nation, I. S. P. (1989a). Group work and language learning. *English Teaching Forum, 27*(2), 20–24.

Nation, I. S. P. (1989b). Speaking activities: Five features. *ELT Journal, 43*(1), 24–29.

Nation, I. S. P. (1991a). Dictation, dicto-comp and related techniques. *English Teaching Forum, 29*(4), 12–14.

Nation, I. S. P. (1991b). Managing group discussion: Problem-solving tasks. *Guidelines, 13*(1), 1–10.

Nation, I. S. P. (1993). Predicting the content of texts. *The TESOLANZ Journal, 1*, 37–46.

Nation, I. S. P. (1997). The language learning benefits of extensive reading. *The Language Teacher, 21*(5), 13–16.

Nation, I. S. P. (2004). Vocabulary learning and intensive reading. *EA Journal, 21*(2), 20–29.

Nation, I. S. P. (2005). Reading faster. *Pasaa, 30*, 21–37.
Nation, I. S. P. (2006). How large a vocabulary is needed for reading and listening? *Canadian Modern Language Review, 63*(1), 59–82.
Nation, I. S. P. (2007). The four strands. *Innovation in Language Learning and Teaching, 1*(1), 1–12.
Nation, I. S. P. (2008). *Teaching vocabulary: Strategies and techniques*. Heinle Cengage Learning.
Nation, I. S. P. (2009). Reading faster. *International Journal of English Studies, 9*(2), 131–144. (a reprint).
Nation, I. S. P. (2013a). *Learning vocabulary in another language* (2nd Ed.). Cambridge University Press.
Nation, I. S. P. (2013b). *What should every ESL teacher know?* Compass Publishing. (Available free from the Compass Publishing website).
Nation, I. S. P. (2014a). *What do you need to know to learn a foreign language?* LALS, Victoria University of Wellington. Available electronically from https://www.wgtn.ac.nz/lals/resources/paul-nations-resources/paul-nations-publications/publications
Nation, I. S. P. (2014b). How much input do you need to learn the most frequent 9,000 words? *Reading in a Foreign Language, 26*(2), 1–16.
Nation, I. S. P. (2018). Reading a whole book to learn vocabulary. *ITL International Journal of Applied Linguistics, 169*(1), 30–43.
Nation, I. S. P. (2022). *Learning vocabulary in another language* (3rd Ed.). Cambridge University Press.
Nation, I. S. P. (2024a). *What should every EFL teacher know?* (2nd Ed.). Compass Publishing.
Nation, I. S. P. (2024b). Re-thinking the principles of (vocabulary) learning and their applications. *Languages, 9*, 160.
Nation, I. S. P., & Bauer, L. (2023). Morphological awareness. *Language Teaching Research Quarterly, 26*, 52–64.
Nation, I. S. P., & Crabbe, D. (1991). A survival language learning syllabus for foreign travel. *System, 19*(3), 191–201.
Nation, I. S. P., & Hamilton-Jenkins, A. (2000). Using communicative tasks to teach vocabulary. *Guidelines, 22*(2), 15–19.
Nation, I. S. P., & Malarcher, C. (2007). *Reading for speed and fluency*. Books 1–4. Compass Publishing.
Nation, I. S. P., & Macalister, J. (2021). Information transfer and topic types. In I. S. P. Nation & J. Macalister (Eds.), *Teaching ESL.EFL reading and writing* (2nd Ed., pp. 145–153). Routledge.
Nation, I. S. P., & Macalister, J. (2021). *Teaching ESL/EFL reading and writing* (2nd Ed.). Routledge.
Nation, I. S. P., & Wang, K. (1999). Graded readers and vocabulary. *Reading in a Foreign Language, 12*(2), 355–380.
Nation, I. S. P., & Waring, R. (2013). *Extensive reading and graded Readers*. Compass Publishing.
Nation, I. S. P., & Waring, R. (2020). *Teaching extensive reading in another language*. Routledge.
Nation, I. S. P., & Yamamoto, A. (2012). Applying the four strands to language learning. *International Journal of Innovation in English Language Teaching and Research, 1*(2), 167–181.

Newton, J. (2013). Incidental vocabulary learning in classroom communication tasks. *Language Teaching Research, 17*(2), 164–187.

Newton, J. (2017). Pronunciation and speaking. In O. Kang, R. I. Thomson, & J. Murphy (Eds.), *The Routledge handbook of contemporary English pronunciation* (337–351). Routledge.

Newton, J., & Nation, I. S. P. (2021). Extensive listening. In J. Newton & I. S. P. Nation (Eds.), *Teaching ESL/EFL listening and speaking* (pp. 60–73). Routledge.

Nguyen, L. T. C. (2015). Written fluency improvement in a foreign language. *TESOL Journal, 6*(4), 707–730.

Oller, J. W., & Streiff, V. (1975). Dictation: A test of grammarbased expectancies. *English Language Teaching Journal, 30*(1), 2536.

Paivio, A. (1971). *Imagery and verbal processes*. Holt and Co.

Palincsar, A. S., & Brown, A. L. (1986). Interactive teaching to promote learning from text. *The Reading Teacher, 39*(8), 771–777.

Palmer, D. M. (1982). Information transfer for listening and reading. *English Teaching Forum, 20*(1), 29–33.

Palmer, H. E. (1916). *Colloquial English. 100 substitution tables*. W. Heffer & Son.

Palmer, H. E. (1925). Conversation. In R. C. Smith (Ed.) (1999). *The writings of Harold E. Palmer: An overview* (pp. 185–191). Hon-no-Tomosha, Tokyo.

Paribakht, T. S., & Wesche, M. B. (1996). Enhancing vocabulary acquisition through reading: A hierarchy of text-related exercise types. *Canadian Modern Language Review, 52*(2), 155–178.

Peters, E., Heynen, E., & Puimège, E. (2016). Learning vocabulary through audiovisual input: The differential effect of L1 subtitles and captions. *System, 63*, 134–148.

Peters, E., & Webb, S. (2018). Incidental vocabulary acquisition through viewing L2 television and factors that affect learning. *SSLA, 40*(3), 551–577.

Philips, S. U. (1972). Participant structures and communicative competence: Warm Springs children in community and classroom. In C. Cazden, V. P. Johns, & D. Hymes (Eds.), *Functions of language in the classroom* (pp. 370394). Teachers College Press.

Pigada, M., & Schmitt, N. (2006). Vocabulary acquisition from extensive reading: A case study. *Reading in a Foreign Language, 18*(1), 128.

Quinn, E., & Nation, I. S. P. (1974). *Speed reading*. Oxford University Press. (Available from Paul Nation's web resources pages)

Radford, W. L. (1969). The blackboard composition. *ELT Journal, 24*(1), 49–54.

Rayner, K., Schotter, E. R., Masson, M. E., Potter, M. C., & Treiman, R. (2016). So much to read, so little time: How do we read, and can speed reading help? *Psychological Science in the Public Interest, 17*(1), 434.

Riley, P. M. (1972). The dictocomp. *English Teaching Forum, 10*(1), 2123.

Robb, T. N., & Susser, B. (1989). Extensive reading vs skill building in an EFL context. *Reading in a Foreign Language, 5*(2), 239251.

Sato, M., & Ballinger, S. (2016). Understanding peer interaction: Research synthesis and directions. In M. Sato & S. Ballinger (Eds.), *Peer interaction and second language learning: Pedagogical potential and research agenda* (pp. 1–30). John Benjamins.

Sawyer, J., & Silver, S. (1961). Dictation in language learning. *Language Learning, 11*(1&2), 3342.

Schmitt, N., & Carter, R. (2000). The lexical advantages of narrow reading for second language learners. *TESOL Journal, 9*(1), 4–9.

Schmitt, N., Jiang, X., & Grabe, W. (2011). The percentage of words known in a text and reading comprehension. *The Modern Language Journal, 95*(1), 26–43.

Schunk, D. H., & Zimmerman, B. (Eds.) (2011). *Handbook of self-regulation of learning and performance*. Routledge.

Senechal, M., & Cornell, E. H. (1993). Vocabulary acquisition through shared reading experiences. *Reading Research Quarterly, 28*(4), 361–374.

Sharan, S. (1980). Cooperative learning in small groups: Recent methods and effects on achievement, attitudes, and ethnic relations. *Review of Educational Research, 50*(2), 241271.

Slavin, R. E. (1980). Cooperative learning. *Review of Educational Research, 50*(2), 315342.

Stahl, S. A., Hare, V. C., Sinatra, R., & Gregory, J. F. (1991). Defining the role of prior knowledge and vocabulary in reading comprehension: The retiring of number 41. *Journal of Reading Behavior, 23*(4), 487508.

Stahl, S. A., Jacobson, M. G., Davis, C. E., & Davis, R. L. (1989). Prior knowledge and difficult vocabulary in the comprehension of unfamiliar text. *Reading Research Quarterly, 24*(1), 2743.

Stevick, E. W. (1959). 'Technemes' and the rhythm of class activity. *Language Learning, 9*(3&4), 4551.

Strong, B., & Boers, F. (2019). The error in trial and error: Exercises on phrasal verbs. *TESOL Quarterly, 53*(2), 289–319.

Suk, N. (2017). The effects of extensive reading on reading comprehension, reading rate, and vocabulary acquisition. *Reading Research Quarterly, 52*(1), 7389.

Sutarsyah, C., Nation, P., & Kennedy, G. (1994). How useful is EAP vocabulary for ESP? A corpus based study. *RELC Journal, 25*(2), 3450.

Swanborn, M. S. L., & de Glopper, K. (1999). Incidental word learning while reading: A meta-analysis. *Review of Educational Research, 69*(3), 261285.

Tarone, E. (1980). Communication strategies, foreigner talk and repair in interlanguage. *Language Learning, 30*, 417431.

Thai, C., & Boers, F. (2016). Repeating a monologue under increasing time pressure: Effects on fluency, complexity, and accuracy. *TESOL Quarterly, 50*(2), 369393.

Thomson, R. I., & Derwing, T. M. (2015). The effectiveness of L2 pronunciation instruction: A narrative review. *Applied Linguistics, 36*, 326344.

Tran, M. N., & Saito, K. (2024). Effects of the 4/3/2 activity revisited: Extending Boers (2014) and Thai & Boers (2016). *Language Teaching Research, 28*(2), 326–345.

Tran, T. N. Y. (2012). The effects of a speed reading course and speed transfer to other types of texts. *RELC Journal, 43*(1), 23–37.

Tran, T. N. Y., & Nation, I. S. P. (2014). Reading speed improvement in a speed reading course and its effect on language memory span. *Electronic Journal of Foreign Language Teaching, 11*(1), 5–20.

Truscott, J. (1996). The case against grammar correction in L2 writing classes. *Language Learning, 46*, 327–369. https://doi.org/10.1111/j.1467-1770.1996.tb01238.x

Truscott, J. (2007). The effect of error correction on learners' ability to write accurately. *Journal of Second Language Writing, 16*, 255–272. https://doi.org/10.1016/j.jslw.2007.06.003

Tsang, A. (2023). "The best way to learn a language is not to learn it!": Hedonism and insights into successful EFL learners' experiences in engagement with spoken (listening) and written (reading) input. *TESOL Quarterly, 57*(2), 511–536.

Tucker, C. A. (1972). Programmed dictation: An example of the P.I. process in the classroom. *TESOL Quarterly, 6*(1), 61–70.

Uchihara, T., Webb, S., & Trofimovich, P. (2022). The effects of talker variability and frequency of exposure on the acquisition of spoken word knowledge. *Studies in Second Language Acquisition, 44*(2), 357–380.

Wajnryb, R. (1989). Dicto-gloss: A text–based communicative approach to teaching and learning grammar. *English Teaching Forum, 27*(4), 16–19.

Walter, K., Dockrell, J., & Connelly, V. (2021). A sentence-combining intervention for struggling writers: Response to intervention. *Reading & Writing, 34*, 1825–1850. https://doi.org/10.1007/s11145-021-10135-8

Waring, R., & Takaki, M. (2003). At what rate do learners learn and retain new vocabulary from reading a graded reader? *Reading in a Foreign Language, 15*(2), 130–163.

Watson, J. (2004). Issue logs. In R. R. Day & J. Bamford (Eds.), *Extensive reading activities for teaching language* (pp. 37–39). Cambridge University Press.

Webb, S., & Nation, P. (2017). *How vocabulary is learned*. Oxford University Press.

Webb, S., & Rodgers, M. P. H. (2009a). The lexical coverage of movies. *Applied Linguistics, 30*(3), 407–427.

Webb, S., & Rodgers, M. P. H. (2009b). The vocabulary demands of television programs. *Language Learning, 59*(2), 335–366.

Webb, S., Yanagisawa, A., & Uchihara, T. (2020). How effective are intentional vocabulary-learning activities? A meta-analysis. *Modern Language Journal, 104*(4), 715–738.

Wei, Z. (2015). Does teaching mnemonics for vocabulary learning make a difference? Putting the keyword method and the word part technique to the test. *Language Teaching Research, 19*(1), 43–69.

Wesche, M. B., & Paribakht, T. S. (2000). Reading-based exercises in second language vocabulary learning. *Modern Language Journal, 84*(2), 196–213.

West, M. P. (1955). *Learning to read a foreign language* (2nd Ed.). Longman.

West, M. P. (1960). *Teaching English in difficult circumstances*. Longman. (The appendix to this book contains the Minimum Adequate Vocabulary for Speech and a classification of that vocabulary).

Wilkinson, D. (2020). Deliberate learning from word cards. *Vocabulary Learning and Instruction, 9*(2), 69–74.

Wood, D. (2009). Effects of focused instruction of formulaic sequences on fluent expression in second language narratives: A case study. *The Canadian Journal of Applied Linguistics 12*(1), 39–57.

Woolrich, B. (1963). Alibi. *ELT Journal, 17*(3), 122–125. https://doi.org/10.1093/elt/XVII.3.122

Yu, S., Geng, F., Liu, C., & Zheng, Y. (2021). What works may hurt: The negative side of feedback in second language writing. *Journal of Second Language Writing, 54*, 1–15. https://doi.org/10.1016/j.jslw.2021.100850

Yuan, F., & Ellis, R. (2003). The effects of pre-task and on-line planning on fluency, complexity and accuracy in L2 monologic oral production. *Applied Linguistics, 24*(1), 1–27.

Zhang, Z., & Hyland, K. (2022). Fostering student engagement with feedback: An integrated approach. *Assessing Writing, 51*, 100586.

Zhou, Y., Yu, S., & Wu, P. (2022). Revisiting praise as feedback in L2 writing: Where are we going? *RELC Journal*. https://doi.org/10.1177/00336882221123100.

Zuck, J. G., & Zuck, L. V. (1984). Scripts: An example from newspaper texts. *Reading in a Foreign Language, 2*(1), 147–155.

# AUTHOR INDEX

Adolphs, S. 108, 306
Allen, V. 37, 306, 309
Al-Homoud, F. 187, 306
Anderson, A. 32, 307
Aronson, E. 34, 306, 311
Ashton-Warner, S. 24, 26, 306
Aubrey, S. 235, 307

Ballinger, S. 123, 300–311, 314
Banister, C. 300, 306
Barcroft, J. 154, 300, 306
Barnard, H. 87, 307
Bauer, L. 103, 136, 138, 143, 281, 283
Beglar, D. 173, 298, 301, 306
Bejarano, Y. 36, 306
Bell, T. 187, 306
Biber, D. 101, 107, 209–210, 306–307
Bismoko, J. 192, 199, 301, 307
Bitchener, J. 86, 216, 300, 302, 307
Bjork, R. 293, 307
Boers, F. 68, 147, 150–151, 153–154, 300–301, 307, 315
Briere, E. 141, 307
Brown, A. 21, 181, 314
Brown, D. F. 32, 87, 105, 307, 309
Brown, G. 32, 101, 307
Brown, R. 65, 307
Brysbaert, M. 197–199, 307
Butler, D. 292, 307
Bygate, M. 45, 48–51, 307

Carter, R. 51, 314
Carver, R. 28, 307
Chang, A. 95–96, 199, 300, 307
Chenoweth, A. 252, 307
Cho, K. 29, 307
Chun, I. 235, 307
Chung, M. 192, 199–200, 301, 307
Claridge, G. 166, 308
Connelly, V. 235, 316
Conrad, S. 101, 307
Cornell, E. 89, 315
Coxhead, A. 64, 279, 308
Crabbe, D. 12, 103, 128, 132, 281, 301, 313
Craik, F. 220, 308
Cramer, S. 199, 308

DaSilva Iddings, A. 35, 311
Davies, F. 84, 222, 310
Davies, N. 32, 308
de Glopper, K. 172, 302, 315
de Jong, N. 154, 301, 308
deHaan, J. 119, 308
DeKeyser, R. 8, 154, 243–244, 308
Den Noortgate, W. 301–302, 312
Derwing, T. 144–145, 301, 308, 315
Desmet, P. 68, 301–302, 312
Dockrell, J. 235, 316
Donkaewbua, S. 65, 307
Doughty, C. 34, 308

Duff, A. 35, 311
Dunlosky, J. 293, 307
Dykstra, G. 230, 308

Elgort, I. 284, 308
Elkins, R. 84, 308
Elley, W. 29, 172–173, 308
Ellis, R. 25, 48, 133, 149, 266, 301, 308, 316

Ferris, D. 211, 308
Flavell, J. 289, 292, 308
Folse, K. 301, 309
Foote, J. 136, 309
Franken, M. 24, 223, 309
Fried-Booth, D. 269, 309

Geng 211, 316
George, H. 35, 238–239, 241–242, 309
Ghadirian, S. 26, 309
Gibson, R. 34–35, 119, 309
Grabe, W. 28, 315
Grant, L 183, 309
Graves, M. 29, 309
Grellet, F. 35, 311
Grimshaw, D. 68, 300, 307
Guthrie, J. 181, 309

Hamilton-Jenkins, A. 119, 313
Harris, D. 81, 309
Harwood, D. 211, 309
Hayes, R. 252, 307
Heynen, E. 68, 301, 314
Hill, G. 36, 309
Hill, L. 81, 251, 309
Hill, M. 301, 309
Hirvela, A. 216, 309
Hoey, M. 222, 309
Holmes, J. 32, 105, 309
Honeyfield, J. 166, 309
Horst, M. 173, 309
Hosenfeld, C. 299, 309
Hu, M. 28, 309
Huang, H. 131–132, 309
Huffman, J. 187, 310
Hunt, A. 173, 298, 301, 306
Hwang, K. 51, 310
Hyland, F. 216, 300, 310
Hyland, K. 205, 207–208, 210, 216, 300, 310, 316

Ilson, R. 82, 310

Jacobs, G. 35, 235, 310–311
Jacobson, M. 30, 315
Jang, J. 144, 300, 311
Jiang, X. 28, 315
Joe, A. 48, 56, 70, 112, 114, 302, 310
Johns, T. 84, 222, 310, 314
Johnson, D. W. 36, 302, 310
Johnson, M. D. 133, 302, 310
Jones, D. 139, 310
Jordan, R. 49, 79, 310

Kalivoda, T. 84, 308
Kato, F. 274, 300, 310
Kennedy, G. 265, 315
Kessler, M. 18, 310
Kite, Y. 173, 298, 301, 306
Kormos, J. 47, 311
Kornell, N. 293, 307
Krashen, S. 7, 20, 29, 172, 302, 307, 310
Kuwada, K. 119, 308

Lado, R. 81, 310
Lai, F. 187, 311
Lambert, C. 47, 311
Langman, J. 275, 311
Laufer, B. 30, 301, 311
Lee, I. 207–208, 212, 311
Lee, J. 144, 300, 311
Levis, J. 143, 144, 311
Liu, C. 211, 316
Lockhart, R. S. 220, 308
Loh, W. 35, 310
Long, M. 32–35, 40, 46, 63–64, 71–74, 76, 80, 82, 105, 114, 119, 123, 126–132, 138–141, 143, 146, 152, 154, 161, 165–166, 170–171, 179, 184–185, 190, 196, 198, 201, 212, 236, 251, 277, 279, 283, 297, 311
Lucker, W. 34, 311

Ma, W. 18, 90, 160, 177, 310–311
Macalister, J. 29, 49, 83, 143, 154, 180, 182, 206, 230, 274, 286, 300, 311–313
Malarcher, C. 169, 193, 313
Maley, A. 35, 311
Mangubhai, F. 29, 172–173, 308
Martinez, R. 183, 311
Maurice, K. 83, 147, 311
McCafferty, S. 35, 311
McCarthy, M. 31, 311
McDonough, S. 123, 302, 312

McLean, S. 187, 312
McQuillan, J. 29, 312
Miller, G. 85, 312
Millett, S. 92, 95–96, 192–193, 197, 199, 300, 307, 312
Min, H. 47, 150, 198, 208, 312
Minn, D. 47, 311
Mondria, J. 160, 312
Montero Perez, M. 301–302, 312
Morain, G. C. 84, 308
Mori 274, 300, 310

Nakanishi, T. 172, 302, 312
Nakata, T. 283, 312
Newton, J. 63, 66, 112, 114, 119, 123, 145, 301–302, 310, 314
Nguyen, L. 252, 314

Oller, J. 85, 314

Paivio, A. 220, 226, 314
Palincsar, A. 21, 181, 314
Palmer, D. 219–220, 222, 225, 314
Palmer, H. 102, 238, 314
Paribakht, S. 185, 187, 302, 314, 316
Paulston, C. 230, 308
Perfetti, C. 154, 301, 308
Peters, E. 68, 301, 314
Philips, S. 34, 314
Pica, T. 34, 308
Pigada, M. 173, 302, 314
Plonsky, L. 144, 300, 311
Port, A. 69, 225, 230, 269, 279, 308
Port, R. 69, 225, 230, 269, 279, 308
Porter, P. 32–35, 311
Power, M. 35, 310
Puimège, E. 68, 301, 314

Quinn, E. 19, 314

Radford, W. 234, 314
Rayner, K. 197–198, 314
Reed, W. 119, 308
Rehman, I. 143, 311
Riley, P. 82, 314
Robb, T. 187, 314
Rodgers, M. 63–64, 108, 316
Rosenfield, C. 34, 311
Rouault, G. 187, 312

Saito, K. 154, 315
Sato, M. 123, 300, 311, 314

Schmitt, N. 28, 51, 108, 173, 183, 187, 302, 306, 311, 314–315
Senechal, M. 89, 315
Sharan, S. 36, 315
Shillcock, R. 32, 307
Sikes, J. 34, 311
Siyanova-Chanturia, A. 300, 307
Slavin, R. 36, 315
Small, J. 235, 310
Solheim, I. 18, 310
Spring, R. 274, 300, 310
Stahl, S. 30, 315
Stevick, E. 2, 315
Streiff, V. 85, 314
Strong, B. 301, 315
Suk, N. 187, 315
Sunitham, W. 123, 302, 312
Susser, B. 187, 314
Sutarsyah, C. 265, 315
Swanborn, M. 172, 302, 315

Tabari, M. 133, 302, 310
Takaki, M. 173, 301, 316
Tarone, E. 32, 315
Thai, C. 139, 147, 150–151, 153–154, 282, 300, 307, 312, 315
Thomson, R. 25, 144, 300, 309, 314–315
Tran, M. 154, 192, 199–200, 315
Tran, T. 154, 300, 315
Trofimovich, P. 145, 301, 316
Truscott, J. 210–211, 308, 315
Tsang, A. 68, 300, 315
Tucker, C. 78, 316

Uchihara, T. 145, 185, 187, 235, 301–302, 316

van den Noortgate, W. 312

Wajnryb, R. 82, 230, 316
Walls, R. 64, 308
Walter, K. 235, 316
Wang, K. 29, 169–170, 313
Waring, R. 7, 65, 159, 161, 163, 165, 172–173, 298, 301, 307, 313, 316
Warren, P. 68, 300, 307
Watson, J. 269, 316
Webb, S. 2, 29, 63–64, 68, 108, 145, 161, 185, 187, 235, 301–302, 311–312, 314, 316
Wei, Z. 302, 316
Wesche, M. 185, 187, 302, 314, 316

West, M. 29, 80, 108, 115, 199, 297, 316
Wilkinson, D. 278, 284, 301, 316
Wood, D. 154, 316
Woolrich, B. 3, 316
Wu, P. 216, 300, 316

Yamamoto, A. 15, 313
Yanagisawa, A. 235, 301–302, 316

Yu, F. 211, 216, 300, 316
Yuan, S. 133, 316
Yule, G. 32, 307

Zhang, Z. 207, 316
Zheng, Y. 211, 316
Zhou, Y. 216, 300, 316
Zuck J. 222, 316
Zuck, L. 222, 316

# SUBJECT INDEX

Note: Several words and phrases, such as *principles, group work, research questions* and *goals*, occur so often in this book that there is no point in putting them in the index – there would be far too many page numbers to list. Nonetheless, I have included the names of the twenty techniques so that reference to them outside their chapter can be easily found.

4/3/2 2, 10, 28, 45–46, 51, 83, 92, 131, 147–156, 248, 250–252, 260, 275, 299, 307, 311, 315

Ananse Tales 230, 233, 235–237, 308
assisted viewing 66
authentic 25–26, 165–166, 297, 311
autonomy 286

blown-up book 64
bolding 4
bottom-up processing 22
brainstorming 36, 129, 208, 266

CEFR levels 229, 280–281
closed captions 66
communication strategies 32, 315
Compleat Lexical Tutor 66, 186
complexity 3–4, 48, 55, 81, 109, 133, 149–150, 154–155, 252–253, 265, 273, 301, 308, 310, 315
content-based instruction 275–276
correction 56, 78, 88, 109, 132, 206, 210–212, 267–268, 302, 308, 315
corrective feedback 72, 75, 85–86, 148, 154, 206, 213, 216, 307

cost/benefit 286
course design 1, 286

delayed copying 79, 81, 251, 309
dictation 2, 9, 13, 18–19, 21, 37, 45, 51, 69, 71–88, 142, 187, 230, 233, 235, 251, 265, 291, 299, 307, 312, 314, 316
dictionary 7, 13, 43, 47, 52, 65, 160, 164, 170, 174, 176, 181–182, 185–186, 214, 270, 290
dicto-comp 83
dicto-gloss 82, 230
dual coding 226

easy listening 2, 10, 61, 89–97
enhancement 4, 153
ESL speed readings 193, 196–197
experience tasks 18–31, 52, 120, 159, 190, 208, 250, 257, 262, 269
expert group-family group 117, 120
extensive listening and viewing 2, 7, 59–70
extensive reading 2, 6–8, 10–13, 15, 25, 29, 41–43, 48, 53, 61–62, 64, 68, 91, 93, 107, 159–175, 177, 179–180, 187, 193–194, 197, 200, 206–207, 223, 229,

## Subject index

264, 272, 290–291, 298, 306, 309–310, 312–316
Extensive Reading Foundation 29, 91, 93, 161–162, 165, 167–168, 170
extensive writing with feedback 2, 205–207, 209, 211, 213–215, 217–218
eye-tracking 75, 175

flemma 281
fluency criteria 89–90, 150, 190–191
formative assessment 210

graded readers 14, 19, 25–26, 29, 41, 65, 67, 89, 91–92, 94–95, 159, 161–163, 165–174, 197, 274, 297, 308, 313
grammar translation 13, 176
Grammarly 132, 216
group work 21, 31–38, 54, 77, 105, 110, 119, 124, 148, 219–220, 226, 230, 239, 257, 269, 276, 300, 311–312
guessing from context 2, 7, 42, 61, 160–161, 177, 179, 181–182, 184–185, 258, 270
guided tasks 18, 22–24, 126, 208
guided writing 2, 9, 82, 208, 229–237, 299

headlines 3, 46, 51, 131
hearing and pronunciation practice 2, 136–139, 141, 143–145, 233, 299
highlighting 45, 132

incidental learning 4, 7–8, 40–44, 56, 60–61, 67, 91, 111–112, 148, 171, 173, 187, 205, 258, 269, 302
independent tasks 5, 17–18, 23, 126, 208
informal conversation 2, 15, 92, 101–109, 115, 128, 130, 136, 206, 233
information transfer 2, 4, 7–8, 22–24, 59, 83, 91, 181–182, 208, 219–228, 234, 291, 312–314
intensive reading 2, 9, 11–12, 61, 63, 66, 69, 71, 73–74, 151, 176–189, 233, 298, 306, 313

keyword technique 41, 53, 228, 277–283, 290

learner training 2, 4, 9, 233, 286–289, 291–294
learning in the wild 67

linked skills 2, 7–8, 10, 15, 45, 48, 51, 120, 131, 151, 187, 224, 235, 251–252, 257–269, 276, 299
listening to stories 89, 91, 93, 307

memory span 81–82, 85, 309–310, 315
movies 59–60, 63–64, 66–68, 103, 128, 316

narrow reading 51, 264, 270, 314
negotiation 8, 32, 35, 38, 42–43, 52, 102, 109, 111–112, 115, 121, 123, 212, 290
notetaking 23, 181, 221

observers 56, 119, 124, 301
outcomes 50–51, 115–117, 125, 177, 269–270, 276

peer feedback 208, 213, 265, 273, 306
peer testing 52, 290–291
performance errors 94, 150, 213
plagiarism 215, 269–271, 274
podcasts 59–60, 69, 126
prepared talks 2, 5, 8, 92, 103, 107, 115, 126–135, 144, 151, 268, 272, 299
problem-solving speaking 2, 8, 42–43, 92, 111–125, 128, 206, 215, 312
procedures 27–28, 117–118, 124–125, 181, 183, 208, 211–214, 218, 223, 260, 264, 303–305
projects 2, 7–8, 10, 132, 168, 269–276, 299
pyramid procedure 49, 51, 79, 117, 125, 264–265, 299

Q->SA+EI 105
quicklistens 89–90, 92, 94–95, 312

read-and-look-up 80
repeated listening 61, 63, 70, 89, 95, 97
repeated reading 46, 51, 152, 196, 264, 307
reporting back 114–115, 123, 125
retrieval 40–41, 53, 103–104, 127, 160, 224, 244, 259, 261, 279, 281, 284–285, 289–292, 299
role play 38, 51, 103, 105–106, 265

say it! 37, 130, 264
say the poem once 47
self-checking 132, 208, 212–214, 306

semantic mapping 26, 28, 49, 181, 208, 219, 225, 228
shared book 59, 94
shared reading 21, 89–90, 94, 315
shared tasks 18, 21, 24, 28, 31, 110, 208
situational composition 208, 215
skill acquisition theory 8, 154, 243–244, 308
songs 59–60, 63, 65, 67, 209
spacing 40, 55, 267, 289, 291–292, 301
speed reading 2, 10, 19, 90, 160, 162, 169, 172, 190–201, 248, 307, 311, 314–315
strategy development 9, 177
strip story 3, 34, 119, 309
substitution tables 2, 233–234, 238–245, 299, 309, 314
survival vocabulary 12, 108, 128, 132, 248

TED talks 59, 64, 67, 95, 308
top-down processing 22, 108
topic types 49–50, 180, 182, 209, 221–222, 226, 313
trial-and-error 11, 52, 290, 315

unexploded dictation 51, 79, 84, 87

varied repetition 14, 43–45, 48–51, 56, 117, 184, 187, 226, 258–259, 265, 302
verbatim repetition 44–46, 49, 51–52, 85, 147–148, 154, 186, 251, 265

VocabProfiler 66
Vocabulary Levels Tests 91, 166, 193–194, 197, 279

word cards 2, 41–43, 162, 174, 180–182, 233, 273, 278–279, 283–285, 289, 291, 312, 316
word families 14, 42, 53, 61–62, 56, 62–63, 66, 70, 108, 160, 165–166, 197, 229, 238, 267–268, 279, 281, 285, 290, 302, 306
Word Family Finder 279
word part strategy 13, 180–181, 277, 279, 283
word parts 2–4, 12, 14, 30, 40, 53, 56, 70, 175, 178, 181–182, 276, 278, 280, 283, 285, 290, 302
words per minute 4, 61, 74, 90, 94–95, 129, 152, 160–161, 169–170, 190–191, 197, 200
writing portfolio 214
writing process 130, 205–208, 215–216, 229, 246

Xreading 65, 67, 91, 95, 161–162, 164, 167–171, 173, 193, 196–197

YouTube 46, 59, 75

Zipf's Law 13